THE BUDDHIST PILGRIMAGE

BUDDHIST TRADITION SERIES

VOLUME 37

The Buddhist Pilgrimage

DUNCAN FORBES

MOTILAL BANARSIDASS PUBLISHERS
PRIVATE LIMITED • DELHI

First Reprint : Delhi, 2011
First Indian : Delhi, 1999

ISBN : 978-81-208-1650-3

MOTILAL BANARSIDASS
41 U.A. Bungalow Road, Jawahar Nagar, Delhi 110 007
8 Mahalaxmi Chamber, 22 Bhulabhai Desai Road, Mumbai 400 026
203 Royapettah High Road, Mylapore, Chennai 600 004
236, 9th Main III Block, Jayanagar, Bangalore 560 011
Sanas Plaza, 1302 Baji Rao Road, Pune 411 002
8 Camac Street, Kolkata 700 017
Ashok Rajpath, Patna 800 004
Chowk, Varanasi 221 001

Printed in India
By Jainendra Prakash Jain at Shri Jainendra Press,
A-45, Naraina, Phase-I, New Delhi 110 028
and Published by Narendra Prakash Jain for
Motilal Banarsidass Publishers Private Limited,
Bungalow Road, Delhi 110 007

Foreword

Forbes has written an excellent travel book, emphasizing the main travel sites of the historical Buddha, from his birth to his decease, mainly in the area of Bihar. Forbes uses fine descriptive power to present his own travel experiences along this same route, while helping the reader with a diagram for each of these centers.

His trip, especially in the mid-1990's starting from North Bihar or South Nepal for the Buddha's traditional birth, is aided by recent archaeological discoveries for establishing certain other centers of the Buddha's pilgrimage. This author also portrays his travels outside this zone established by the Buddha, mainly in Nepal and in Hong Kong.

Forbes was sometimes helped by a guide, and sometimes by other informants, who allowed him to evade certain situations which could have been disastrous. Fortunately he knows scholarly facts of the Buddha's life to combine with the travel accounts. This is certainly a commendable work.

Alex Wayman

Preface

I might never have gone on my Buddhist Pilgrimage if I had not seen the great stupas of Bodhnath and Swayambhunath in Katmandu, and if I had not been to Lumbini when it was still called Rummindei. I felt the peace of that distant and hallowed place, and I planned my travels without knowing that others were organising groups to do much the same.

Of those who helped me on my way the Venerable U. Nayaka was generous with his time in Kushinagara, as was Swami Ananda Chaitanya Das in Rajgir. I also thank my son, Anthony, for arranging the material in such a way that it will, I hope, be read with pleasure, and even with profit.

To Him the Way, the Law, apart,
Whom Maya held beneath her heart,
Ananda's Lord, the Bodhisat.

Introduction

For a thousand years and more the places where the Buddha of our present age lived and moved were lost to view. The once magnificent monuments commemorating the most significant moments in the Buddha's life had either crumbled away and decayed to such an extent that they were no longer recognised as such, or else had disappeared completely from sight.

In recent years, beginning at the end of last century, many of the sacred sites have been rediscovered. Some are still in dispute. Others still remain hidden. As recently as 1995, as a result of excavations under the Mayadevi Temple at Lumbini, a stone marking the Buddha's birthplace was brought to light on top of the platform on which the temple stands. But the stupas of the Great Renunciation have not yet been found.

In this book I recount my experiences and adventures as a pilgrim bound for the traditional, time-honoured sites of the Buddha story by the modern means of the twentieth century. At some sites, such as Vaishali and Pava, I found little to see. But at others, such as Bodh-Gaya and Shravasti, there was a great deal. Indeed, I saw that Bodh-Gaya, Shravasti and Kushinagara had become the veritable building-sites of a Buddhist renascence.

A lone pilgrim might be considered to be lonely. But that was not my experience. Some fellow-visitors - at Nalanda, for instance, or at Sarnath - were doubtless simply tourists. But the majority were probing the past on a spiritual journey in the present, and those with whom I established contact were not reluctant to tell me how and why they had become involved in the doctrine of the Buddha. Their tales seemed to me to be a living counterpoint to the dead bricks of the stupas, and although I have not revealed their identities, they know who they are.

A pilgrimage should be a joyful experience in spite of the trials and tribulations of travel. The memory of it should remain with the pilgrim for the rest of his life and should not be over-burdened with the weight of scholastic interpretation. I have, therefore, eschewed the diacritical marks that some scholars use in transliterating Indian names into the Roman script, and instead written such names as, for instance, Shravasti and Kushinagara in accordance with the usual usage in India today rather than with the Pali language of the distant past.

List of Photographs

Maps and Plans

Contents

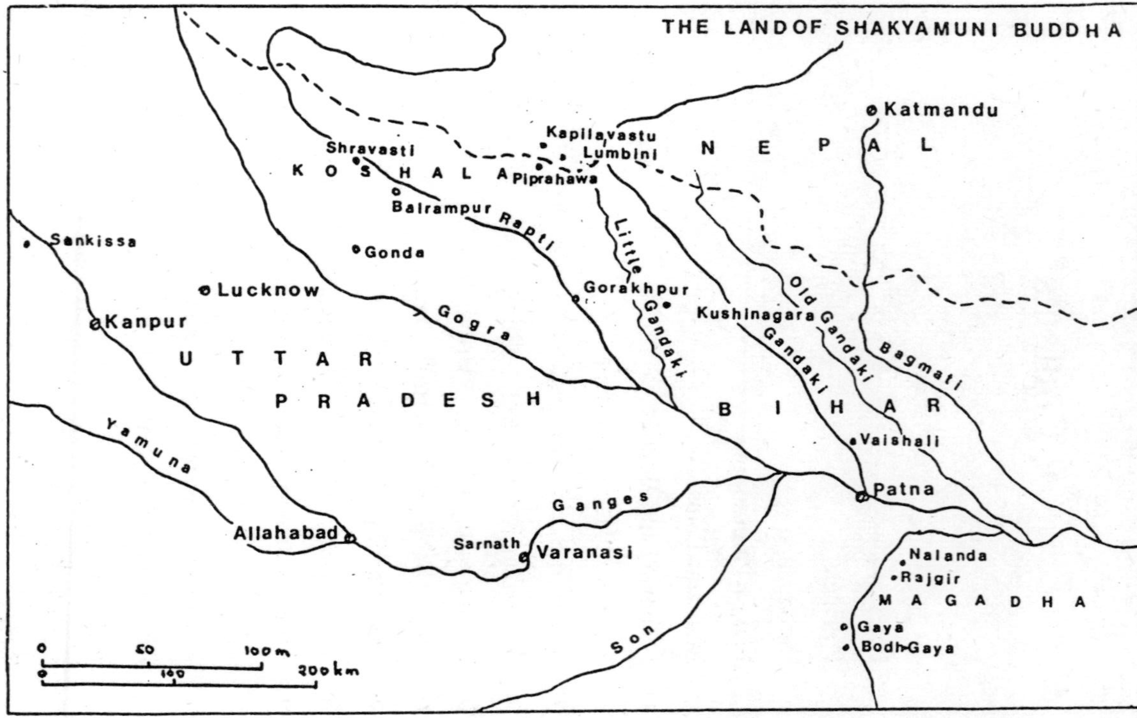
THE LANDOF SHAKYAMUNI BUDDHA
Katmandu
NEPAL
Kapilavastu
Lumbini
Shravasti
KOSHALA
Piprahawa
Balrampur
Rapti
Sankissa
Gonda
Little Gandaki
Lucknow
Gorakhpur
Kushinagara
Old Gandaki
Gandaki
Kanpur
Gogra
Bagmati
UTTAR PRADESH
BIHAR
Vaishali
Yamuna
Patna
Ganges
Allahabad
Sarnath
Varanasi
Nalanda
Rajgir
MAGADHA
Gaya
Bodh-Gaya
Son
0 50 100m
0 160 200km

1

Following the Buddha

There have been many Buddhas in the past, and will be in the future. A thousand is not an unusual number to see painted on the walls of monasteries in Ladakh, or represented in rows of golden statuettes as in the Temple of a Thousand Buddhas at Shatin in the New Territories of Hong Kong. For a Buddha is simply an Enlightened One, who has broken out of the cycle of birth and rebirth to remain in the spirit world. And in the aeons of eternity there has been time enough for many to achieve that goal.

The Buddhas have also been seen and represented in many forms. I have seen one with no less than a thousand arms. Others have many heads, three eyes. Some are benign, others fierce in aspect. Some people say that they are products of the imagination, others that it is through the imagination that we see them. Buddhas have also marked certain places with their footprints, and great temples have been built over indentations in the rock, as at Saraburi in Thailand, which are in the form of feet of superhuman size.

But there is only one Buddha in the recorded history of our world, and he is never represented in any but human form, standing or else seated in the Indian way with his feet tucked up over his thighs, or more rarely reclining as in the posture of his last hours on earth. Indeed, in the generations immediately following his decease he was not figured at all, and the wheel of the doctrine and the swastika of well-being were the symbols of the faith.

Of this Buddha we know much, more than we know of Jesus Christ although he lived six hundred years before the Jewish Messiah and in a more distant land. Though their ministries both commenced when they were about the same age, in their thirties, his lasted forty-five years, Jesus' only three. The literature about the Buddha's doings and sayings is immense. The sutras, which are the records of his teachings, make up only one of the three baskets, the Tripitaka, which contain the essence of Buddhist thought and practice. Yet these scriptures were largely unknown to Europeans until dedicated scholars undertook the task of translating them from the Pali of Sri Lanka and from the Chinese and Tibetan in the late nineteenth century.

Likewise there was considerable doubt about the locations of the places where the Buddha had been and taught until nineteenth century antiquarian interest and twentieth century archaeology moved in to resolve many of the doubts. For under the destructive blows of Mohammedan fundamentalism and Brahminical revival Buddhism had been almost obliterated in the land of its origin and only flourished abroad.

Before this destruction of monasteries and scriptures took place Chinese pilgrims wrote good descriptions of the holy places of Buddhism, which have been proved to be accurate by modern investigators. But it is only in the last thirty years that extensive excavations, largely carried out by Indian and Japanese archaeological teams working in partnership, have brought to the light of day the more problematic of the sites made memorable by the Buddha's life.

The Buddha's family name was Gautama and his given name Siddhartha, and because he was born a Shakya he was later known as Shakyamuni, the Shakya sage. After his

Enlightenment another name was given to him. He was called the Tathagata,"He who has thus arrived." Indeed it was only after the Enlightenment that he could be said to have become a Buddha.

His life is not a mystery, though nothing definite is known about his youthful years. He was born at Lumbini,now in Nepal, and brought up at Kapilavastu, said by some to be in Nepal by others in India. He fasted nearly unto death at Uruvilva in the Indian state of Bihar, achieved enlightenment at nearby Bodh-Gaya and preached his first sermon at Sarnath near Benares. He visited Rajagriha, the capital of Magadha, many times and spent many rainy seasons at Shravasti, capital of Koshala, the state that included the land of the Shakyas. He often went to Vaishali near Patna, where the Second Buddhist Council was held a hundred years after his death, and he died at Kushinagara, which is nowadays said to be near Gorakhpur in Uttar Pradesh. Later on, a great Buddhist university was founded at Nalanda near Rajagriha

I determined to see for myself these places, most of which had been buried in obscurity for hundreds of years. Many of them are still hard to get to. But a pilgrim should expect to have to face hardships on the way, and I was to find that the moments of exhilaration that I experienced, and the glimpses that I had, or thought I had, of some enlightenment far outweighed the rough going of the road.

The modern Buddhist pilgrimage takes in Lumbini and Kapilavastu, Bodh-Gaya and Sarnath, Rajagriha, Shravasti, Kushinagara and sometimes Vaishali, eight places that are revered in the Buddha story. But only two of them, Bodh-Gaya and Sarnath, were known with any certainty a hundred years ago.

The traditional Buddhist pilgrimage, as depicted in a stone carving of the Gupta period, took the pilgrim to Pava instead of Rajagriha. This is where the aged Buddha ate the tainted food that led to his death at nearby Kushinagara.

But where was Pava? Where, for that matter, was the Anoma River, which the Buddha reached, and some say crossed, on his flight from Kapilavastu before divesting himself of his worldy trappings? Where are the monuments that commemorated the spot where he dismissed his charioteer, the place where he had his long hair cut off, the site where he doffed his princely garments? They were seen by the Chinese pilgrims and are yet to be rediscovered.

Where was the River or Well of the Arrow, for which Kim's lama was diligently searching in Rudyard Kipling's immortal work? The Chinese pilgrims give directions. Should we not follow them?

I tried to follow them whenever I was in doubt, and this was one reason why I chose to travel alone. But when I saw the pilgrim groups—the Japanese, the Singapore and Malaysian, the Taiwanese, even the Anglo-Americans with the excellent Shantum Seth accompanying them—I wondered why it was that I chose the single path. For India is and always has been the land of pilgrims, and nearly all of them travel in groups, led by their pandars, both for company and for mutual protection.

Yet always you will see, too, a loner from time to time tramping the road with pilgrim staff and scrip, bound for some distant goal, perhaps responding to a vow once made, perhaps simply involved in a personal obsession, determined to see with his own eyes some magic place that he has been told of, and to be present there in his own body.

I suppose that I, myself, was like these loners, obsessed with seeing the places where the Buddha had been, so obsessed that I even tried to rediscover some of those that had been hidden for nearly a thousand years. It was un-Buddhistic, no doubt, since such an ego-trip glorifies the self that rightly does not exist as a whole and fills the space that Buddhists say is void.

The Heart of Wisdom Sutra, which is based on the Buddha's sayings during one of his sojourns in Shravasti, clearly states that Form is Void and Voidness is Form. So that feelings, discernments, formative elements and consciousness are also void.

Yet here was I not only bent on tracing the places the Buddha graced with his presence but on writing about them too.

2

The Birthplace – Lumbini

The land of the Shakyas was close to the outworks of the Himalayas in Northern India, between the Rapti river and the Sewalik hills. On a clear winter's day you can see the mountain range like a white line on the horizon. But in the heat haze of summer nothing rises above the level of the trees. Indeed the Terai country of these borderlands between Indian and Nepal is all a flat alluvial plain, watered by the numerous rivers that emerge from the mountains. So any hillock or mound of more or less regular shape is bound to have been made by man.

Here, in the sixth century BC, the Shakya people lived in their village democracies under the aristocratic government at Kapilavastu. The Buddha's father is often referred to respectfully as a maharaja. But it is more likely that the Shakyas had a republican form of government. If this is so the raja was simply the elected chief, himself subject to the government of the state of Koshala at Shravasti,

In any case the Shakyas certainly saw themselves as a distinct clan, one of the many Aryan groups that had entered India from the north-west. They were sometimes at loggerheads with their neighbours, the Koliyas, who lived to the east of them. But the Koliyas were not far away, hardly more than a two-day trip from Kapilavastu, and from this we can see that we are talking about small chieftains in their modest castles, nowadays called kots, rather than great kings.

The river that divided them, and sometimes upset them in water disputes, was the Rohini, which is even today a common name amongst Indian girls. It flows north to south some twenty-five to thirty miles east of Kapilavastu, an inconsiderable stream except when swollen by the summer spate, and like all the rivers of this region, it ends its life in the much bigger Rapti.

It was on her way to this river that the Rani Maya gave birth to the Buddha-to-be, and it happened thus. Maya was the daughter of a Koliya chieftain and one of the two wives of Shuddhodana,the Shakya raja. For many years both wives had been childless, and it was not until she was forty-five years old that Maya became pregnant and hoped to give her husband a son. Her hopes were not without foundation. For she had dreamt of a white elephant, an episode that is reproduced in pictures in countless Buddhist temples and in stone on many Buddhist monuments. This was held by the wise men to mean that the child would be male, and that he would become a great man in some way, either as a ruler or a philosopher.

It has also prompted some to propose a virgin birth for the Buddha, since the elephant had appeared to penetrate the sleeping lady in a kind of mystic impregnation. This would enhance the status of Maha Maya, Great Maya, like that of the Virgin Mary, and Shuddhodana would be merely the Joseph of the story. The fact that, for so many years, he had been unable to father a child on either of his two wives made him apt for such a role.

In those days it was customary for pregnant women to return to their parental homes for their confinements, and Maya was no exception to the rule. She set out with her retainers, no doubt carried in a palanquin. As we now know, Lumbini is some twelve miles east of Kapilavastu, and if she reached the grove of trees there and the lakeside on the same day as she had set out she would certainly have been tired. It could not have been much before nightfall, and the party would have wanted to rest and spend the night there before going on into Koliya territory. It is said that she carried the future Buddha in her womb for ten months as smoothly as oil in a monk's bowl.

Then it happened. The exact year has been the subject of scholarly argument. But South-east Asia and the Mahabodhi Society consider it have been 624 BCE. Legend has it that the sun was shining and birds were singing in the trees beside the lake.

Maya's time had come, and she gave birth standing up, effortlessly and some say from her side, holding the branch of a sal-tree above her head. For women to give birth standing up is a practice that is not as uncommon as those accustomed to the maternity wards of modern hospitals might suppose. But what happened next was certainly unexpected. The baby stood up of his own accord and immediately took seven steps. This scene too has been depicted many times. But perhaps the most ancient of all the depictions is the sculptured relief that has been at Lumbini itself longer than anyone knows.

My own starting-point for Lumbini was Varanasi, which is easily accessible by air from Delhi. To old-timers it was Benares, holiest of Hindu cities and old before London was even thought of. But it was destroyed so ruthlessly by the Moslem conquerors of the twelfth century that little remains there which can be dated to Pre-Mogul times. With a population that has multiplied more than four times to over a million since the time when Murray published the second edition of his Handbook for Travellers in India, Ceylon and Burma in 1894, its narrow streets are abominably overcrowded.

Yet the railway divides the place neatly into two unequal parts. South of the tracks the city seethes with traffic. But north of them, in the cantonment, hotels and bungalows stand in their own gardens, and the pedicabs cruise the quiet roads, where a white man walking on his own sticks out like a sore thumb. Indeed a pedicab tricyclist will soon convince you that it is not right and proper for you to be walking even though the autumn weather is delectable and there is no one in the way. So up you climb onto the pedicab and down you sit, looking at the nape of his neck as the cab rumbles along in and out of potholes.

I was on my way to Varanasi Junction railway-station to book a sleeper on the night train to Gorakhpur, and I doubt if I could have done it without my pedicab driver's help. He took me on visits to three different offices, all far from each other, and at the last of them the clerk had run out of paper. So nothing could be done until he had obtained a further supply of that quite valuable commodity, which had to be signed for in accordance with the regulations.

Having reached this point I might even then have lost my place at the window, since no one had told me that it was not enough just to ask for a reservation and pay for it. One had first to fill in a form stating what one wanted, and sign the form and hand it in before anything could be done, and I had not such a form. But luckily a person standing behind me had several and kindly offered me one from his hoard, which I was able to replace when my faithful tricyclist returned from yet another office to which he had gone to get one.

So I paid a hundred and two rupees, a mere £2.50 in my calculations, for the overnight journey and received a green piece of paper in exchange. I hoped it would entitle me to a non-air-conditioned first- class berth on the No. 76 Passenger due to depart at 23.30 hrs. I felt pleased, and I paid my tricyclist well when he dropped me back at the Hotel India in the cantonment. In other words I gave him the equivalent of about 80 p. I then found that I had plenty of time to spare ahead of my late departure.

However, the Hotel India was not at all a bad place to spend it in. At Rs. 175, or less than £4 a night one might have expected it to be rather basic. But that was not at all the case. My excellent room on the ground floor, with ablutions en suite, was a good place in which to relax and plan my onward travels, and the restaurant was clean and tidy, and quite habitable once I had persuaded the waiter to slow down and stop the electric-fan.

I thought I was going to be the only person eating in the restaurant until three Chinese people entered, one a thick-set man of the fields with a huge moon-face and still wearing an enormous peasant hat, the second a woman as thin as a poker in a straight up and down blue denim dress and still wearing her white floppy sun-hat, and the third hatless in white shirt and grey trousers. What could they be doing, I wondered, but visiting Buddhist places? For them the Chinese side of the menu came into play with dumpling soup and noodles. For me it was egg curry, and the egg was a duck's.

I thought, then, of what the Buddha usually ate. The short answer is that he took what people gave him. He and his monks went out with their begging-bowls, to which the pious people contributed with rice and vegetables. Once each bowl was filled with sufficient food for a meal the monks begged no more. The begging round was in the morning and the meal at midday. After that, the monks ate no more on that day. It was enough to keep them alive and healthy, but often not enough for them to take part in tiring manual labour.

Such was the rule, still adhered to in South-east Asia, and such the dependence on the local people that two consequences followed. Firstly, there had to be people near the monastery and secondly they had to be willing to fill the bowls. If the population faded away, or became so impoverished that they could spare nothing, the monastery, called the vihara, had perforce to dwindle too. This may well have been the cause of the disappearance of the viharas in the deserted regions that the Chinese pilgrims visited.

As far as diet is concerned, after he had espoused the Middle Way the Buddha saw no reason for particular austerity. He was perfectly willing to be present at feasts given by prominent people in his honour at which, in the words of the sutras, 'choice food, hard and soft' was served. But there is little doubt that he was a vegetarian, as were all Shamans. So it seems strange to me to speculate as to whether the Buddha's fatal meal at Pava might not have been some sort of pork dish.

As always when in India I followed the vegetarian rule, though ducks' eggs were far from being my favourite food.

When I left the Gup Shup restaurant it was still light. But though the bank next door to the hotel was open, and there were bank-clerks in it, it was too late for business with the public. Yet I felt that I needed more cash for the remote places I intended to visit, where credit-cards or traveller's cheques would be of little use. So one of the bank men helpfully referred me with a nod to the next building along.

Sure enough I had only to walk in that direction for someone to usher me into a bare room on the ground floor. Change a hundred dollars? No problem at all. A stack of one hundred-rupee notes was soon found, and thirty-two of them were handed over to me plus a fifty-rupee note for good measure. Back I went to the hotel to pay my bill.

"I'll pay cash," I said to the receptionist.

"Oh no," said he. "You must use credit-card."

"And what if I haven't got a credit-card?"

"You must be having one credit-card," said he. "You cannot have cash if bank is closed."

"Oh yes, I changed some money," said I.

"It is not permitted. Here in Uttar Pradesh it is not allowed."

"Indians pay cash," I said. "Why not me?"

"Well, where is your receipt for money-change? No having money without receipt."

"Oh that," I said. "I think I have it in my room."

So into my room I went and found tucked into one of the pockets of my bag the currency-exchange voucher that I had been given in Delhi.

"Here it is," I said to the receptionist. "I told you I had it."

Whereupon he rather reluctantly accepted my cash, noting down on his copy of my bill the reference number and date of the voucher before giving me my receipt.

I was flustered by these negotiations. I felt that I should have taken the plunge and been travelling like a true pilgrim, bare-foot, sleeping rough with a small cloth bag containing all my necessities. My Sahib's luggage, even though reduced to one modest terrylene bag with a travel-agent's logo splashed across it, still seemed to be too much.

As if to vindicate these thoughts, when I returned to my room I found that I had left my room-key inside it on the other side of the self-locking door. Back at the reception desk I called myself a fool.

"Where is the room-boy?" said he, and as if by magic the room-boy appeared.

I then expected to be back in my room in a matter of seconds. But what the receptionist gave the room-boy was a blue plastic bucket containing about a hundred keys. Some were in bunches on rings, some were separate with labels attached. Some had wooden squares with numbers on them. Some had neither labels nor squares, and others had little brass maps of India attached, no doubt the logo of the hotel, which I had not seen before. Out of this bucket the boy was expected to produce the right key to open my door.

He tried. He tried again and again, looking for keys of convincing size and shape. But not one of them fitted. Other members of the hotel staff joined us, wanting to be helpful and forming a vociferous group that was generous with its advice. I was beginning to despair, imagining No. 76 Passenger pulling out of Varanasi Junction whilst I was still waiting to get into my room.

Then from behind the group came a short, dark man I had seen earlier sweeping the corridor with a grass broom. He plunged his hand into the bucket, pulled out handfuls of keys and let them trickle out between his fingers. There seemed to be no sense in it. But suddenly he stopped, picked one out of his hand which had neither ring nor label nor wooden square attached to it, inserted it into the lock and opened the door instantly. I was amazed. I wanted to give him bakhshish. But when I turned to him to do so I found that he had melted away as silently as he had appeared, like a Boddhisattva doing good without thought of any reward.

Back in my room I got everything ready. It was still early. But thinking that it would be a good thing to get to the train in good time to secure my place, I left the hotel with over an hour to spare. My middle-aged tricyclist had gone, and it was another, younger man who pedalled me through the dark streets. He had a zebra-striped muffler wrapped round his neck against the cold night air and a woolly khaki cap on his head, for it was November and though the days were warm and sunny, the nights were chill. The muffled cyclist took me by back streets that I had not seen before, and landed me up in a very short space of time at the end of a muddy alley, where he expected me to leave him.

"All right," I said. "But where to go?"

"There," he grunted in a creaky, grumbling voice. Leaving me on his pedicab, he disappeared into a grog-shop and I saw him no more.

My bag had wheels. But the wheels were not much good on the rough, rutted ground, across which shapes shrouded in loose, grey-white garments passed and repassed like spirits risen from the dead. Somehow I bumped the bag along. For I had been dumped at the back of the station, and no porters were to be seen until I had crossed two sets of tracks and climbed up and down a bridge.

Then one of the men in red appeared, one of the Indian railway-porters who seem to know far more about the trains, their times and their platforms than the station-officials. This man took me to Platform 3, and there he left me as I was still too early. The train was not standing in the station as I had hoped, since it did not originate in Varanasi. It was coming from Allahabad and was expected to be late.

Every Indian railway-station platform is a village in itself, and Platform 3 was no exception. There were people sitting in family groups in rings round their belongings. There were bodies lying on the platform with sheets pulled right over their heads. There were men in turbans carrying baskets and bundles on their heads, and steadying themselves with stout wooden staves. There were people sucking up tea from little earthenware cups and throwing the cups down on to the line when they had emptied them. And there were the begging poor, since for them there is no question of needing a platform-ticket to get on to the platform.

There was no seat unoccupied, and I did not feel like squatting as others were doing. So I sat on my bag. The wait would have been interminable if it had not been for Mr.Deshpande, newly appointed manager of the Bank of India in Gorakhpur, who seized two wall-seats for us just as they were being vacated and kept me distracted with his conversation.

Mr Deshpande, neat in a glittering brown safari-suit, had left his family behind in Benares and for the time being was occupying bachelor accommodation in Gorakhpur. He complained of poor pay and lack of pension, and offered me any assistance I might need there. Meanwhile it became known that the platform had been changed because the train was running late. So once more a porter was summoned, not for Mr Deshpande, who only had a small attaché-case, but for me, and off we went over the bridge to Platform 6, where eventually the train crept in.

Most Indian trains are immensely long, twelve to sixteen or even twenty coaches being not uncommon, and they travel immensely long distances of a thousand miles or more. In comparison the night train to Gorakhpur was quite short, as was the distance to be covered. Even so, there were heads peering out of glassless windows and bodies leaning out of doorways far along the platform, and I relied entirely on my porter and Mr Deshpande to find me the right place. Find it they did, and they also found that the first-class coach was practically empty. I went into a two-berth compartment expecting Mr Deshpande to join me. But at that point he disappeared and I was left alone, reflecting that I need not have gone through all the bother of making a reservation after all.

In this I was wrong. No ticket without reservation is the rule, as the conductor explained to me before leaving me to settle down for the night in a room that looked like an iron cell and certainly dated back to the days of the Raj. I was glad I had brought my pocket-torch, since the light-switches had no protective cover whatever and consequently a misplaced finger would have ended up on the live wires.

The train slid out of the station incredibly slowly. It went slowly enough for some passengers to leap back on to it again from the platform and for others to pay platform-vendors for their tea and samusas. I thought it would soon pick up speed. But it never did, and when it might have done so on the lonely single-track line in the early hours of the morning, it went even more slowly because of fog.

I did not sleep well. I had no bedding, and it was cold. What has all this to do with the Buddha? I thought as I woke, or rather failed to sleep for the fiftieth time and the train lurched to a halt with nothing but a black void outside the windows.

Then I saw the lights. There were hundreds of spots of light, of fire flickering in the darkness as the Buddha lights are said to flicker on Omei mountain in China. The fog lifted a little, and the bigger lights showed women dressed in scarlet saris, sitting by small fires with saucered candles around them in amongst the whitewashed masonry of memorial shrines. And there was a thin sound of music, like a tune played with tissue-paper on a comb, which came from rustic pipes.

A monk who later befriended me told me what these women must have been doing. It was the auspicious sixth of the month Shathi, perhaps a kind of halloween, and they had cut their children's hair and were laying it on the graves for their prosperity. In the grey of the late dawn we came to a station called Deoria, where I saw girls chewing sticks of sugar-cane, which they also do on this particular occasion. A blind man tapped the windows of my compartment with a stick, offering his tin begging-bowl, and this also was the way of the Buddha.

In due course, long after our scheduled time, the train reached Gorakhpur Cantonment, where a railway official, who had been travelling in the compartment next to mine, kindly stopped me getting out. Indeed I might have got down on to the platform if it had not slowly dawned on me, like the slow dawn seeping through the murky window-panes, that I had been on this train before, and that nothing had been done to it in the intervening forty years.

On that occasion I had reached Gorakhpur Junction at the proper time of 5.30 a.m. and my business had been with the Gurkhas and their recruiting depot. This time it was nearly eight o'clock. I was worn out, and when I emerged from the train I was easy meat for a tallish. thin man in a long white shirt with shirt-tails flapping over his knees, who captured me by the simple means of seizing my luggage and striding rapidly away from the train with it.

Of course I was glad to leave the train. But I was hardly happy to trot along behind this ball of fire, who claimed to know exactly what I needed and where I was going. The trouble was that he was right. I was going to Nepal and I did need some transport to get there. It was a fair guess. For now that motor-roads have been built from the Nepalese border at Sunauli to Pokhara and Katmandu, Gorakhpur is a common place of departure for back-packers and other travellers intending to go up into the hills.

It is really a simple matter to walk across the station concourse to the bus-stop and board a bus heading north. But this is not what my captor, Sher Khan, had in mind. He took me across the road and suggested that I should check in at the Raj Hotel (Rs. 60, the equivalent of £1.50 a night). When I objected to this, he took my luggage into the office of Himalayan Travels and Tours (P) Ltd., where a warm-hearted, heavy-eyed gentleman called for tea and told me it would be no problem for him to arrange all my onward travels. In fact he was there just to do that very thing.

"Where you from?" said he. "Germany?"

I was to hear that question a hundred times in the next fortnight, and no one ever suggested that I might be British. It was as if the British had left India never to return.

"No," I said, "And I'm going to Lumbini. What about the Himalaya Hotel in Bhairewa?"

"Why not the Yeti?" he said.

"Why not the Himalaya?"

"Better stay in the Yeti."

"If you say so."

So it was money up front in return for a voucher to stay in the Hotel Yeti for one night and the cost of a telephone-call, with instructions to meet Mr Ajay at the Hotel Manta in Sunauli and the promise of free transportation to be arranged by Mr Ajay from Sunauli to Bhairewa.

"What about a car? No problem. Lumbini, Kushinagara, Piprahawa, Shravasti. Where you want. No problem."

"What about a bus?"

"Not so good for you, I think."

"Never mind. I'll take the bus."

"So. No problem. I fix that for you too."

"Where's the bus-stop?"

"Just here."

I finished my tea, which was brewed the Indian way, the tea and the milk together. A bus appeared.

"Is it this one?" I said.

"Not this one. I will tell you. Why not take car?"

I went to the station restaurant and breakfasted there, the only customer, on toast and tea. When I returned to Himalayan Travels Private Ltd. there was another bus standing outside the office.

"Is it this one?" I asked.

"No problem. I will tell you."

I went over to the bus and asked the driver where he was going.

"Nepal?"

"Yes."

So, against the wishes of Sher Khan, I retrieved my luggage from the office and went and sat in the bus. Sher Khan ran after me.

"You must wait, Uncle," he said.

"I'll wait in the bus," I answered.

"Then no problem. Give me money for keeping the luggage."

I gave him bakhshish. I had not expected to find Muslims in this part of India. But, as I was to discover, there were many, even across the border in Nepal, with their white mosques and minarets decorating the landscape. After all we were not far from Lucknow, the ancestral home of India's Shiite Muslims.

People climbed into the bus in ones and twos. The young bus-boy put my bag on the roof and off we went. But it was only down the street and back again to drum up business with loud blasts on the horn. We returned to the original bus-stop where, just as if we had been waiting only for them, a group of three Austrians plus an Indian guide climbed aboard and moved into a semi-circle round the engine in the front compartment beside the driver. They had plenty of trekking kit, and the bus-boy tried to make them put their baggage on the roof like mine. But he did not succeed. A booking for first-class travel had been made and money had been paid. So the door between us and them was shut, and that was that.

In fact they were more cramped than I was, and the ride did not prove to be as uncomfortable as Sher Khan had told me it would be. The price was Rs. 22, less than 50 p. for the fifty-mile journey, which took nearly three hours because of the frequent stops on the way to pick up and put down passengers. They did not even have to be scheduled stops. You could wave the bus down anywhere and you could ask the driver to put you down anywhere, not infrequently away out in the countryside. At stops in populated areas street-hawkers came forward, even climbing on to the bus if the bus-boy would let them. They tried to sell peanuts, either loose and mixed with a relish of dried onion or done up in a cone of newspaper, which passengers would troublesomely want to inspect before buying. Some biscuit-sellers were forbidden entry. But one peanut-vendor was allowed to travel on the bus to the next stop in return for a handful of nuts.

However, the bananas were the greatest attraction. The banana-sellers, who were mostly girls, were definitely kept outside the bus. The fruit was fresh and succulent in spite of the fact that many of the banana-skins had a mottled, unhealthy look about them. They were sold in bunches. But when I asked for just one I got it and found that it was deliciously fresh and tender. As I ate it I watched the harvested fields go by. Most of the rice was in, and the stalks were being gathered into sheaves. Some of the sugar was still standing and so were some other crops. But sheaves of rice and canes of sugar, and even rice itself, were drying out on the sides of the road, and in some places sugar-canes were actually laid across the road to be crushed by the wheels of lorries and buses.

Having passed the great Gorakhnath temple and emerged from the crowded city, the bus roared steadily down the straight road, slowing only to negotiate the frequent sleeping policeman, quaintly called ripples, which were placed wherever ribbon development had created a populated area. The road ran through noble avenues of ancient trees, which must have been there for hundreds of years. I had been told that these northern parts of Uttar Pradesh and Bihar were impoverished. But the land did not look like that to me. If there was poverty, it was not famine, though the number of mouths to feed constantly increases.

Sitting where I was in the ordinary passengers' front seat, with more leg room than I would have had further back, I became on quite intimate terms with the seventeen-year old bus-boy, not to be confused with the bus-conductor, an older, clerkly man, able to read and write, who was carrying a sheaf of tickets and a money-wallet. It was the bus-boy's job to start and stop the bus, which he did by banging on the loose metal of the passengers' door, and if the driver did not respond to that, by yelling out *chaloji* for 'go' or *rokhiye* for 'stop!' He also had to monkey up on to the roof to fetch or deposit luggage, and to shout at people in the street to persuade them that they wanted to get on the bus, or at people who had got off the bus to talk to friends or to relieve themselves to warn them that the bus was about to start up again, backed up by the driver roaring his engine.

It was a full-time and necessary job. But the conductor was busy too. He had to sell tickets and to record on those tickets how much he owed the passenger if at the moment of sale he did not have sufficient change, for a shortage of small change was always a problem. He also had to record his sales of tickets in a sort of account-book, which took quite a lot of time. Although he left the shouting to the bus-boy, he himself was not idle.

I did not know what to expect at the end of this bus-ride. But I need not have worried. There were pedicab men eager to pedal a white man, and thus hopefully a good payer, across the border with his luggage. They were free to do so. For everybody except obvious foreigners moved freely back and forth. This made me think that the smiling Nepalese immigration official, with his colourful, flowered Bhadgauni topi on his head, was more concerned with a useful source of revenue than the security of his country. I paid £30, or it could have been $40, for a single-entry visa and was waved through the customs. I then headed for the Hotel Manta.

This hotel was only a few yards further up the road. Standing on the left-hand side, it was in a good position in a country that still drives on the left to catch the back-packers and others who intend to go by bus up into the mountains. Mr Ajay was not there. But Jim Parker was. He was a young man from Woking, sometime waiter, would-be actor, who had been drifting about with a friend but had somehow lost him, and was not quite sure what he was going to do next after he had, hopefully, recovered from a bout of Delhi belly.

It was pleasant sitting in the sunshine outside the hotel beside the beer-fridge, and asking and answering the questions everyone puts, 'Where you from? Where you going?' The sun shines, the lady of the house brings cold beer, and if Mr Ajay isn't there it doesn't matter much. But he does come eventually, and he and I crush ourselves into one of the ancient jeeps that ply the road between Sunauli and Bhairewa.

Strictly speaking the correct name of this place is Bhairahawa, though it is as short as Barewa on my 1953 Survey of

India map. But now a significant change has taken place. We are in Lumbini Zone, and the little town, which is the starting-point for the mountain trails, is called Siddharthanagar in honour of the Lord Buddha. I have, indeed, arrived. Mr Ajay, who is a lean, nervously active man, tells me that I cannot go to the Hotel Yeti as it is full.

"I didn't want to go there in the first place," I answer.

"You will go," says he, "to Hotel Himalaya."

"What about the phone-call I paid for?"

"Give me your voucher."

I gave the voucher to him, and at a certain moment he called on the driver of the jeep to stop. Out we got, and a boy dressed in a khaki suit ran up to take my luggage.

I knew nothing then of the Hotel Yeti. But the Hotel Himalayan Inn (P) Ltd. did prove to be a good choice. The bell-boy was the son of a Gurkha officer who lived in Delhi, and he himself hoped to join up when he was old enough, whilst the manager could not have been more helpful in getting me a jeep to visit Lumbini. There was a group of Taiwanese at dinner, and after my own dinner of malai kurma I looked at the stickers on the glass of the restaurant door. One of them in particular caught my attention. It was 'Hyecho Adventure Tours Ltd., Seoul, Korea—To the Holy Land'.

I walked outside. New Road, in which the hotel stood, was just a dusty, straight funnel for the buses and lorries—for the buses to Pokhara, which take four or five hours, and the overnight bus to Katmandu, which had left at 5.30 p.m. and if all went well would reach the capital of Nepal at between 2.30 and 3 a.m., as if anybody would want to be thrown out into the street at that unearthly time. Heavy goods vehicles were pounding along too. One of them had eyes painted on it in front and behind, and on its tailboard were written in English the words, 'Use dipper at night. God bless you!'

Next morning I too went to the Holy Land. There was fog again, and a jersey and windcheater were hardly enough to

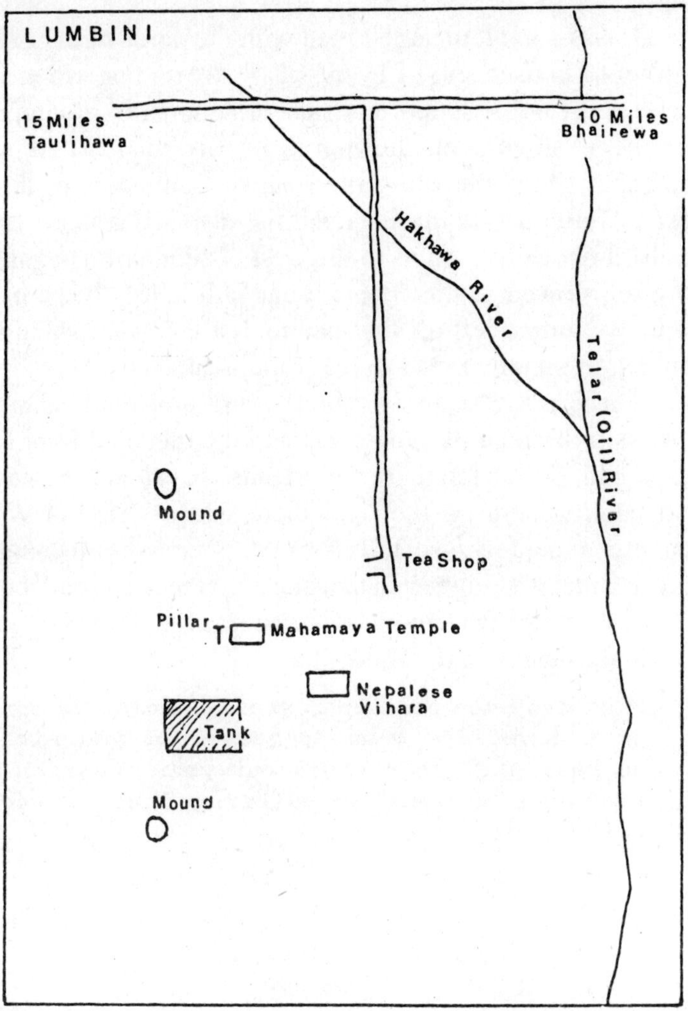
LUMBINI
15 Miles
Taulihawa
10 Miles
Bhairewa
Hakhawa River
Telar (Oil) River
Mound
Tea Shop
Pillar
Mahamaya Temple
Nepalese
Vihara
Tank
Mound

keep out the cold, since the jeep was open to the wind in front, whilst its side-door had to be kept in place by hand. To begin with Dunga Bahadur, my driver, was as dour as the weather. But he gradually thawed to me when I spoke to him in my rusty Nepali.

It was a good metalled road with the name of every little group of houses and of every small stream that we crossed written in English letters on roadside signboards, though none of them tallied with the names on my map. There were frequent signs indicating the road to Lumbini too, though there were no side turnings and the distance was not great, only about twelve miles to the west of Siddharthanagar. But the fog slowed us down, and it had still hardly lifted by the time we turned left off the road to Taulihawa down another stretch of metalled road to reach the sacred site.

Then, as we swerved round a family of ducks that was crossing the road, the fog lifted and the metalled road came to an end. On the left there was a teahouse called the Lumbini Social Club and on the right there was a little hut with a counter and a few postcards for sale. There was no charge to go in. But it was suggested that one might make a contribution to the Lumbini Development Trust, since a placard opposite the hut proclaimed the following:

> Much has been done to restore Lumbini as one of the world's great centres. If you wish to help the great endeavour your contribution can be sent to either office listed below
>
> Lumbini Development Trust
> Lumbini
>
> Lumbini Development Trust
> Katmandu

The master plan for this development was depicted on another placard and, in miniature, on a postcard. It included a circular sacred garden round the Mahadevi temple, the

Ashoka pillar and the Sacred tank, and an avenue called the Central Link leading away from it to a Flame of Eternal Peace, which was already built but not yet lit. Here would be the Lumbini Center, the Cultural Center and tourist accommodation, whilst on the other side of the Central Link there would be the East . Monastic Zone and the West Monastic Zone separated by Lumbini Square, with the little Hakhawa river joining forces with the Telar, the Oil river, in the light of the rising sun to the east.

It was a brave prospect, and work was already under way rebuilding the Mahadevi temple. But I was glad that, so far, little more progress than that had been made. The old name of the place, Rummindei, which had persisted even after it had been pinpointed as being the site of Lumbini, was gone for good. All the same the place still had a rustic, faraway look about it, which the fact that at the time I was the only visitor did nothing to dispel.

At the time of my previous visit, bumping along a rough track from Paklihawa, the recruiting centre for the British Gurkhas close to Bhairahawa, it had seemed like the end of the world, or the beginning, a place of immense calm. There were just the three stupas, the sacred tank, the old Mahadevi temple, the new Nepalese temple and an abandoned ancient steam-roller, which had been called into service to make the way smooth for the Buddha Jayanti celebrations of 1956. I had walked about with the three young Gurkha soldiers I had brought with me, and the saffron-robed bhikshu of the temple, with whom we had speech, had been the only person in sight.

Even quieter must it have been for a thousand years until 1896, when archaeologists were permitted to enter Nepal to investigate the Ashoka pillar which was re-erected at that time. It was found to have an inscription on it which was written in the Brahmi script that had fortunately been deciphered fifty-nine years before.

The language of the inscription is Magadhi, named after Magadha, the kingdom to the south of the Ganges with its capital at Patna, which became the nucleus of Ashoka's vast empire. Thus Magadhi, by the time of Ashoka, had grown in importance to become the lingua franca of that part of the world, or the Hindustani of the time. It was the language that was most widely understood by the common people. Although the inscription is quite short, it is long enough to convey the following information:

> King Piyadasi, the beloved of the Devas, in the twentieth year of his reign, himself made a royal visit. Shakyamuni Buddha having been born here, a stone railing was built and a stone pillar was erected. The Lord having been born here, Lumbini village was freed of tax and entitled to the eighth part.

Some authorities have offered 'relief' as an alternative reading to 'railing' and it is tempting to think that the stone relief is still in existence as well as the pillar. For although it has been tentatively dated to about the second century CE, the black stone representing Maya holding on to the sal-tree as she gives birth looks so worn down by time that it would not be surprising to be told that it was carved in the pre-Christian era.

This stone relief was the first thing within the sacred area that I was to see, as it had been removed from the precincts of the Mahadevi temple where it had been for many years, and placed in another brick building nearby, so that the modest little temple, which had once looked like a cube of white sugar in shape and colour, could be rebuilt. The relief had been cleaned, and only a vestige of the red paste with which it had been coated by worshippers remained. So it was possible to see that the face of Maya no longer existed at all, and that the surface of the stone was flat from the head to the feet of the figure. But the arm held up above the head was clear enough, as was the stone tracery representing the branches of the tree behind the head.

Next to the ancient relief had been placed a modern version. It was pretty enough. Maya was a wasp-waisted beauty, attended solicitously by her servants, whilst the baby Buddha, already on his feet, had his right arm raised to match his mother's, the hand of which was clinging to a convenient branch. This was the one to which those who must do such things were directed to plaster with their red sindur paste, whilst the venerable statue enjoyed an honourable retirement behind a glass screen.

The difficulty was that a piece of Buddhist lore had been absorbed into the vast Hindu pantheon, and gentle Maya, Maha Maya, or Great Maya to many Buddhists, had been elevated still further to Maha Devi, the Great Goddess, and worshipped as such. Indeed, as the woman in canonical yellow and red showed me, puja was still being offered with flowers and plants and paste to the other unrecognisable objects from the temple connected with childbirth.

If there were three stupas at Lumbini, it would not be an unusual pattern. As it is, only two are clearly visible, one 150 yards to the north of the Mahadevi temple and the other equidistant to the south. Neither appear to have been excavated and both have curiously out-of-place place constructions on them. The one to the south has a circular brick tower on it, which is about ten feet high and has a conical cap. The one to the north has water-tanks placed on top of it, and there is a garage-like store-room gouged into one side of it. Maybe they were not stupas at all, but simply piles of earth.

The third stupa was opposite the pillar. For the temple is on a man-made eminence enclosed in brick walls about ten feet high and then up a further terrace of steps. It was in order to excavate this stupa that the temple had been demolished and was being rebuilt. Excavations have produced additional evidence for a stupa. For it was the custom for pious individuals to erect subsidiary stupas around the main ones like coronas of satellites round a sun, and the bases of such a ring of small stupas have, in fact, been brought to the surface recently.

Facing the stairway leading up to the temple stands the famous pillar. It is an extremely well-preserved example of its kind, except for a split near its base which was observed by the Chinese pilgrim, Hiuen Tsiang when he visited Lumbini in the middle of the seventh century. He said that it was surmounted by a stone horse, which presumably faced the stupa. But although a blackened, bell-shaped capital was discovered by the pillar, the horse has not been found. The stone railing, if that is the correct interpretation of the inscription, is no more. In its place there is a modern iron railing keeping people far enough away from the twenty-foot pillar to prevent them defacing it. I found the railing draped with Buddhist flags.

From here it was only a stone's throw to the temple. But a policeman stopped me walking up the steps to the temple platform because of the work in progress there. It was a necessary precaution. A dozen labourers under the orders of a foreman, but each one adding his own shouts to the foreman's commands, were trying to lift a heavy wooden beam on to the new brick walls to form part of the roof. They tried and failed, recoiled and tried again. In the midst of all the hubbub I would certainly have risked being trampled under foot.

Judging from its size and shape it looked as if the new building was not going to be very different from the old one. Hopefully it would not be long before Mayadevi's image would be back in its rightful place and properly protected there.

It is hard to imagine what the horse might have been looking at from the top of the pillar. The stupa would probably have been of a lower elevation than those vast white hemispheres that we can see today in the Nepal Valley, in Sri Lanka, in Thailand and in Myanmar. But it is unlikely to have been finished simply in bare brick. The brick surface would quite likely have been enclosed in a plaster of lime cement. Then surely there would have been some kind of monument at the apex of the stupa, perhaps built of brick, perhaps of wood, but probably not of stone. Building in stone was rare in the plains of India before the current era.

I went to the other side of the sacred tank and inspected a great tree, which had been conscripted into the service of religion, for the spirits of the trees and snakes existed even before the Buddha. In the alcove between two buttresses of its roots three shelves had been built. On the broadest of them, at ground-level, there was the standing bust of a baby which, in the context, must surely represent the Buddha. On the next shelf, in what one person examining my photograph told me looked like a television-set, there was a reclining golden figure. Surely this was the Buddha child, for legend tells us that, as her pregnancy advanced, Maya's body became transparent and the child could be seen distinctly in her womb like an image in a crystal casket. But on the top shelf the image was so plastered with red paste that it was impossible to tell what it represented.

Clearly, however, it was all connected with the cult of Mahamaya or Mahadevi. The noticeboard says, 'Sacred Tank. Mahadevi bathed here before giving birth to Buddha.' And Hiuen Tsiang says, 'Lumbini is on the bank of the River Telar where an Ashokan pillar with a split in it, the Mayadevi temple, the Sacred tank and a few stupas are situated.'

So at the time of the Chinese pilgrim's visit the temple was already there, though Mahadevi was still known as Mayadevi. Now there are the Nepalese and Tibetan temples as well. In the grounds of the Nepalese temple there is a memorial to 'Shree Darmaloka Mahashavir 1890-1967 CE, who dedicated his life to the renovation of Lumbini and establishing the Theravada school of Buddhism in Nepal.'

The eyes on the tower of the Nepalese temple gaze at you as you pass, and the curl between the eyes looks like a question-mark. Indeed, some questions will never be answered. For instance, to what does the 'eighth part' refer in the inscription on the pillar? Some have seen it as a tithe of an eighth of the produce of the village instead of the usual quarter. But this is not freedom from taxes. Is it the eighth part of the Buddha's remains? If that were the case, the remains must have been amongst those redistributed by Ashoka, and there may still be an urn to be discovered under the Mahadevi temple.

3

The Home – Kapilavastu

The year of birth of the Buddha has been much discussed. The earliest surviving records were written several hundred years after his decease, and the evidence is not unanimous. This is why some European scholars have proposed the year 566 BCE for that great event, two generations later than the date that is established in South-east Asia.

They arrive at this figure by referring to the date of accession to the throne of the great Buddhist Emperor of India, Ashoka, which appears to have taken place in 268 BCE. Two Sri Lankan chronicles state that Ashoka became Emperor two hundred and eighteen years after the Buddha's decease, which would thus have been in the year 486 BCE. We also know that he was eighty years old when he died, which brings us to 566 BCE for his birth.

Nevertheless the year 624 BCE has prevailed, bringing us to 544 BCE for the year of the Great Decease and 1956 of the Common Era for the 2,500th anniversary of that notable happening. In that year the Buddha Jayanti celebrations were both heartfelt and widespread throughout East Asia.

After giving birth Maya did not continue her journey to the parental home at Devadaha, but returned to her husband in Kapilavastu with the child. Three days later a sage named Asita inspected the baby, and on the basis of certain marks on

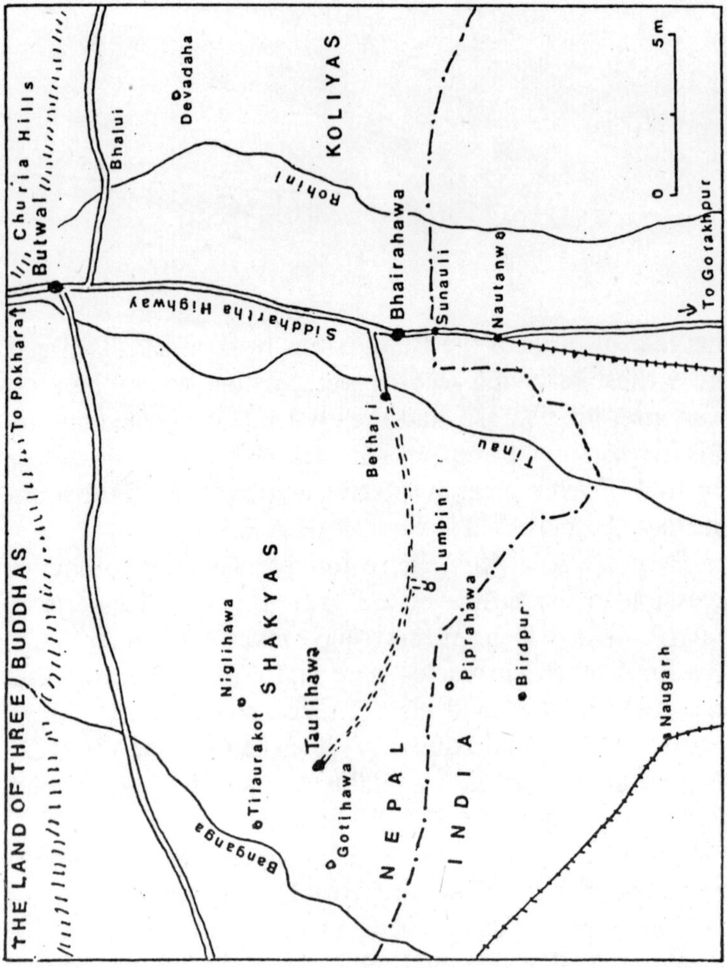
THE LAND OF THREE BUDDHAS
Churia Hills
Butwal
To Pokhara
Bhalui
Devadaha
KOLIYAS
Rohini
Siddhartha Highway
Bhairahawa
Sunauli
Nautanwa
To Gorakhpur
0
5 m
Bethari
Tinau
Lumbini
SHAKYAS
Niglihawa
Taulihawa
Tilaurakot
Gotihawa
Banganga
NEPAL
INDIA
Piprahawa
Birdpur
Naugarh

his body foretold a future for him as a Buddha. Old Asita wept to think that he would die without the chance of witnessing this supreme occurrence. But like St. Simeon seeing the infant Jesus, he rejoiced that his eyes had seen the Lord.

Four days later the Brahmin priests performed the naming ceremony and called the child Siddhartha. They also prophesied a marvellous future for him. But they were unable to specify whether it would be in the spiritual field or as a mighty king, a *Chakravartin*, he who turns the wheel.

However, all this did little for Maya except to give her a sense of awe at having produced such a wonderful child. On the same day, seven days after she had given birth to him, she died. Pajapati, Maya's younger sister and Shuddhodana's second wife, took over the role of mother to the infant. She had recently given birth to a boy, who was named Nanda. So the two boys became like twins to her.

Yet at home in Kapilavastu Raja Shuddhodana was not at all keen on having a Buddha for a son. He was a kshatriya of the martial class and he wanted his sons to be true to that class as well. So young Siddhartha was brought up as a kshatriya and taught the martial arts, such as archery. He married a courtly lady named Yashodhara whom he won, according to some accounts, in a test of skill at arms against rival suitors. She bore him a son called Rahula.

This was the kind of life the Buddha-to-be led until he was twenty- nine years old. And it was led almost exclusively within the town of Kapilavastu, since he was actively discouraged from going out of the city-gates into the wide world.

After the visit to Lumbini I intended to go to the site of the Kapilavastu which lies within the borders of Nepal. But first I was curious to see what remains of the Devadaha, or Devdah as the locals call it, to which Maya did not return. As the capital of the Koliyas it must have been a place of some note.

The fog still persisted as my driver and I drove northwards along the road the truckers take to Katmandu or Pokhara. No mountains were visible, and at that stage one could have been forgiven for thinking that the vast Indian plain would go on for ever, even into Nepal. But thirty miles on, at Butwal, wooded hills emerged from the mist ahead, the foothills that lie like a backdrop to the Buddha's homeland.

The roads divide in Butwal at the statue of King Mahendra in a crown plumed with bird of paradise feathers arching backwards over the royal head. Straight on to Pokhara on the Siddhartha Highway, but turn right for Katmandu along the broad Mahendra Highway, which runs the whole length of the country through fields and forests in the low lands. After the muddle of India it is fine, neat country with rice-fields endlessly irrigated by the waters from the hills, producing two or three crops a year, or great sal forests where once the tiger roamed.

Three miles from Butwal and just short of a place called Bhalui we reached the river which, unlike many, such as the Gandaki and the Rapti, has not changed its name in the last two thousand five hundred years. It is the Rohini, noted in the Buddha story as the line dividing the Shakyas from the Koliyas.

This very same river was cited in verse when, after the Buddha had renounced the palace life, his father sent emissaries to him to try to persuade him to return home:

This is the delightful season.
  Neither too hot it is, nor yet too cold.
Let Koliyas and Shakyas see you
  Cross the Rohini on the westward road.

The river was running between low cliffs of yellowish clay. Its width could be judged from the span of the cantilever bridge, which is 31.40 metres long according to a notice at the roadside, and it looked as though at this point, emerging from the hills, it had never changed its course as the Rapti and

Gandaki had done. But when a river is in spate it is hard to tell exactly what it will do. A short distance downstream there once stood one of the most famous and considerable of the Buddhist stupas. It was the Ramagrama stupa, which contained the Koliyas' portion of the Buddha's bodily relics and was seen by the Chinese pilgrim, Hiuen Tsiang although by that time the surrounding countryside was deserted. According to tradition it had been guarded by a Naga king, but was subsequently washed away by flood waters so that little remains today.

Driving slowly, eyes alert to look for lanes leading off to the right, we went beyond Bhalui for three miles until our attention was rewarded by the sight of a small wooden sign tacked to a tree, which said 'Devadaha 3 km'.

It proved not to be the most direct route, since a smaller river, the Bhairimai Khola, lay between us and our destination, if what we eventually found was indeed what I was looking for. However, there was a ford which we were able to negotiate, followed by a planked bridge scarcely wide enough for our wheels, which was soon to be replaced by a new bridge, already built but with as yet no approach road.

The village that we reached at the T junction on the other side of the bridge was called Pipraya, abbreviated from the Piprahiya that appears on my map, a sheet that is now unobtainable at the Sales Office of the Survey of India in Delhi as it is classed as restricted for reasons of national security.

It was a school holiday, and as usual there was a student standing about who was prepared to help us on our way. His name was Krishna Prasad Prajuli. A teenager in the second year of secondary school, he came with us to the next village, where the most prominent landmark was a large, white rectangular building which was, in fact, his school.

The name of the village was Kerwani, also marked on the map I was not supposed to possess. But of Devadaha there was little to see. Alongside the school some rectangular sections, now flooded had been dug out, and beyond the village there was an area of grass-covered hummocks which looked to me to be worth investigation if that had not already been done.

But the claim of Kerwani to be built on the site of ancient Devadaha is really contained inside the roughly circular fence that encloses the rustic holy places. Of these there are two. One is a more or less open four-sided pavilion which contains a gilded cobra, a representation of the Naga spirit. The other is a more enclosed shrine with only one doorway, which is the temple of Bhawani Mata, that is the Mother of the Blessed Lady.

Clearly the grandmother of Shakyamuni Buddha is intended. The picture is reinforced by the temple treasures. They are stone figures carved in the same black basalt as the ancient relief of Maya giving birth that can be seen at Lumbini. Inside the building there are two standing figures facing the door, with several smaller figures on either side, the stone splashed here and there with worshippers' red. Outside there are much the same number of figures in high relief ranged against the wall on either side of the door.

What these figures portray it is hard to tell. But certainly they are far from being village work, and there is no reason why they should not date back to high antiquity, when Devadaha was still a significant town. That has all changed. But outside the town there has probably been little change in the manner of life, except for the use of donkey engines to drive the threshing machines that husk the rice.

The people are Tharu, who have a resistance to the malignant form of malaria called the *aul*, for which these regions of the Terai were once notorious. They are probably not descended from the Koliyas since the Chinese pilgrim, Hiuen Tsiang, noted that the region was practically deserted when he visited the Ramagrama stupa. It could be that malaria had taken its toll and people were unwilling to risk repopulating an area that was known for its 'bad air'.

That was a pity since the land I saw was abundantly fertile, well watered and now ably managed. As soon as one crop of rice or mustard is raised another is planted. Krishna Prasad took me to his house to meet his father, a man who did not look old, but whose bristles on his chin were already white. I was given tea in a metal beaker and shown the fields behind the house, the small vegetable plot and the great pile of rice straw, ten feet high, that would be used to feed the three buffaloes and two cows, the great providers of milk.

After a few minutes a girl came walking down the track with a huge load of rice-straw on her back. "That is my sister," Krishna Prasad said. "She carries. I read."

Indeed, he did read, even Japanese from a book left, no doubt, by some searcher after the Buddha's tracks like myself. He also showed me some money he had been given, banknotes from Singapore and from the Lebanon. So I, myself, gave him a United States dollar, which my driver carefully inspected to make sure that I had not mistaken it for a hundred dollar bill.

However, the money that interested me was a coin shown to my by the miller who lived on the other side of the track. It was a copper coin three-quarters of an inch in diameter and not far short of a quarter of an inch thick. On one side there was a figure mounted on an elephant, and on the other an almost obscured standing figure with no discernible inscription. Surely the coin was old, but strangely enough the copper was not in any way discoloured.

The pop-pop of the donkey-engines of the millers faded into the distance as we returned to the main road by the more direct route. My mind formed a picture of the life of the Koliyas, hardly different from that of the Shakyas. It consisted of a town of no great size surrounded by a flat countryside with scattered villages,cut into sections by the rivers flowing down from the jungle-clad hills. In the town there would be a modest royal palace, which would be occupied by the elected raja and his family, and a wooden moot-hall such as the Anglo-Saxons maintained in England in their time, but in India called a darbar hall. Such a one can still be seen in the neighbourhood today.

The next day I set out with Dunga Bahadur for the Nepalese Kapilavastu to see for myself, as far as it was possible after more than two thousand five hundred years, what the young Buddha's home may have been like. My driver had now fixed a piece of green plastic flex to the frame of his jeep to save me the trouble of continually hanging on to the door. With this he tied me in, the only drawback being that he had to run round and untie it whenever I wanted to get out and walk about.

Beyond the turn-off to Lumbini the road to Taulihawa degenerated into a rough track, which was good enough for jeeps and buses but shattering for the rare cars. However, the sun was shining, bright-blue or grey kingfishers were darting about, and men and women with huge bundles of rice-straw on their heads were walking in single file along the road, prepared to scurry off it onto the verge at the sound of our approach.

Taulihawa is one of the many *hawas* in this part of the Terai. The word *hawa* means 'air' in modern Hindi. But in this case it signifies an enclosed place, a yard, as it were, as in 'farmyard', and is probably cognate with the old English word *haw*.

But this particular hawa, like Bhairahawa, has been differently described. In the past it was abbreviated to Tauliya with or without 'Kot' added to it, which also means an enclosed and protected place. On the other hand the actual site of ancient Kapilavastu is now referred to as Tilaura Kot, though the name is not recorded on my Survey of India map.

In any case after we had bumped along for fifteen miles from the Lumbini turning I was left in no doubt that we had reached the town. Painted on the wall of the house that faced us as we turned into the busy main street were the words, 'Welcome to Taulihawa. San Miguel beer. One of the world's best beers'.

Shortly after that we passed under one of those white archways of Himalayan peaks that the Nepalese like to construct for visiting royalty to pass under. Possibly Taulihawa itself will be named Kapilavastu in the future, since it is now the seat of Kapilavastu District headquarters, which we passed after making a sharp turn to the left. Then, passing the Sunshine English Boarding School and another sign which said, 'Tuborg beer wherever you are', we headed northwards for another couple of miles until we came to the little museum on our left and the track leading to the antiquities on the right.

These antiquities are contained within a rough ellipse about 1,700 feet in diameter from north to south and 1,200 feet from east to west. The circumference is thus a little over a mile, which is a good deal less than Hiuen Tsiang's estimate of fourteen or fifteen Chinese *li* for the city wall. Before the recent excavations were undertaken as a joint venture between the Nepalese and a Japanese team, the whole area was under thick jungle, which had remained there down the ages because of the impossibility of cultivating land that was so cluttered up with building-bricks.

A small Japanese group was just leaving as I arrived, and as soon as they had gone all five custodians of the ruins, dressed in their official khaki tunics and trousers, came forward to help me. I did not need so many. But when the number had been whittled down to one, I came to be very glad of his assistance as he showed me things I would not otherwise have found.

The first thing to be seen was the western gateway, which was close to the entrance leading through the perimeter fence

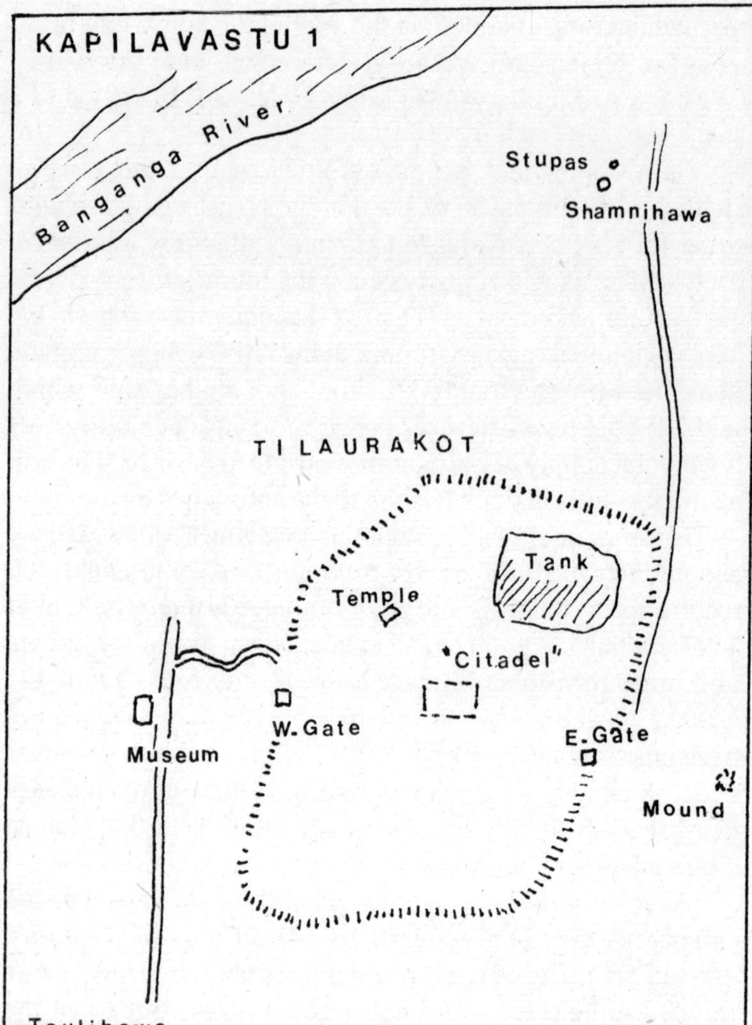
KAPILAVASTU 1
Banganga River
Stupas
Shamnihawa
TILAURAKOT
Tank
Temple
"Citadel"
W. Gate
E. Gate
Museum
Mound
Taulihawa
2 Miles
0
500
1000 ft

and was strangely higher than the present level of the surrounding ground. It was flanked by two brick bastions. From their height it was easy to see the ten-foot wide defensive wall, which once encircled the city, and the depression in the ground left by the twenty-two foot wide moat.

It was less easy to see the nineteen-foot wide road, paved with bricks, which led to the so-called citadel in the middle of the town. The reason was that only sections of it had been cleared of grass and soil. The rest of it was still hidden under foot, parts of it still used as a forest track by the local people, who are supposed to stay outside the perimeter wire but do not always do so.

At the site itself, at the rough centre of the town, the 'Citadel' was more cautiously called an 'Ancient Structured Complex'. An area of about a hundred yards square had been cleared, some brick flooring had been uncovered and brick walls a few inches high had been pretty well restored. One brick had the actual imprint of a foot on it, which must have been made before the brick was baked.

There were four gates to this town, which had clearly been carefully planned, one at each of the cardinal points of the compass. But only the western and eastern gateways, on opposite sides of the central complex, have so far been excavated.

I found the eastern gateway, which is the one furthest from the entrance, the more interesting simply because it was the more evocative. It is known in the story of the Buddha as the Mahabhinishkramana Dwara because it is the gateway through which he left Kapilavastu and the worldly life of his youth in what is known as the Great Renunciation.

It is similar to the western gateway, and similar objects to those discovered in and around the western gateway were discovered there. They included terracotta human and animal figurines, coins, beads, bangles, sherds of painted grey pottery and northern black polished pottery, and a seal with an inscription on it written in the Brahmi script, which is the same script as Ashoka used on his proclamatory pillars.

Opposite this gateway, and some might say significantly about two hundred yards to the east of it, there stands amongst the rice-fields a hillock with bushes and trees on it which can hardly be anything other than an as yet unexcavated stupa.

There seemed to be no point in trudging over the fields to this hillock. But there was a good reason for taking the path northwards from the eastern gateway, which runs alongside and outside the perimeter fence. The custodian who had become my guide told me that in that direction lay the stupa that actually had been excavated.

We skirted the edge of the jungle, surprising a troop of red-bottomed monkeys that had been gleaning in the nearby rice-field. They scampered back into the trees, all except the male leader of the troop, who remained on guard and ambled slowly back into the woods only when we got quite close to him.

For about half a mile we stepped softly along the grassy track amongst the rice-fields in the sunny not hot, not cold stillness, passing ancient trees and a woman who gave me the *namaste* greeting as we went by. Ahead lay a longish thatched, white-walled farmhouse. But before we reached it my guide pointed to the stupa on our left.

It was a large circular, brick structure some twenty-five feet across and gently rising to about six feet above ground level at the centre, where an indentation in the brickwork probably marked the setting for some kind of monument. Being used to the great hemispherical stupas of Katmandu and Sri Lanka, I was rather disappointed. But stupas exist in a great variety of shapes and sizes, the only common feature being that, apart from square plinths and sometimes square towers, they are nearly all circular.

Stupas also used to be referred to under a variety of names. The Pali word *tope* was often used instead of *stupa* and is still frequently used in writing about the famous Sanchi Tope. In the north they were called *chortens* and in the south they were described as *dagobas*. But nowadays these memorial monuments, whether they contain the ashes or relics of the great deceased or not, are all usually referred to as stupas, using the Sanskrit word for them irrespective of their architecture.

As my guide and I walked round and on and about this low-lying stupa and a small satellite stupa nearby, a little group of farmers, weatherbeaten men and women, gathered to see what we were up to. We discussed the stupas, and the custodian told me what these local inhabitants must have known perfectly well, that there are five ruins in the vicinity of Kapilavastu which have been identified as stupas.

They are the two stupas that we had been looking at, the unexcavated one that I had seen to the east of the eastern gateway, another at Dehrahawa to the west, and a fifth not far away at a place called Chatrakot. Apart from the two at Shamnihawa, where we were standing, none of them have so far been excavated.

As well as the five stupas there are five pillars, or vestiges of pillars in the locality, which are commonly attributed to Ashoka. One of them is at Niglihawa three miles north of Kapilavastu, and another is at Gotihawa six miles to the south. The Niglihawa pillar that I saw in photographs is lying at about a sixty-degree angle to the surface of the earth, with an unknown length buried below the surface. and only about five feet above the ground. The inscription is said to refer to Kanakamuni Buddha.

The pillar at Gotihawa has been excavated to a considerable depth and appears to refer to Karakuchanda Buddha who, like Kanakamuni, is one of the three Buddhas who are said to have appeared in our own era before the time of Shakyamuni. It used to have a shapeless, roughly circular stone on top of it, which is now on the verandah of the little museum but hardly seems, in fact, to bear any relation to it.

All this evidence appears to lend strength to those who identify Tilaura Kot with Kapilavastu. Furthermore the Chinese monk, Fa Hien, who travelled in India between 399 and 414 CE, says that Kapilavastu lay less than a *yojana* to the east of the birthplace of Kanakamuni Buddha, and that less than a *yojana* to the south of that was the birthplace of Karakuchanda Buddha.

If a *yojana* is reckoned to be the equivalent of six to seven miles, these distances would fit some of the stupas quite well, though Fa Hien does also tell us that the stupas were erected at the places where these earlier Buddhas were said to have attained nirvana as well as where they were born. A particular place called Nabigha is mentioned as the birthplace of Karakuchanda Buddha. This cannot now be located. But the distance he gives us of twelve *yojanas*, or about seventy miles, from Shravasti would fit Tilaura Kot very well, except that the south-easterly direction that Fa Hien gives would be more appropriate to the site just across the border, where the Indians have their own Kapilavastu, in which they believe equally strongly.

Meanwhile the good folk of Taulihawa and Kapilavastu District in Nepal claim all five Buddhas—the three earlier ones of the current era, the Mahabhadra Kalpa, including Kashyapa as well as Karakuchanda and Kanakamuni, Shakyamuni Buddha and the future Buddha, who they confidently expect to appear in the same region.

In any case the Kapilavastu in which our Buddha was brought up, was destroyed in his own lifetime. It is said that Prasenajit, King of Koshala, sought the hand in marriage of the daughter of one of the Shakya noblemen. But the Shakyas despised him for being outside their clan and sent him a slave-girl instead. The king remained ignorant of their deceit, and in due course the son of this union, named Virudhaka, became king in his turn. But the Shakyas knew about it, and when Virudhaka went to visit them they called him a base-born fellow. Whereupon he became so enraged at the insult that he went back to Shravasti and sent his army to sack the town.

When Fa Hien went to Kapilavastu over eight hundred years later he found the area desolate. 'The country of Kapilavastu,' he says in James Legge's translation from the Chinese, 'is a great scene of empty desolation. The inhabitants are few and far between. On the roads people have to be on their guard against white elephants and lions, and should not travel incautiously'.

It is interesting to note that lions were still roaming the plains of India at that time in a region that later became famous for its tigers, and that white elephants were not so rare as they are today. Fa Hien says that in Kapilavastu 'there was neither king nor people. All was mounds and desolation. Of inhabitants there were only some monks and a score or two of families of the common people. At the spot where stood the old palace of King Shuddhodana there have been made images of the prince, his eldest son, and his mother. And at the places where that son appeared mounted on a white elephant when he entered his mother's womb, and where he turned his carriage round on seeing the sick man after he had gone out of the city by the eastern gate, topes (i.e. stupas) have been erected.'

When I read the last sentence of this passage there immediately came into my mind a photographic image of the hillock that I had seen in the midst of the rice-fields to the east of the Gate of the Great Renunciation. For the story is well-known. The Buddha-to-be became increasingly satiated and discontented with his life of pleasure and restricted existence within the city. So one day he managed to get out of it.

It was then that he saw the sick man and realised that life had its sufferings as well as its delights. He saw a blind man and a dead man too, and all three sights made such a profound impression on him that he found it impossible to carry on with his carefree style of life any more.

Fa Hien also states, adding the fabulous to the believable, that 'the places were also pointed out where the Rishi Asita inspected the marks of Buddhaship on the body of the heir-apparent; where, when he was in company with Nanda and others, on the elephant being struck down and drawn on one side, he tossed it away.'

This is a reference to an elephant that the Lichhavis of Vaishali sent to the young Siddhartha. His cousin, Devadatta, killed it out of jealousy, and his half-brother, Nanda, found the carcase blocking one of the gateways of the city. When Siddhartha saw the body of the elephant he picked it up by its tail and threw it over several fences and ditches, creating a great dent in the ground where it fell.

This Herculean miracle is only one of several which, Fa Hien tells us, provided the focal interest of the spots where they were said to have occurred. In another superhuman feat the Buddha-to-be shot an arrow a distance of thirty *li*, which would be about four miles, and at the point where it struck the ground a spring gushed forth, which was turned into a well to quench the thirst of travellers. Evidently the locations of these miracles were still being shown to pilgrims in the Chinese monk's time. It was the well or river for which Kim's lama went searching up and down India.

The Chinese pilgrim, Hiuen Tsiang, who visited India after Fa Hien in the seventh century, confirms that the towns of the Shakya country had been destroyed and were deserted. He says that there were ten deserted cities in the Kapilavastu country, but they cannot be identified today with any confidence. He allocates to the Shakya people a territory of 4,000 *li* in circumference. That would be about 600 miles at six or seven *li* to the mile, which is the reckoning that seems to accord best with Hiuen Tsiang's own calculations.

However, there are many uncertainties in trying to locate places from the evidence of the Chinese pilgrims, in particular Fa Hien, who visited India in the fourth century of our era, and Hiuen Tsiang, who went there in the seventh century, and it may well be asked why we have to place such reliance on the evidence of these Chinese visitors. For it is hard to believe that no accounts of the places they visited ever existed in the Indian languages.

The short answer is that such accounts probably did exist. Hiuen Tsiang refers several times to 'The Records of India'. But such was the ruthless barbarity of the conquest of Middle India by the Moslem fundamentalists that the manuscripts went up in flames along with the Buddhist cultural centres. So the accusation often voiced by nineteenth century scholars in the West that ancient Indians had no idea of historical perspective or factual description may well be quite unfounded.

This is why we have to find evidence for the wonderful great days of Indian Buddhism in Chincse, Tibetan and even Sri Lankan records. It is the latter, which western scholars began studying when Sri Lanka was still the British colony of Ceylon, that have been the most important in presenting the picture of Buddhism that was once pre-eminent in Britain and still prevails though not to the same exclusive extent.

Sri Lanka was colonised by Aryan people from Northern India at about the same time as the Buddha lived. The Singhalese Great Chronicle states that Vijaya was the leader of the first wave of immigrants. His name simply means 'victory' and the date of his landing on the island has been calculated to have been 543 BCE.

The islanders were converted to Buddhism in the third century BCE by Mahendra, a son, or some say a brother, of Ashoka, and from that time to this day the Singhalese have preserved their old traditions and Buddhist way of life. The Singhalese monks have also preserved their Buddhist literary canon, which was written in Pali, a language which may have been the ancestor of modern Singhalese and is thought to have been the language that the Buddha actually spoke.

Thus it came about that the key facts of Buddhism have appeared under two guises in the West, in Pali and in Sanskrit. Kapilavastu is Kapilavatthu in Pali, Shravasti is Savatthi, Siddhartha is Siddhattha. The Dharma, which is the doctrine of Buddhism, is the Dhamma in Pali, and stupas are topes. These differences in spelling and pronunciation may not appear to be very great. But they have frequently confused people and led them to think that commentators on Buddhist subjects either cannot make their minds up about the spelling or are writing about different things.

It is not clear historically whether Pali preceded or succeeded Sanskrit. But the linguistic evidence certainly points to the latter conclusion. It is not difficult to see, in the above examples, some of the rules for conversion from Sanskrit to Pali.

Pali does not like consonant clusters, like the 'st' in *Shravasti* and in *stupa*. So it drops the 's'. It does not like the 'r' in consonant clusters either. So it drops that too, giving us *Savatthi* instead of *Shravasti* and *Dhamma* instead of *Dharma*. The Sanskrit, to use a linguistic term, has been derhoticised, which means that Pali has lost many 'r' sounds in certain well-defined linguistic circumstances. It is like modern English compared with Middle or Scottish English. The 'r' in many English words like *heart* and *part* is no longer pronounced.

Pali, therefore, was a descendant of early Sanskrit as Italian is the child of Latin. As it was current in the wide realms of Koshala, which covered an area more than twice the size of England, it would have been natural for the Buddha to speak it.

Yet we do not know for certain which language the Buddha spoke in delivering his discourses, though it is a safe guess that it was one of the Indo-European dialects of Northern India, called Prakrits, that had developed from a common ancestor, which was later formalised as literary Sanskrit. In this book I use the Sanskrit version of names wherever possible, and in a transcription which reflects their probable pronunciation. I use, for example, 'Sh' in *Shakya* and *Ashoka* rather than the accented 's' of more scholarly works. This, after all, is what one sees on noticeboards and in other writings, even train timetables, in India today.

The fact that the extant records from before the time of Ashoka are extremely scanty does not help us. But this does not mean that they did not exist, only that they have not survived.

In all probability the Buddha wrote nothing himself. The tradition was for religious teachers to speak out and for their disciples to memorise their sayings. Indeed, one of the most important functions of the monks was to pass on the Buddhist lore orally without altering it, proclaiming the sutras and other works in the murmuring, muttering tones that one can still hear in viharas today.

Yet the people were by no means all illiterate. In fact one account of the Buddha's life states that he learned to write as a boy, using a scratch-marker on sandalwood. Palm-leaves were available then, as they were in more recent times, to make the pages of a book. But they were also perishable.

The literal meaning of the word *sutra* is a thread as in our word 'suture'. It may perhaps indicate the thread joining the palm-leaves together as well as the thread of a discourse. Furthermore the Pali canon was collected in what became known as the *tripitaka*, or 'three baskets'. One might keep a collection of books in a basket but not, I think, an oral tradition.

Frankly, we do not know how soon after the Buddha's death any of his sayings were written down. The earliest Buddhist writings that have come down to us do read like passages that are meant to be learnt by heart. The repetitiveness of the prose and the resonance of the verse are typical. We must also remember the long tradition in India of passing on religious lore and epic poetry orally. It was considered to be a surer, more lasting and simpler way than relying on scribes, and it made the lore available, if such were considered appropriate, to the illiterate majority. Like the Indian storytellers, who relate their stories, word perfect, to the villagers, the Buddhist monks will have declaimed the Buddha's words and the Buddha stories from memories made prodigious by constant repetition.

So it is often said that the words, 'Thus have I heard' which introduce many of the sutras, indicate that they were handed down for many years in a purely oral tradition. Yet 'Thus have I heard' could equally well be an appropriate introduction for a scribe taking down dictation.

These are the sorts of questions that serious students of Buddhist historiography have to face. My task was easier. It was simply to observe and consider what I saw. After looking at the two stupas to the north of Kapilavastu I and my guide went back into the forest to see the vestiges of the large tank which lies inside the northern part of the city wall. It had hardly been touched and was still obscured by undergrowth and a thick covering of lotus-leaves. So it was a difficult feat to imagine Siddhartha bathing there amongst the girls who were thrown his way to try to tie him to the life of pleasure.

This tank, to use the Indian name for such artificial lakes, would have been fed by the Banganga, one of the larger rivers that flow into the Rapti. In the Buddha's time it probably ran closer to Kapilavastu than it does today, keeping the moat full.

Making our way back from the overgrown tank past the 'citadel' we came upon a group of people picnicking outside a small brick building, which proved to be a rustic shrine. There was a man in a blue shirt and a blue-check dhoti, and another in a white shirt with a towel draped round his neck.

There were two women in red saris decorated with gold thread, and there were numerous children—at least ten as far as I could count them.

A third man, the most important of the group, was dressed entirely in white. He was sitting on one of the mats that were placed on the ground, and he had a book in front of him of the traditional kind. It consisted of oblong loose sheets of paper printed from wood blocks and bound together, when not in use, between two wooden boards.

He was the pujari, and his was the task of reading from the scriptures and leading the rites of worship. Beside him were the accessories of his calling. They were laid out in silver chalices and included the red powder to pay homage and mark the foreheads of the congregation, the butter to turn the powder into paste, the leaf-fronds and flower petals, and two of those strange, striated egg-shaped fossil stones called saligrams, which are found in the Gandaki river. They welcomed us amiably enough, and the pujari intoned from the book and blew a mournful note on his conch-shell to attract the attention of the goddess.

One corner of the brick building was built on to the trunk of an aged sal-tree. Its sides and front had niches for statues that were not there. Grass was growing on the roof.

Inside, it was hard to see what the cult objects were, since the larger stone image was almost entirely obscured by festoons of jasmine petals, whilst the smaller stones had thick coatings of red sindur paste on them. But I also saw crude models of animals, and as well as the flowers there were coloured flags hanging down from the ceiling.

"It is Sonemai," my guide said, and the pujari nodded. But who was this Sleeping Mother, There was no clue to that. Yet with the way my thoughts were running I wanted her to be some distant folk memory of Mother Maya. Some call her Somaya Mai.

In the little museum I read that the man-made deposit at Kapilavastu goes down to a depth of nearly ten feet. As at the nine cities of Troy there are nine distinguishable layers of this deposit. Distinct periods covered by these layers have been calculated to be 800 to 300 BCE, 200 to 100 BCE, and 100 to 200 CE. This appears to indicate that Kapilavastu, if such it be, was reoccupied after it had been ravaged by the King of Koshala and continued to be inhabited, on and off, for another six hundred years.

It is recorded that monks were still showing visitors the holy places of the Buddhists in Fa Hien's time. But there are only two Buddha figures in the museum, both of them carved in stone. One is a head, and the other is a seated statue in the pose of the *bhumisparsha mudra*, that is with the right hand lowered to call the earth to witness. They are both only a few inches high. Apart from them there is also an assortment of coins and fragments of pottery, and there are photographs of the royal visit of the King and Queen of Nepal.

Here I said farewell to my self-appointed guide, taking care to give him bakhshish out of sight of the others, and my driver and I left Tilaura Kot. Dunga Bahadur was not in a good mood. Clearly he thought that I had spent longer amongst the ruins than a good tourist should, and he complained that he had not yet had his food.

"Neither have I," I said. "Let's go and look at the pillar at Niglihawa."

He refused, saying it was not in his contract to do so, and I could do nothing about it. He also refused to give a lift to a monk, who was plodding down the road in front of us. He was wearing the regulation three pieces of cloth—the yellow garment with the russet cloth over it and, no doubt, the piece of underwear beneath—and I would have liked to talk to him, as he was the only monk I saw in the vicinity of Kapilavastu. But Dunga Bahadur was like a horse bolting for its stable and could not be stopped.

When I got back to the Himalayan Inn the Taiwanese people had gone. But there were new guests. There was a family who had driven down from the hills—an ex-army Englishman with his Nepalese wife and children. There was a group of six Japanese men and women. And there was Gregor.

Like me, Gregor was on his own. So it was natural that we should come together. When I told him I had just returned from Lumbini, he wanted to know how I had got there and what I thought of the place.

Gregor had the mild Scottish accent of the Western Isles, and the sun had reddened his soft skin into scarlet patches. It had also bleached his fair Celtic hair, which would have hung down in waves to his shoulders if he had followed the fashion of the back-packers. But he was too old for that, already filling out the waist of his trousers and the khaki shirt he wore hanging outside his trousers the Indian way.

As we sat down to eat together I told him a fair-skinned man like him ought to wear a sun-hat. But he hardly noticed my advice.

"Tell me about Lumbini," he insisted. "What's there to see? What were your impressions?"

"It doesn't take long to get there," I said. "And there's not a lot to see. I hope you won't be disappointed."

"I'll never be that," he answered.

"It's very peaceful."

"It must be."

"But what brings you here anyway. Are you a Buddhist?"

"I don't know. I think I am," he said. "I've not studied it much yet. It only started a little while ago."

"What did?"

"It was like this," he said. And then I knew that he had been wanting to tell his tale to a stranger from the moment we met. I studied the long printed menu. He hardly looked at it. "Vegetable curry for me," he said. "I never eat meat now.

Not in India anyway. Well, you wanted to know how I became a Buddhist. It was in Singapore. I used to visit Singapore a lot, and that's where I met the Don. I was representing an English company. Publishing. Books. Specially text-books and school-books. English is still the language there."

I thought of the formula phrase 'Thus have I heard' that starts off so many of the Buddhist Jataka stories, and I settled back to listen.

"His name was Don and people called him Don. But what he liked to be called was The Don, because his full name was Don Alvarez, and actually I don't know whether it was Don short for Donald or Don like a Portuguese Don. Anyway, he was The Don to me, and he bought books from us for his shop, and we became good friends.

"But he never asked me to his home. Well, he could have done. As far as I knew he lived by himself in one of the old houses that hadn't yet been bulldozed to make flats. His wife had left him and gone to Australia, or so he said, and he had a son he never saw. But he was a good talker and we spent a lot of evenings together. He said his own family lived in Madeira. Wine people. You know, those flat bottles like flasks. He'd tell me which to drink and which was rubbish. I believed him. Of course I wanted to believe him. That was the point. There was Adelina.

"Adelina Wong Tsze Ting worked in a bank. But she helped Don with his accounts as well. And now you're going to say she was his girl. But that wasn't quite true. Or I thought it wasn't. I wanted to think it wasn't. Adelina lived with her parents and brothers in a small flat in Ang Mo Kio. That's one of the new towns they built. High-rise flats. But not like ours at home. The Chinese manage to live peacefully in those rabbit warrens.

"I never went to her place. I was in a hotel of course. The Royal. Not too expensive but one of the best. Nice swimming-pool, and Adelina was a great swimmer. Breast-stroke, backstroke, dog-paddle, butterfly, you name it she did it. So the thing was to come to my room after work, have a swim and then go out to dinner. You could eat at the Royal, of course. But we liked to go down to the seaside and eat baked crabs at Pasir Panjang, or maybe baby squid on the East Coast, or oysters down by the Padang."

As we sat waiting for Ram, our little, slow waiter, to bring us our vegetable curry, I thought I saw an unbuddhistic mist come over Gregor's eyes as he contemplated the seafood delights of Singapore.

"The Don," Gregor began again. "The Don. See, I'm still calling him The Don when he was really plain Donald. Don didn't run a car and always insisted on paying the taxi hire. It was impossible to stop him. It was often hard to pay for a meal too. Why's he so generous? I thought. He must love me. But what does it matter? He likes to do it. I was the big man from the UK. And well, he was in books. That was the link between us. He was writing a series of books himself. New ideas for learning English.

"Adelina's English wasn't bad either. She'd learnt it at the Salvation Army. But sometimes her pronunciation let her down. It could be a big laugh. One day we all went to the races. 'You go to be' with me?' she says. Big laugh. She meant 'bet' not 'bed'. So she giggles and hides her face. I liked that.

"It's all done on the word-processor," The Don said. He showed me some sheets of his book for adult learners. 'You read it. Tell me what you think. It's all programmed. Programmed learning.'

"I said it looked good. It had to be good because my mind was on Adelina. We were all in my room together. Adelina and I had been swimming. The Don not. He just liked to sit under a pool umbrella watching us. 'She's into dancing too,' says The Don. And sure enough she comes out of the bathroom with nothing on and starts to dance.

"That was it for me. The Don says he's going downstairs for a coffee and leaves us to it. After that I wanted her again. She liked me. I liked to think that. But she wouldn't make a date. It was the three of us together as before, laughing and joking but me looking at her and always thinking when's going to be the next time. And every time they'd drop me off at the Royal and then he'd drop her back at her family flat and go on back home alone, so he said.

"And then the books he'd written. I didn't think they were much good. But I didn't say so. I didn't want to upset him. So I said the opposite. And one day Adelina said, yes, she would go on a weekend with me, and we went off to one of the islands across the Straits. Tropical paradise. After that there didn't seem to be any way I could do without her.

"I'd praised The Don's books, and when I went back to London I took them with me. I could have told him they wouldn't publish. But I didn't. I was thinking of Adelina and the hold he had over her. Like Svengali. I was going to break it. Well, by now I thought she loved me.

"After three months I went to Singapore again. I'd already booked a trip to Bali for the two of us. I didn't tell The Don. This was just arranged between Adelina and me writing letters to each other. But when I got to Singapore and phoned her up from the Royal she wouldn't see me. Just kept making excuses. I was wild. I saw The Don again. He didn't mention his books, just made excuses for Adelina. When he looked straight at me I thought he was enjoying himself.

"Yes, I was wild, and he knew it. I phoned her up, wrote her letters, reread the letters she'd written to me. No good. Like the books. She was doing what he wanted, I was sure of it now. True the books had been turned down. But I thought we were all friends and it wasn't so important. She had written love letters to me. I raged about it, couldn't sleep, guts twisted, tight jaw, you name it.

"Then one day I was out near one of the Buddhist temples and I saw people going in and out. So I went in too. It was midday and it was cool in there. And there was the Buddha at the other end of the hall. All gold. Sitting with his hands one on the other. And laughing.

"He was really only smiling. He wasn't one of those pot-bellied laughing Buddhas. But to me his expression seemed to be laughing. I kept looking and then I started laughing too. People turned to look at me and smiled. I laughed my head off and I went on laughing in the street outside the temple. And that was the beginning."

"And then?" I asked.

"I knew I was just like a hungry ghost."

"And that's how you came to be here?"

"I wanted to see where it all began. And I had a dream too. I was in the middle of the ocean. Rough sea. I was struggling not to drown. She was in it too. Not helping. Holding my arms tight. Then the laugh. The sea went smooth, and I was swimming. But not on the level. I was swimming downhill to the beach. Imagine that. Swimming downhill!"

That swimming downhill seemed to have impressed Gregor even more than the laughing Buddha.

"You won't see a lot at Lumbini," I said. "But it'll mean a lot. You can take my sun-hat if you like."

4

The Great Renunciation – Piprahawa

After the Buddha-to-be had seen the sick man, the blind man and the corpse of the dead man, he became more concerned than ever about the nature of life, and more perturbed than ever before about the way he was living his own life. The reaction of Raja Shuddhodana was to redouble the pleasures that were offered to him. But this did not stop him meeting a monk in the vicinity, who convinced him that a change in his life was inevitable.

In our age of kinks and perversions and pleasure in violence the pleasures of Siddhartha Gautama appear to have been rather innocent. Frolicking with the dancing-girls would seem to sum them up—an activity that was perhaps not accidentally in direct opposition to the ascetic ideal of the monkish life.

We can see it all on the greatest picture gallery in stone that has ever been created or is ever likely to be built. The huge stupa at Borobodur in Central Java, which was restored from a ruinous condition less than twenty years ago, has the whole of the Buddha's life, up to the moment when he preached his first sermon, illustrated on it in a hundred and twenty stone reliefs. They follow the legend related in the Lalitavistara, which was probably composed in the first century BCE. Here we see the typically generous-bosomed, broad-hipped Indian dancers trying to beguile Siddhartha, and here too we see what follows.

One night after an evening of song and dance, everyone fell asleep—everyone, that is, except for Siddhartha. He remained awake, his mind deeply disturbed by the apparent pointlessness and futility of life, and by the problems of suffering and death symbolised by the three unfortunates that he had seen. Peering at the dancing-girls, he found them lying asleep in ungainly postures, legs apart, arms flung all ways, hair awry, snoring. It is a picture that would not unduly worry a modern devotee of orgies. But to the young nobleman it was one of utmost ugliness.

Siddhartha's mind was made up. He sought out his charioteer and told him to saddle his horse. Then he went to see his wife, Yashodhara, and his son, Rahula. In what is perhaps the most poignant moment of the whole story he had it in mind to say goodbye to them. But they were both asleep and did not awake in his presence. Sadly he left them undisturbed.

Then, in the middle of the night, he left Kapilavastu by the eastern gate riding his white horse, Kanthaka, and accompanied by his charioteer, Chandaka. We can read about this in the Mahabhinishkrama Sutra. He left at midnight. There was a full moon and a clear sky. So he found no difficulty in riding off into the night. There is no mention of a second horse. So Chandaka must have run along with him. Indeed in some portrayals he is shown hanging on to the horse's tail.

At dawn Siddhartha stopped, dismounted and sent his horse back to Kapilavastu with his charioteer. The scene has been portrayed many times in paint and stone, not least at Borobodur. In the hallowed scene the poor horse, Kanthaka, is so overcome with grief that he hangs his head far enough for his muzzle to touch the ground. This is the truly great renunciation, the cavalier parting from his trusty steed. Some say that it was not long before Kanthaka died.

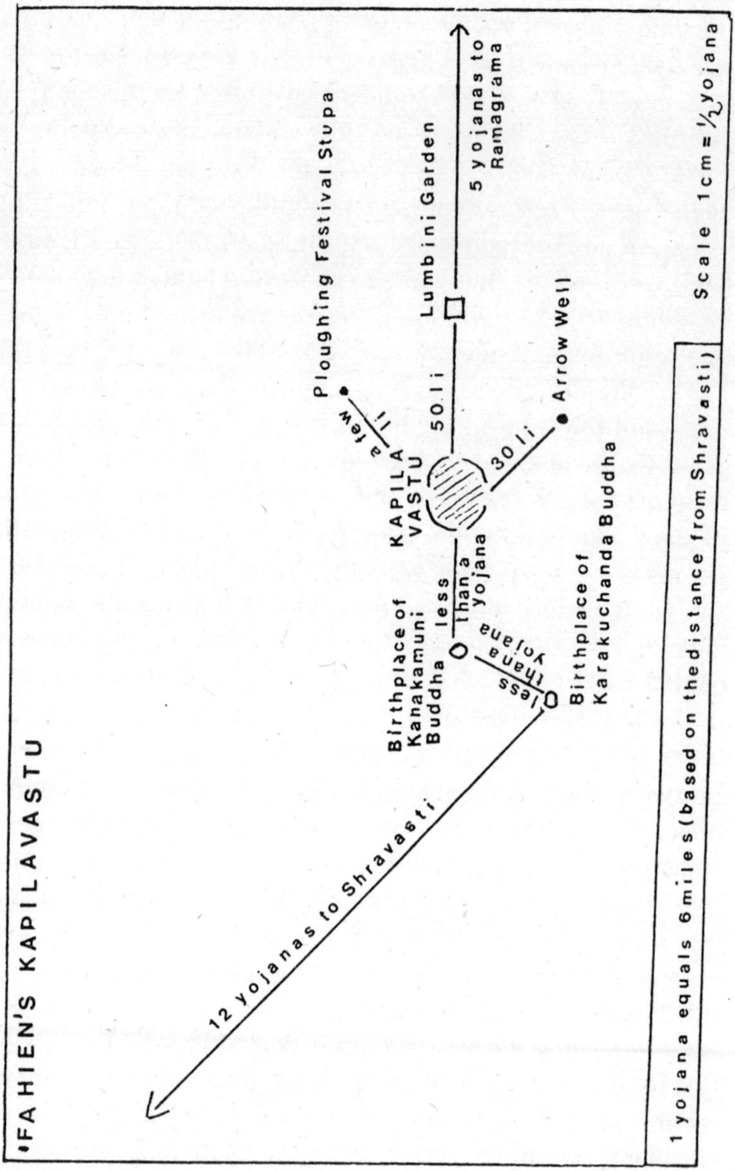
FAHIEN'S KAPILAVASTU
Ploughing Festival Stupa
a few li
KAPILA VASTU
50 li
Lumbini Garden
5 yojanas to Ramagrama
30 li
Arrow Well
less than a yojana
Birthplace of Kanakamuni Buddha
less than a yojana
Birthplace of Karakuchanda Buddha
12 yojanas to Shravasti
1 yojana equals 6 miles (based on the distance from Shravasti)
Scale 1 cm = 1/2 yojana

We are told that this farewell took place beside the River Anoma. It is not certain where this was. But if it was at dawn next morning, five or six hours after they had left the city, unless there was superhuman intervention it could not have been at any great distance from Kapilavastu with Chandaka running behind Siddhartha on foot.

It is hardly to be doubted that they were heading east or south-east since, after sending back his horse and groom, Siddhartha carried on in a south-easterly direction until he reached the country of Magadha. Piprahawa, the place I went to see next, lies nine miles south-south-east of Tilaura Kot, the Nepalese Kapilavastu.

It should have been a simple matter for Dunga Bahadur to drive me there from Taulihawa. If all went well we might have reached the place in half an hour. The Piprahawa site is so close to the frontier that the village of Pipra is shown on my map as actually being inside Nepal.

But unfortunately this was not possible. The road that crosses the border at that point, such as it is, does not constitute a recognised route, and no facilities exist there for entry into or exit from either country. Naturally the frontier there is hardly a barrier for the local people, who live similar lives on either side of it. But a foreigner in a vehicle cannot behave in the same way. At the very least, if he were to try to cross the frontier at that place and got away with it, he would be wrong-footed with regard to entry and exit stamps on his passport. In any case, I could not imagine Dunga Bahadur being willing to try it on for me.

So there I was back in the Himalayan Inn wondering how best to get to the Indian Kapilavastu, which is Piprahawa. Would I have to back-track to Gorakhpur? Could I catch the puffer-train on the metre gauge line to Nautanwa and carry on from there? After seeing one of the line's stalwart little steam locomotives pulling a train northwards on the section

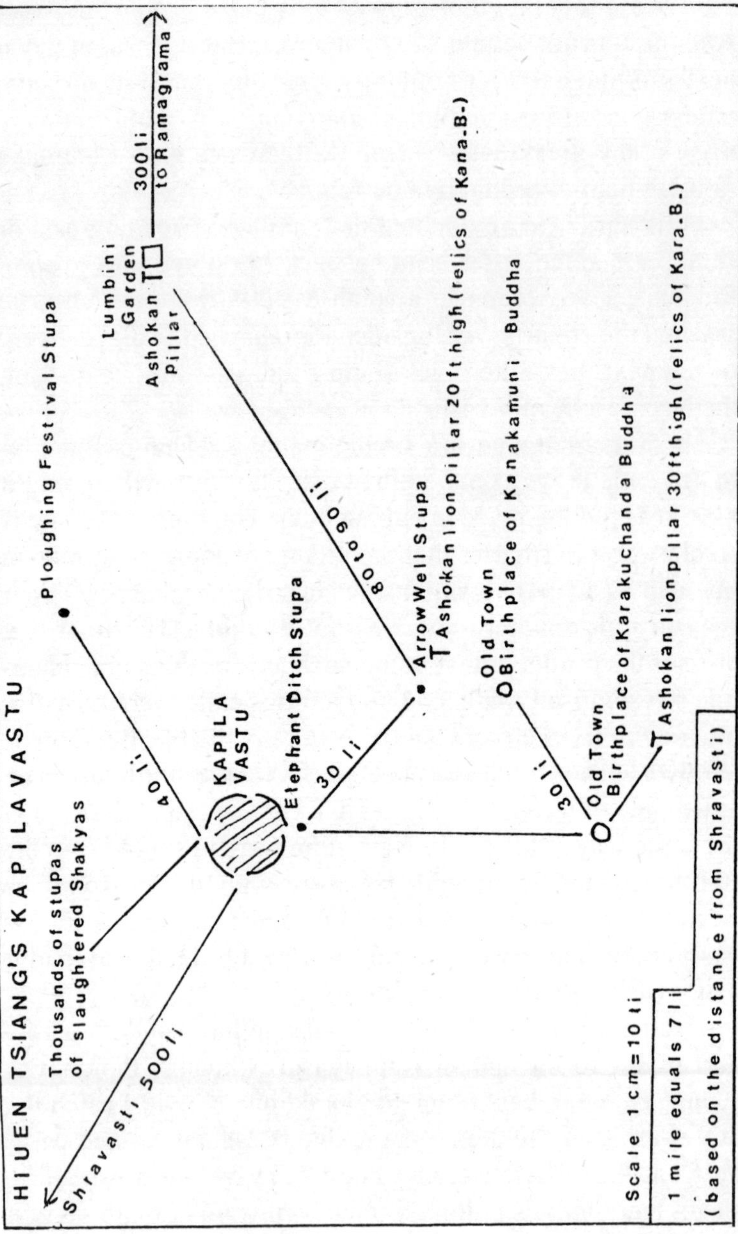
HIUEN TSIANG'S KAPILAVASTU
Thousands of stupas
of slaughtered Shakyas
Shravasti 500 li
40 li
Ploughing Festival Stupa
KAPILA
VASTU
Elephant Ditch Stupa
30 li
Arrow Well Stupa
Ashokan lion pillar 20 ft high (relics of Kana.-B.)
80 to 90 li
Lumbini
Garden
Ashokan
Pillar
300 li
to Ramagrama
Old Town
Birthplace of Kanakamuni Buddha
30 li
Old Town
Birthplace of Karakuchanda Buddha
Ashokan lion pillar 30 ft high (relics of Kara.B.)
Scale 1 cm=10 li
1 mile equals 7 li
(based on the distance from Shravasti)

where the line runs parallel with the road to Nepal, I was quite keen to do this.

But the difficulties loomed large in my mind. After changing trains at Pharenda to get on to the Gorakhpur-Gonda loop of the former Oudh and Tirhut Railway, would I get off at Bridgmangunj or Naugarh, and would I be able to get transport at either of these places if I did? Nobody I spoke to knew the times of the trains, how long they would take, or whether they would be so crowded that it would be impossible to get on one.

"No problem," said the manager of the hotel. "I can arrange car for you. Wait one minute."

It took longer than that of course. But soon after nine o'clock in the morning a Sikh, who was dubbed the Sirdar, appeared with an Indian Suzuki land-rover type vehicle called a Maruti. In the bargaining process I had reduced the price of hiring it from two thousand Nepalese rupees to one thousand five hundred Indian rupees, realising only later that it was really no reduction at all Once again money had to be paid up front, this time not to the Sirdar and certainly not to the driver but to the hotel-manager who had arranged the deal.

This was all the same to me. But the question became 'Where would I end up that night?' We telephoned the Nepalese frontier-post and were informed that I would not be allowed into the country a second time on my single-entry visa, even though I had only obtained the visa a couple of days ago.

"So that's that," I said. "I'll stay on the Indian side."

Back at the border the Sirdar got out of the car on the Nepalese side and disappeared into the Punjabi restaurant next to the Niranjana hotel, which I assumed was named after the river that flows past the place of the Buddha's enlightenment. However, Sunauli, the name of the frontier conurbation, means 'golden', and how that nondescript, straggling conglomeration, too big for a village and too small for a town, ever got such an elegant name it is hard to tell.

After negotiating the frontier-posts my driver stopped again. "What for?" I asked. "One minute," he said. And five minutes later a thick-set, bustling man emerged from an alleyway and joined us. At first I thought he was a man going our way who had made a private arrangement with my driver, and I was prepared to get annoyed. But he turned out to be the owner of the vehicle, and quite naturally one of the first things he said to me was, "How much you pay?"

Having nothing to hide I told him. Now it was he who got annoyed, not with me but with the Sirdar. "He only give me six hundred," he said. "I do it for eight hundred all day no problem."

Of course the trick was that I had already paid. So off we went, as by now it was clear that he was going to come with us, and soon we were quite a happy trio. A few miles down the road we stopped for refreshment at a roadside teahouse, and the drinking of the tea and the eating of squashy, round white cakes made of rice and milk seemed to forge a friendly bond between us.

I knew the road as far as Nautanwa, the railhead. This was also a hamlet that had become a town of perhaps ten to twenty thousand inhabitants but still behaved as if it were an over-sized village. After Nautanwa we turned right to pass through a place called Lotan and another called Muhara, skirting the border of Nepal where it dips southward in the loop made by a small river.

So we drove on in the endless way of Indian roads, which always seem longer than they actually are. There were pigs and their piglets, which had to be eased off the tarmac, clearly not in Moslem country, and there was rice-straw and even rice-grain thrown across the road to dry out. We stopped several times at check-points to pay tolls, five rupees a time, and we stopped once beside a lake which had on it a flock of brilliantly white heron-like egrets.

"Photograph," said my friend Dirba, and like a good tourist I complied. But most of the time he was making calculations about the cost of petrol and time, and telling me how cheaply he might extend the hire of his car for me to continue my journey to other places, even as far as Shravasti.

I should have listened to him. But his pressurising put me off. In his jersey of dark blue, red, white and green bands he looked too much like a hustler, and I felt that he would simply be pushing me to get a move on all the time.

We turned right at Birdpur which, like Bridgmangunj, Campiergunj and even Forbesgunj must have been named after one of the old opium, indigo or sugar planters. But Mr Peppe it was who had owned the estate a few miles north of Birdpur, on which the Piprahawa stupa is located.

Mr Peppe decided to excavate this stupa and in doing so he found, in January 1898, the important reliquary urn which is part of the Indian claim to possess the authentic Kapilavastu. There is a photograph in *Buddhist India* by T. W. Rhys Davids, published in 1903, which shows the stupa after Peppe and his men had been at work. Called in *Buddhist India* a tope, the stupa looks like a great pile of brick rubble with a few trees growing actually on it and a deep trench gouged right through the middle of it.

The picture is very different today, since there was quite recently a complete restoration of the stupa. One would also have to go a long way to see the urn, which was soon removed to the Calcutta museum, whilst the ashes found in it were presented much later to the King of Thailand.

The lid of this famous urn was found to be inscribed with words which translate as, 'This urn for the relics of the exalted Buddha is the donation of the Shakyas, his bothers and sisters, their sons and wives.' It is still the oldest Buddhist inscription to have been discovered anywhere, and as is the way with such writings, the precise meaning of it has been much disputed.

The inscribed urn, with its relics of bone and ashes, was one of five vases found in the stupa, and the inscription was not easy to decipher, which may account for the fact that different sources give different versions of the text. Firstly, it was written in the Brahmi script, which was current at the time, and not in the Nagri of classical Sanskrit. Secondly, the consonants were roughly written, whilst many of the vowels were not written at all. The long vowels were expressed as signs hanging on to the consonants, as is the case with a number of the vowels of the Hindi script that is current today.

However, the urn was an object of the greatest interest to students of the historical Buddha, as not only did it provide the earliest epigraphic evidence to come to light, but it also appeared to pin down the home of the Shakyas to that particular place. It was known from the literature that, after the Buddha's death at Kushinagara, his bones and ashes were divided into eight portions, which were distributed amongst the peoples who had been involved in his ministry and had accepted his message. Each portion was buried in a stupa. But only two of them have so far been discovered, one at Piprahawa and the other at at Vaishali. So it was with considerable anticipation that I looked forward to seeing what this renowned stupa and its surroundings actually look like today.

After we had passed Birdpur I did not have long to wait. There was a broad new road built with Japanese help, and fifty miles from Sunauli we came upon the Buddhist flag, On the right stood the Piprahawa Guest-house, a government project that was not yet open, and on the left there was a signboard saying, 'Piprahawa. Ancient Kapilavastu. Stupa which yielded the corporeal relics of Lord Buddha'.

This signboard was on the right of the entrance to the antiquities. On the left of the gate there was another sign which said, 'Warm reception to the coming tourist at

Kapilavastu, Birth-Liew (sic) of Lord Buddha on behalf of Siddharth Ideal School, Manager Wazid A. Khan. Add. Dharmpur - Birdpur No 7, Kapilavastu, Siddharth Nagar (U.P.)'.

How Mr Khan had been allowed to erect his erroneous advertisement there, I do not know, and I did not stop to enquire, as the stupa was directly in front of me up a gradual incline within the Archaeological Department's fence. I thought of the photograph in Buddhist India and tried to see the stupa as it had been before Mr Peppe got to work.

It was impossible. The general elevation was the same. But there the resemblance ceased. The lower course, up to a height of about four feet, had become a square instead of a circle, and the upper, circular parts had been recreated as a series of concentric rings diminishing in height as well as in circumference towards the top. The sides of the square were about a hundred feet long. But the height of the stupa was only about twenty feet.

So although this stupa was a good deal larger than the restored stupa at the Nepalese Kapilavastu, its elevation was in roughly the same proportion to its base. I wondered how firm the evidence had been on which the reconstruction had been undertaken. And this was not without reason, for some of the rebuilding that has been and is being done at a number of the sites is based on the flimsiest of indications found on the ground.

Yet the intermingled dark and light-red brick, amongst which it was hard to tell the new from the old, gave the stupa an attractive, dappled appearance which blended well with the surrounding grassland of rough pasture. And rough it was—rough enough to be simply waiting for further excavation.

Meanwhile it was good to see the work that had been done so far. The stupa is not the only thing to be seen within the large square enclosure. On the right, on the way up to the stupa, there is a large oblong complex, bigger than the stupa itself, which is some two hundred yards long with brick flooring in parts and brick walls up to four feet high, which suggest the cells of a monastic court. Its most unusual feature is a square, brick-lined pit about thirty feet wide and the same depth, divided at the bottom into two sections.

As I was peering into this hole three young schoolboys, smartly dressed in tunic-suits with rubber flip-flop sandals on their feet, came up to me and started a conversation with the usual question, "Where you from?"

They were some of Mr Khan's students on holiday for the day, and one of them, named Mobarak, said he was learning Farsi, the language of the Persians. But he could not speak it. They offered me some specks of burnt, blackened grain, which they wanted me to believe had been retrieved from the ground after a lapse of about 2,500 years.

However, they laughed when I refused the gift, and followed me whilst I looked at the other sights. On either side of the stupa, to the north and south of it and also to the west of it, other ruins, more or less circular in shape, had been uncovered and tidied up. They appear to be the remains of smaller, subsidiary stupas. Some distance to the east and close to the perimeter wire, there is another rectangular complex.

I spent some time at this eastern edge of the antiquities, distanced from the boys and from would-be guides. There was a mango-grove to the north of the remains of the brick building, and in the centre of the grove I found a circular brick well about five feet across and filled with earth to within two feet of the surface. But there were bricks breaking the surface of the ground in scattered places all over the enclosure, many of them crumbled under foot. Indeed, at some vulnerable points of the restored buildings, such as the edges of pathways and the corners of walls, even new bricks had been knocked about.

The white-clad custodian gave me two visitors-books to sign, and after that my driver, Bhagwan, and I drove the few hundred yards to the frontier-post, where Dirba had already gone to talk to a friend. We found him with Police-inspector Narendra Shukla, who was in his office dispensing rough justice in a land dispute.

The office had an earth floor, a thatched roof and sides open from a height of about two feet so that, in the hot weather, the room would be open to every available breeze. Inspector Shukla was seated at a table addressing a grizzled peasant who had a group of three or four people with him. Beside the low wall stood his Enfield motor-cycle with a tool-box that was decorated with a pair of lips and the words, 'Don't kiss'.

"A woman has been left a widow," he explained, "and this man is claiming the land."

He did not tell me what his judgement was. But it seemed to be accepted respectfully by the elderly plaintiff. Documents were signed and handed over, and tea was ordered.

"Is there much crime around here?" I asked the Inspector, thinking of tales I had heard of atrocities in North Bihar.

"No crime," said he. "The whole district is peaceful and happy in the Lord Buddha."

Then he told me that there was, in fact, a way to get to Taulihawa without going back to Sunauli. You had to go back along the Birdpur road, carry on in the direction of Naugarh, then turn right for Chilia and from there head north again for the border crossing.

It was too late for me to take advantage of this new information. So I was anxious to leave in order to go and look at more of Piprahawa before Dirba got impatient and decided that it was time to go. But I felt obliged to wait for the tea, which was a long time coming. Then Inspector Shukla decided that he would come with us, as he himself was ready to go back to Birdpur.

It was good that he did so. Otherwise it would have been easy to miss the way, as neither Dirba nor Bḥagwan had any clear idea of where the second site was. Or perhaps the truth was that they just wanted to get back home without waiting about any longer.

In fact it was on the same side of the road as the stupa, but further back from it, and one had to go along a brick road for about a quarter of a mile, which would have been motorable by our Maruti if workmen had not been in the middle of repairing and rebuilding the culverts that carried it over several small gullies. The bricks were definitely not old. They had been manufactured by the Swastik Brick Company in one of the many brickyards that were to be seen whenever one drove about the countryside. For bricks it has to be. There is absolutely no stone in the plains of India. So if stone is required for building or for statuary, it has to be brought from elsewhere at considerable expense.

'Garwaria Mahal. Ancient Kapilavastu. Where Shakya Palaces are exposed'.

Thus announced the signboard, and up the road through the rice-fields in open grassland like that of the stupa site, I saw a large complex of brickwork on a slight elevation. But first, on the right, the track passed a large square enclosure with walls up to about four feet high and a well inside it, which was very like the supposed monastery court near the stupa.

The 'palace' in this part of Kapilavastu 2, as it is now often called, is a great deal larger than the 'citadel' in Kapilavastu 1. The difficulty is that the layout of this palace is just the same as that of the monastery court that I had already seen and of those that I was to see later at Nalanda. In this case the walled enclosure is about a hundred and fifty feet square with outer walls rising to some twenty feet above the ground. Inside the enclosure there are twenty-eight rooms, or perhaps cells, with walls five feet thick and eight feet high, one of which was being rebuilt as I watched.

Well, perhaps palaces were like that in the Buddha's day. But the evidence from writings and from works of art such as the reliefs found on the railings and gateways of the Bharhut stupa in Central India gives a rather different picture. Typically a raja's palace would have an outer court with perhaps two inner courts, one for public audience and the other for private recreation. Between them there would be a building of two or more storeys. The upper storey would be smaller than the lower one so that there would be a terrace on which it would be possible to walk or sit. In addition, in a republic such as that of the Shakyas there would be a moot-hall, in which the leaders of the community would debate long and hard until they reached a consensus on the right course of action to take.

The 'palace' at Garwaria is surrounded by mounds of brick rubble covering at least as large an expanse as the stupa site. The uncultivated grassland stretches into the distance, showing that Kapilavastu 2 must have been a good deal larger than Kapilavastu 1.

I picked up two fragments of northern black polished pottery before responding to Dirba's shout and gestures pointing out the path for me to take to leave the site. On the way back three young children, girls this time, offered me little black grains in their little brown hands, as the boys had done. Again I refused to take them, and they laughed, telling me to give them money anyway.

Going back in the Maruti I pondered the problem of the Kapilavastus. If one takes the logical view that the stupa site and the palace site at Piprahawa are two parts of a whole, Kapilavastu 2 must have been, at some stage of its life, much bigger than Kapilavastu 1. So what is the sense in regarding Tilaura Kot as Kapilavastu rather than, for example, one of the other eight 'cities' of the Shakyas that are named in the Buddhist texts. They are both practically equidistant from Lumbini, where the birth took place.

The sense appears to lie in the gateways of Kapilavastu 1 that have been excavated, the central complex big enough for a modest palace, the city wall and the stupas, both excavated and unexcavated. The question of the city wall of Kapilavastu 2 has not yet been properly addressed, and a lot more excavation to trace the city plan has to be done before the claim for it to have been the Buddha's home town can be proven. I myself am not yet convinced that a palace really has been found.

Yet the inscribed urn that was discovered two years after the inscription on the pillar at Lumbini was recorded, is strong evidence that Kapilavastu 2 was indeed the capital of the Shakyas at the time of the Buddha's death or not long after it. Furthermore, during the the final investigation of the stupa before the trench was filled in and it was rebuilt in the early 1970s two more urns containing bones were discovered, and in the same period some terracotta plaques and the lid of a vase were found during the partial restoration of the ruined monastery beside the stupa. Inscriptions on the plaques referred to Kapilavastu by name.

The monastery there appears to have been built in the second century of our era: But the stupa was found to have two skins, an outer skin having been built to enclose the original one. It was within the original skin that the seven vases or urns were discovered, five by Mr Peppe and two in 1972.

In any case the fact that Kapilavastu was sacked by the King of Koshala during the Buddha's own lifetime has led to a convenient way of settling the claims of both sides. It is possible to say that both Tilaura Kot and Piprahawa were the Buddha's Kapilavastu. Yet we can see clearly what Kapilavastu 1 might have looked like in the Buddha's time, but not Kapilavastu 2, where most of what we see today probably belongs to later centuries. Looking at it another way, we have to admit that the tradition that Piprahawa had been

Kapilavastu must have been a powerful one to encourage such great monastic activity there, even if it is only the monastic remains that we are so far able to see.

Indeed, although much has been done to rediscover the locations of the places of the classic Buddhist pilgrimage, many are still in doubt. But a hundred and fifty years ago, in the middle of the nineteenth century, none at all were known with any certainty. Thus it was still possible in 1854 for an Oxford professor to read a paper to the members of the Royal Asiatic Society in London maintaining that the supposed life of the Buddha was a myth and the 'Buddha himself merely an imaginary being'.

It was only after the travel books of the Chinese pilgrims, Fa Hien and Hiuen Tsiang, had been translated into French and English that serious attempts to pinpoint these places on the map of India became possible. This was because it was the usual custom of these pilgrims to give the distance and direction of each place from the previous one as they progressed. Fa Hien used *yojanas*, one to six or seven miles, and Hiuen Tsiang used *li* at six or seven to the mile.

Buddhist Records of the Western World, containing translations by Samuel Beal of both pilgrims' travels, was published in 1884, closely followed in 1886 by *A Record of Buddhistic Kingdoms*, which was James Legge's annotated translation of Fa Hien's book. But clearly General Alexander Cunningham had access to Beal's work previous to those dates as he relied heavily on it in writing *The Ancient Geography of India*, which was published in 1871. He also had access to Julien's *Houen Thsang* which was a French version. But unfortunately he did not have access to the Ashoka pillar at Lumbini, which indicates the Buddha's birthplace beyond reasonable doubt, or the stone marking the birthplace of the Buddha that was discovered in 1994 during the excavations under the Mahadevi temple that were under way at the time of my visit. Nor had he seen the inscribed vase that was discovered by Mr Peppe at Piprahawa and was described in the *Journal of the Royal Asiatic Society* in 1898.

Without this knowledge Cunningham, who was Director-General of the Archaeological Survey of India from 1871 to 1875, led his reader from Sahet-Mahet, which he correctly surmised to be Shravasti, more south-south-east than south-eastward for five hundred *li*, as stated by Hiuen Tsiang, to propose a place called Nagar, far to the south of the River Rapti, as the site of ancient Kapilavastu. This was more than fifty miles south of the positions of the present two contenders for the honour.

As the birthplace of the Buddha is reported by both pilgrims to have been quite close to Kapilavastu, Cunningham could not have done this if he had known about the inscribed pillar at Lumbini, which was subsequently re-erected by the Nepalese government. But as a consequence he placed Ramagrama, the populous place where the Koliyas had enshrined their share of the remains of the Buddha, about fifteen miles west of Gorakhpur, since Hiuen Tsiang had said that it was three hundred *li* east of Lumbini.

The Anoma River, which the Buddha crossed to abandon the trappings of his princely life, was then equated with a small river called the Aumi, or sometimes merely the Ami, which runs parallel to the Rapti south of Gorakhpur, since the Chinese pilgrim had said that the stupas of the Great Renunciation were a hundred *li* to the east of Ramagrama.

The rediscovery of the undoubted birthplace of the Buddha in 1896 put these calculations out of kilter. With this new information three hundred *li*, say fifty miles, eastward from Lumbini take us beyond the Rohini River and as far as the Little Gandaki.

Now the word 'Anoma' itself, means 'No name' or without name or fame. Some have proposed that the significance of the word is 'nameless' is the sense of illustrious. But 'nameless' as of little account makes better sense. Clearly it was a small river. The legend says that his horse jumped it. Exaggeration perhaps, but the Little Gandaki, in comparison with its big brother, the Sapt Gandaki, then called the Narayani, would be of little account.

A hundred *li*, say seventeen miles, east from Ramagrama on the Rohini River do indeed take us to the Little Gandaki and hereabouts, the Chinese pilgrim tells us, stood the stupas of the Great Renunciation.

There were three. Firstly, there was the stupa marking the spot where the Buddha dismissed his charioteer, named Chandaka or Channa. Secondly, there was the stupa at the point where he had his long hair cut off and his head shaven, and thirdly the stupa where he doffed his princely garments and donned the mendicant's rags.

Japanese people have been searching for the remains of these monuments, so far without success and probably without the benefit of the restricted four inch to the mile map. I suggest that Budhadeh and Chanda between Siswa Bazaar and Nichlaul on the Indian side of thc border might repay investigation. They lie respectively west and east of the present course of the Little Gandaki; and they would satisfy the legend that on that fateful night the Buddha-to-be passed through the territories of three rajas before leaving his horse and charioteer. Thus, starting amongst the Shakyas he got clear of the Koliyas and into the land of the Mallas.

Whilst I was trying to keep my mind clear enough to think about these points, Dirba returned to the attack about hiring his car to carry on to Shravasti.

"You will be at the Maya Hotel tonight," he said. "No problem."

"I'll go by train," I said, thinking of the old steam locomotives. "I'll catch it at Naugarh."

"Train no good," he said. "Very slow. Very too much crowd."

"Never mind," I said. "I shall like the train. I'll get off at Balrampur."

"Much problem for you, I think."

In spite of Dirba's argument Bhagwan did drive us down to Naugarh and we did reach the railway-station. But then my nerve failed me and I had to admit that he was right. I was defeated by the sheer density of the Diwali crowds.

We had forced our way through a seemingly impenetrable grey-white mass of people down a seemingly endless rutted lane on the far side of Naugarh, which could hardly be called a road, and we had at last arrived at the station approach, over which a stucco Buddha presided. I had then got out of the Maruti and peeped into the station, where I had seen not an inch of empty floor-space either in the station-hall or on the platform. So I had seen no chance of getting a ticket, not that that mattered much, or of finding out what time the Kapilavastu Express was expected, or of getting on it when it did arrive, or of knowing at what time of night it was likely to reach Balrampur.

So I surrendered, but not to the extent of continuing for another hundred miles to Shravasti in the Maruti. We went back to Sunauli, where Dirba took me to the hotel owned by his brother. It was called the Sanju Lodge, and it was up the alleyway from which he had emerged when I first saw him.

I think I had the best room in that hotel for the equivalent of less than a pound. It was on the third floor, above the general level of flies and mosquitoes, and it had a good outlook over the roofs of lower dwellings and into the countryside. Doors gave access to these roofs, on which there was domestic activity that could never have been seen from down below. Women hung their washing there, men smoked, children played hopscotch.

My bedding ration was one sheet, one pillow-case and one blanket. But I had a shower and toilet-room en suite which, according to the Sanju Lodge representative's visiting-card, was 'Attached Bath Room with Running Hot & Cold Water'. The water certainly did run. In fact I could not stop it running, and whenever anyone used the wash-basin in the living-room outside my bedroom waste water from there ran in my shower-room too. But it was not hot.

Dinner was a casual meal. You ordered it for a particular time. But the cook had no watch and was not particular about preparing it for that time. Back-packers appeared in twos and threes. There were some New Zealanders, who were worried about a girl in their group who had had to return to Katmandu to straighten out a problem with the expiry date of her visitor's visa. There was an Australian couple and there was a young man from Germany. It could have been a youth hostel, since they all kipped in a unisex dormitory, in which the beds were so close together that it would have been hard to drop a guide-book between them.

The Sanju Lodge 'Behind the Indian Immigration Office, Sonauli, Dist. Maharajganj' also claimed to have 'Prompt Room Services' and 'Neat and Clean Room'. I can vouch for that too. The room was neat because there was nothing in it except the bed, and it was cleaned, in return for bakhshish, by a nearly naked man the colour of old mahogany and dressed in a simple loin-cloth, who worked over it with a bunch of grass. The room-boy, too, was ever eager to run errands for a few rupees, and it was only with difficulty that I dissuaded him from bringing my vegetable curry to my room, for it is characteristic of Indian gentlemen that many of them prefer to eat in private.

But I did not avail myself of 'Bus and Train Ticket With Reservation From Sonauli To All Over India And Nepal' or of 'Car & Bus Reservation To All Over India & Nepal', although Mr Sarush, the manager, did his best to persuade me to do so. I went back to Gorakhpur the way I had come, by going down to the bus-stop next morning and getting on to a bus.

5

Fasting near to Death – Uruvilva

Siddhartha's Great Renunciation of the life of pleasure and attachment led him to a mango-grove near a village called by some Anapiya. It has not been rediscovered. Here he spent a week coming to terms with his new life as a *shaman* before setting out in a south-easterly direction.

Nowadays a *shaman* is thought of by many as being a Siberian or even a North American medicine-man. But the word is Indian, *Shaman* or *Shramana*, as the Buddhist texts show. They survive in Nepal to this day, not necessarily wandering mendicants but men who are considered to have closer than normal contact with the spirit world.

We are not told clearly why Siddhartha chose to go south-east. Possibly there were two reasons. One might have been that the main highway to Vaishali and the River Ganges followed that direction. The other may have been his wish to meet a well-known Rishi of the Kalama people, named Alara, who was residing near Vaishali beside the highway.

It was on this road that emissaries from his father caught up with him. For when Chandaka, the charioteer, got back to Kapilavastu and broke the news of Siddhartha's adoption of the life of a *shaman*, the raja was much distressed. So he sent his wisest minister and his chief Brahmin to him to try to persuade him to change his mind.

It was to no avail. The new *Shaman*, who was already in touch with other religious men, proceeded on his way. He had no possessions now apart from the eight things necessary for a monk—the three garments of his dress, the alms-bowl, a razor, a needle, a water-strainer and a girdle. In such a state he came upon Alara Kalama close to Vaishali.

Alara became his guru for a while. But the Buddha-to-be was not satisfied. To his mind Alara's teaching, wise though it was, did not go far enough or get at the root of his problem. So he went on his way on foot again and found another teacher, Udraka. The outcome was the same.

Siddhartha continued in the same direction as before. It must have been the dry season since, in the wet weather, the rivers become almost impassable and nearly all travel comes to a halt. It must have taken time too, as he travelled many miles through the land of the Mallas and the land of the Licchavi, crossed the mighty Ganges and went on up into Magadha, where he will have had his first sight of hills again after leaving his home country.

On that first journey the Buddha's goal was Rajagriha, capital of the Magadhas. Even Bimbisara, King of Magadha, went to see him upon Pandava Hill. But the Buddha, dissatisfied with his second teacher as he had been with the first, journeyed further southward from the Rajagriha locality to a place called Uruvilva, or some say Uruvela.

Uruvilva was near the Niranjana river, where it joins the Phalgu on its way from the south to the Ganges. By all accounts the forest thereabouts was pleasant enough, with lofty sal-trees, clumps of bamboo and shady groves surrounded by undergrowth. Monkeys would have been common, and are often included in pictures of this episode of the Buddha's life, whilst the truly wild beasts would have kept themselves to themselves.

To Siddhartha all this was nothing. For he had now come to believe that the only sure way towards self-realisation was through fasting and concentration on emptiness. He was following the yogi ascetic's path, trying to free the mind by subduing the body. He suffered loneliness within himself, though he was not alone. He had been followed from Kapilavastu by five ascetics, whom he had previously encountered on a visit to the banyan-grove outside the city, where such people habitually gathered. These men stayed with him and fasted with him.

In our day we have encountered fasting near to or unto death by Mahatma Gandhi and by members of the Irish Republican Army. These fasts were politically motivated. But the Buddha's fasting was purely for personal reasons, since he saw it as a way to unveil the ultimate truth. The great grey-black statue that stands in the central position in the Lahore museum shows what he must have looked like when hardly an ounce of flesh remained on his body.

Some of the accounts of this period of his life are given in dramatic detail. One says that he lived on one jujube fruit, one sesame seed and one grain of rice a day. Another says that he ate cow-dung and even his own excrement, and frequented a charnel-ground, where those bodies that were not cremated were thrown to be consumed by the beasts.

For six years Siddhartha fasted in the forest and in caves. He then reached a crisis point in his mental development, coming to realise that this severe fasting was simply weakening all his faculties and not advancing his awareness of the truth. The change came with Sujata. She was a village-girl, daughter of a man who owned cattle. One day she came close to him with her cows, and seeing his pitiable condition she offered him rice boiled in milk. The rice-pudding was accepted, and thus the fast was broken. A stupa, still unheeded and unrestored, marks the location of her house. The courtyard of a temple commemorates the event.

To get to this place I had first to go to Gaya, which is a good two hundred miles from Gorakhpur on the other side of the great river. I spent the night in the Chanakya Hotel, Patna, sharing it with two cricket-teams, one from Zimbabwe and the other from Sri Lanka, which were competing with India for the Heroes' Cup. It was a good hotel, as it should be, named after a great king, and the only trouble I had there was with a swarm of green fleas that came into my room when I opened my window for some fresh air.

Beside the gateway of the hotel there was a booth containing an effigy of the delectable raven-haired Lakshmi, the presiding goddess of the Diwali festival, and a lot of noisy music was coming out of the loudspeakers above her head. I hurriedly closed the window, squashed as many of the fleas as I could catch, and went to bed.

Next morning I planned to catch the 9.05 DMU Limited Stop to Gaya, a distance of about sixty miles. But there were problems. My porter at Patna Junction told me the 9.05 was not running, took me to another train, which was standing empty at platform 5, and sat me in it. I had a first-class ticket and there were no first-class compartments in this train. So back went my porter to the first-class ticket-office to cash in my ticket for Rs. 99. He then had to go to the second-class ticket-office, which was in a completely different building, to get another ticket costing fourteen rupees, and I went with him since a fellow-passenger told me not to trust him with the money.

Back we went to platform 5. My bag, which my porter had been carrying backwards and forwards on all these errands, now appeared to be stuck firmly to his head. I then waited patiently for the 10.30 departure, though I became worried when the train did not fill up. After a good while my porter came back, running this time and in a great hurry, to tell me that the 9.05 was going after all.

It did go, nearly without me. In fact it was already in motion when he bundled me into the rearmost carriage, and he had to run alongside it to catch the money I gave him for his complicated services. This train was as jam-packed as the other had been empty. To start with I could not even sit, and it was only when a kindly old man made a small space for me in a corner that I was able to huddle down into a sitting position on my bag.

Passengers came and went at every station. But the crush never grew less. Then came the milkmen with their four-gallon kerosene-tins of milk, which slopped from side to side of the open containers with the motion of the train, slopping the straw about that was floating on it as well. Each of the milkmen had a yoke with which to carry his two tins, and the yokes were cleverly hooked on to the strap-hangers' straps that dangled from the roof of the carriage. One of them climbed up the wall to lie out of the way on a luggage-rack.

Yet I was somehow at peace with all these brown bodies around me of people who seemed to be quite devoid of malice. Outside in the bright sunlight were the open plains with the harvest in and sheaves of rice-straw laid out on the ground to dry off in the sun. Presently two crags appeared on my left, rising almost vertically out of the level land. They were part of the northernmost limits of the Vindhya range, and one of them had a summit that was shaped like the hooded head of a vulture. I felt sure, wrongly as it turned out, that it must be Vulture Peak, which was often climbed by the Buddha for the sake of the cool air.

I was now resting reasonably comfortably in my corner and prepared to sit out the three-hour journey that I anticipated. So when the train slid into Gaya Junction after little more than two hours, I was pleasantly surprised. Gaya is a place of pilgrimage in its own right because of the footprint of Vishnu that is in the heart of the town. But my recommended hotel, which was opposite the station and close enough to it for my red-uniformed porter to carry my bags there himself, was a reminder of the Buddha story.

The Ajatsatru Hotel, Station road, Gaya is named after another King of Magadha, the son of Bimbisara. According to the legend he got tired of waiting to inherit the throne and starved his father to death. Much later the parricide called on the Buddha, who was by then well-known. Bearing the weight of his misdeed, he sought relief for a bad conscience, which the Buddha gave him.

In spite of its royal name the Ajatsatru was not an expensive hotel. Rs. 65, or less than £1.50, cash in advance, would get you a room for night, though a 'luxury tax' of 3% was added to the bill. There was actually no luxury in my room at the end of the first-floor corridor, overlooking the station and all the little food-stalls in Station Road. But there was Leslie.

I made a mistake when I first met Leslie, as I tried to tip him for carrying my bags up to my room. He let me know firmly that he was not a tippable class of person, and as head-waiter, or steward, of the Sujata restaurant downstairs anything he did for me he would do out of his personal wish to help me and persons like me.

Leslie was tall, lean and dark. He wore blue jeans and a coloured shirt, and he spoke in a warmly intense and protective manner. When I told him I wanted to go to Bodh-Gaya he explained that the cheap way was to take a pedicab to a place called the Zilla School, and from there get a place in a motor-rickshaw. He had a strong desire that I should not pay more than was absolutely necessary, and I suppose that, relative to his tiny salary of Rs. 150 a month, saving ten rupees here and five rupees there would be a significant economy. He did not like pedicab pedallers or motor-rickshaw drivers to get more than the proper fare.

Leslie's mother still lived in Dhanbad, the railway centre further down the line to Calcutta. Many of his relations had gone to Australia and England. But he and his mother were of the few who had got left behind. He was not happy in his work, and his real pleasure in life was helping Australians,

New Zealanders and the rare Britishers who appeared in the hotel. In this way he felt he had contact with the world that he admired.

Leslie had been working at the Blue Lagoon in Benares. But he had fallen foul of some men he called villainous people, and moved on. His immediate ambition was to cycle across India to Goa, where he was sure he would be able to pick up a much better job in one of the tourist hotels. He was working out his month, and then he would go. Perhaps he would take some of the money his mother had saved for him, perhaps not. He showed no nervousness about pedalling 1,500 miles, more or less, across the sub-continent. So I told him he should do it before the hot weather descended on him. Wherever possible he would spend his nights with people of his own kind. And if not Goa, then Australia.

I took Leslie's advice and transferred from pedicab to motor-rickshaw outside the Zilla or District School. But I had not the heart to push my pedaller off with no more than the five rupees that Leslie had specified, and when it came to bargaining with the controller of the rickshaws I found it impossible to beat him down to the amount that Leslie had said was the correct fare. I got the rickshaw-driver to remove the tarpaulin hood from his vehicle so that I could see where I was going, and off we went.

I was travelling alone in some state on one of the two benches of the rickshaw that would ordinarily accommodate at least six people. So it was not long before somebody tried to leap aboard. It was not hard to do that, since we were bumping in and out of potholes in the long, straggling urban street at only about ten miles an hour. Was it nine, twelve or fifteen kilometres to Bodh-Gaya? Different sources gave different answers. My driver merely went by time, saying it would take about three quarters of an hour.

The next two hitchhikers were not turned away. One of them was a thick-set Australian accustomed to travelling in the bush, and the other was a Nepalese young man, who was for ever smiling. The latter's head was shaven like that of a Buddhist monk, and he also had a red Hindu *tilak* mark on his forehead. On the pocket of the jacket of his jeans there was the head of Kitchener with the words, 'I want you'. I received these two travellers, drifters, pilgrims, tourists or whatever as my guests, which did not stop my driver extracting a fare from them when we reached our destination. It was not my business.

We had been travelling for some time alongside the Niranjana river, which some authorities call the Niranjara, and now in the centre of the Bodh-Gaya bazaar, where two roads meet outside the white, cigar-shaped tower of the Hindu temple, instead of going on to the Buddhist Mahabodhi I was asking where the Sujata temple was.

Nobody knew. I bought the *Land of the Blessed One Tourists' Bodh-Gaya Guide*. On the back of it was the *Buddhgaya Tourist Map* with the Sujata temple clearly marked, and a tree beside it. It was on the other side of the Niranjana.

I had not expected that. But now, although the river had completely disappeared behind the houses of the town, it seemed logical to follow the road that led upstream past the Hindu temple and look for a crossing-point. My motor-rickshaw would have been of no use here. The crowd was packed so tight that all motor-transport had been brought almost to a halt and even cyclists were walking their bicycles. Squeezing between the wheel of a lorry and a sweet-potato stall or sidling through a narrow gap in a group of women or creeping between a wall and a drain to avoid a bicycle, I slowly worked my way forward.

I was flagging badly when the narrow bazaar thinned out and I found a lane on the left beside some stacks of timber, which led to the river-bank. The river was immensely wide, broad enough, I thought, to be both the Niranjana and the

Phalgu together. But it was also shallow. What would have been a vast rush of water in the rainy season, was now a large number of rivulets winding their ways between wide stretches of sand. People were coming up out of the river, and others were half-way across it. I spoke to a middle-aged, bandy-legged man who was plodding up the bank with the aid of a crooked stick, and asked him about the Sujata temple.

"Yes," he said. "You see that white building over there."

Far away there was indeed a white speck under the line of green trees on the opposite bank. "Is that it?" I asked.

"Not that. Past that."

"*Dhanyabad*. Thank you."

I took off my shoes and socks, rolled up my trousers and went ahead. The streams looked deeper than they were. So although I expected each one to wet me to the thighs, none in fact came up above the knees if one picked one's way carefully along the ridges of sand in the clear water. With my sights steadily on the white house I eventually reached the powdery dry sand on the other side, put my shoes on again and stopped to survey the scene. A secondary-school student came striding up behind me on his way home from school.

"Sujata temple?" I asked.

"Oh yes. This way," he said.

From that moment Banwari became my guide. He would have us take tea in his family house. But I wanted to see the Sujata temple first. So we pushed on through the village and picked our way along the narrow path between the rice-fields, the potato-plots and the cauliflower-patches on the other side of it.

"There are many millers in this village," said Banwari, using the word *myal* for miller, which sounded strangely similar to the English. "But we are poor people."

"You don't look poor," I said. "Good harvest. Plenty of rice and vegetables."

"Not enough."

"Too many children I think."

"What to do? It is a problem."

Presently another white building came into view. It was a Shiva temple with Shiva's trident on its tower. Behind it there was a courtyard, and it was in this courtyard under the banyan-tree that Sujata was honoured for giving succour to the Buddha.

On the far side of the brick courtyard there was a tableau of half life-size plaster figures. The central figure was the Buddha, not looking particularly emaciated and decorated with white scarves. To the left of this figure, symbolically crowned, was Sujata with a white calf beside her, offering rice-pudding from the kneeling position, and to the right of the Buddha there was a maidservant standing behind a cow. The whole display was inside a box made of concrete, with iron doors that could be closed and locked if need be. On the inside of one of the doors there was a notice which said, 'This is the ancient place where Sujata of the village of Senani (Bakraur) had offered milk-rice to Siddhartha under the Banyan tree'.

There were flags decorating the tree above the display-box, and in front of the cow there was a red donation-box together with a ledger in which to enter the amount of the donation. It all looked very modern. But there were two ancient Buddha statues there also, placed one on either side of the display, each stone block containing the statue being no more than two feet high. These little statues, bearing traces of ancient worship, seemed to me to be the reason for the identification of the site for Buddhist veneration.

The temple Brahmin came and joined us. He was a handsome fifty-year old man, and he told a long tale concerning incidents in the Mahabharata in connection with the temple, which left me none the wiser.

On the other side of the banyan-tree an extension to the temple courtyard had been built up in brick above the surrounding fields and the nearby watercourse. Here, back to back with the first tableau, there was another display. In this one the figures were life-sized and, I thought, more dignified in appearance. Both were seated, the Buddha slightly above Sujata, who was sitting sideways on to him proffering the bowl of rice-pudding. Both had those white, alabaster-like translucent skins for which the Burmese images are noted. The Buddha had black hair going up to a top-knot, and a purple sash. In his lap, by hands in the meditation pose, there were flower-petals left by visitors.

Here also there was a donation-box, and there was a sign which said, 'Donated by U Bokyaur + Daw Tin Myint, Daugters [*sic*] Mar Mar and Wai Wai (15) Aung Min Gaung Paya Road, Windermeir [*sic*] Yangon, Myanmar. May all beings share out merits equally with us 21-4-93'. There was another sign saying, I imagine, the same thing in Burmese, and the bricks had been supplied by the Swastik Brick Co. logo a swastika.

Beyond the parapet of the brick-wall enclosing the Burmese courtyard the fields stretched away in flat squares and rectangles with trees and copses breaking up the monotony. A quarter of a mile distant there was another statue of the Buddha also put up by U. Bokyaur of Windermere, Rangoon and his family. It marked the route to the Dungeshwari mountain, which I could see four miles away sticking up out of the horizon like a withered thumb.

There, in a cave, the Buddha for some time practised his severe austerities before he saw that this was not the true way, and thence came a band of sturdy men and women, dressed in maroon homespun which looked far too hot for an autumn in Bihar. They were from Ladakh behind the Himalayan ranges in the remote north-west of the Republic of India. They were hot and tired from their trek, joined us for a moment, kissed the donations ledger but did not donate, and went on towards the Tibetan monastery where they were staying.

Meanwhile two other students joined our group. The Brahmin called for tea, and we sat through the afternoon, spending it as lazy, hot afternoons should be spent, in the shade of a tree discussing matters of importance such as the recent cricket-matches between India and Zimbabwe and between India and Sri Lanka, and talking about modern literature, asking which of the Indian authors writing in English had international status and if so why.

The tea was a long time coming, and as soon as I had drunk the guest's cup I proposed to leave. Banwari led the way back, soon followed by a group of begging children, and so we returned the way we had come. But at a certain point we turned right instead of left along a path that led us to a small hill.

In fact it was quite a large hill for a flat alluvial plain, and I was sure it was not a natural one, though cattle were browsing on its grass and on the rice-straw that had been thrown out for them. Scattered trees were growing on it too, and broken brick was visible where feet on well-used paths had worn the grass away. It must have been about two hundred feet across by sixty feet high, and it could only have been a stupa age unknown.

Banwari confirmed it. "Sujata's house was here," he said.

We walked on. Another man, sitting on a string-cot outside his house, called out to us to take tea. But the sun was going down. I did not want to cross the river in the dark. So, giving Banwari some money to buy books, I bade him farewell on the sand at the water's edge.

Some authorities say that it was under the very same tree beside which Sujata fed the Buddha that he found enlightenment and it has to be said that, when Hiuen Tsiang visited Bodh-Gaya in the seventh century, they were showing a stupa to the south-west of the Bo-tree outside the temple compound but on the same side of the river, and claiming that this was where Sujata had lived.

At that time the stupa in Bakraur was called the Stupa of the Scented Elephant in commemoration of a Jataka story about the Buddha in a previous life. According to this story the *Ghandahasti*, the Scented Elephant, was blind and her son, who was really the Tathagata as a Bodhisattva, looked after her. He frequented a pool, where he gathered sweet lotus-roots for his mother and collected water in his trunk for her to drink.

One day the young elephant came upon a man who was lost in the forest and guided him back to the right road. The man went to his king and told him that he had found a wonderful scented elephant in the woods. Whereupon the king went and captured the elephant-cub, although when the man pointed it out to him both his arms fell off as if they had been cut off by a sword.

In the king's elephant-stables the captive elephant went on hunger-strike, and his keeper was obliged to go and tell his sovereign that the marvellous beast would neither eat nor drink. The king went himself to the stables and asked the young elephant why he would not take nourishment. The elephant replied that his mother was blind and without his help must by now have existed for days without food or water.

"How can I have any appetite when my mother is suffering like that?" he asked.

The king was moved to pity and ordered that the young elephant should be set free.

Be that as it may, other authorities confirm that the Buddha had to cross the river as I was about to do. The river was also called the Lilanjana, and it must have been deeper when Siddhartha crossed it because we are told that a grass-cutter, named Sotthiya, gave him some bundles of grass with which he made a sort of raft to carry him across. So it is not clear whether Uruvilva, said to have been an assembly area for Bimbisara's troops, was on the right bank or the left bank of the river. Perhaps it was on both, with the parade-ground on one side of the river and the forest on the other.

I waded back towards a point on the bank which was a good deal further downstream from the spot where I had first entered the river. Naked boys were splashing about in the deeper part and running back to a stepped terrace, which would fulfil the functions of a ghat when the river was higher. Sitting on the bottom step of the ghat there was a tall, thin man dressed in blue jeans and white trainers, whose knees were almost up to his chin.

The man had on a green jungle hat. Nevertheless the low, westering sun lit up the flat side of his long face with an orange glow, and his blue eyes, which appeared to be gazing unblinkingly across the river, shone like opals. Even when the naked boys plucked at the skirt of his grey bush-jacket to gain his attention, he never moved. But when I got close to him and across his field of vision, he called out to me.

"That river's not deep."

"You can go across if you want to," I said.

"Buddha was over there?"

"They say he was there fasting."

"I guess I'll go tomorrow. Too late now."

He took his hat off and smoothed his hand back over a head that was thinly covered with straight, fair hair.

"Yes. Better go in daylight," I said.

"He broke his fast over there?"

"So they say."

"I'd sure like to see that place."

I nodded and moved on, emerging from the river, as I had intended, by the bus-terminus. Then I took a seat in a waiting bus that was bound for Gaya. But before I did so I glanced back at the white man sitting on the ghat, and saw that he had resumed his motionless gaze. The brown boys, tired of trying to get him to react to them, had moved away and were splashing each other in the stream again.

The bus filled up. Someone tapped me on the shoulder to tell me I was sitting in a seat reserved for ladies, a point that the ladies themselves would not have dared to make. So I moved back to a narrower place, where it was not possible for me to sit without turning my legs sideways into the aisle. The cleaner banged the metal door for the driver to start, the conductor took fares but gave no tickets, young children travelled free.

Night fell, and the stops of the bus became more frequent, not only to let passengers on and off but also because we encountered chariots with modelled figures on them, nearly life-size, dragged by young men and surrounded by groups of prancing male devotees. The four-armed betinselled, garlanded beauties in red saris represented Lakshmi, the goddess of the festival of lights. Lakshmi, the people's queen of wealth and prosperity, her neck adorned with a chain of marigolds, was carried down the street on her cart with an ecstatic enthusiast whirling a heavy stick to make room for her. Even the bus-driver dared not push his bus past, and as Lakshmi was reduplicated more than a dozen times our progress was painfully slow.

It was only when I got off the bus opposite the District School that I noticed Mr Ambedkar. I would not have noticed him at all if he had not approached me, since I had been near the front of the bus and he had been at the back. But he touched my arm in an almost furtive way as I turned to look for a trishaw, and at first I thought he must be trying me for a tip.

His shoes were battered, and his black umbrella had a broken spoke in it, whilst the all-embracing shirt that flowed over his lower garment looked definitely off-white. Yet his dark face was full of warmth as he addressed me, and his red lips, coloured not by lipstick but by betel-nut juice, pouted at me as might those of a lover.

"So we are both pilgrims," he said. "I saw you at the temple asking about Sujata. Also coming from the river."

"I didn't see you," I said.

He spread his hands. "I am just, how you say, one of the crowd. But you..."

"One of a different crowd."

"Yes, yes. But we both follow the Buddha. Let us walk."

And so, ignoring the importunings of the trishaw-wallahs, we made our way together towards my hotel.

"Our people used to worship sticks and stones," he went on. "But that was in the old time. Then many took up with the Christians. I did not do that. My god was a goddess. Goddess Kali. Black face, many arms. Lakshmi too. Money goddess. Like the girls on the carts.

"Some Buddhist images have many arms," I said.

"Perhaps. Bhot and such places. Well, it does not matter. You are here for a special reason?"

"Not so special," I said.

"I am here for special reason. I did not know about Buddha until I had some trouble. Because Buddha, you know, they were forgetting in this country. Then they found him again. He was here all that time, and nobody was knowing it. And now they say all the Buddhas were here at Bodh-Gaya sitting under that tree."

"I'm going to see that tomorrow," I said.

"You want to hear my trouble?"

"Not really," I said, again thinking that I was going to be touched for a never-to-be-repaid loan.

"Well, I'll tell you. I had a good job. Not government job, but good job. Happy family. Every day I go to office, sit at desk. My employer, Mr Das Gupta, also sits at desk. Of course, bigger desk. But same room. He comes and goes, I stay. Office man. One day he goes out, I stay. Then Mr Bannerjee comes into office. He also office man. Another office. He comes in and he says, 'Mr Ambedkar, I put these papers in Mr Das Gupta's desk.' So he puts them in the drawer of the desk. But ..."

Mr Ambedkar paused for emphasis, His mouth chewed although there was no *pan* in it.

"He puts papers in drawer. *But*, but he takes money out of drawer. Hundreds rupees, five hundreds rupees. He not care. He even shows them to me. Smiles. Yes. Laughs. Puts the money in his pocket and goes out of the room. So you see! You see!"

"Your boss accused you."

"Exactly. I said no. It was Mr Bannerjee. He was not believing me. Mr Bannerjee is Brahmin, and I...Well, he was not even letting me speak. The sack, I got into it. You imagine! In India we have no, what you call industrial tribunal, so I got right into the sack. I said to Mr Bannerjee, I will kill you if you do not confess. But he just laughed again.

"So my poor family was starving. I was forced to work as sweeper. Yes, you are not believing me. I was sweeping the steps of Karaya Mansions in Calcutta, and my wife was *aya*. What next? Kali told me to take my revenge on Mr Bannerjee. But I did not do it. I could not do it. The Buddha tells you, What matter? Every bad deed brings its own suffering. You do not have to revenge it.

"So I followed the Buddha. The four truths tell us how to avoid suffering. That is what the Buddha found out under the tree. The Buddha said all men are equal. Mr Ambedkar, same name as me, he was our great leader. One friend got me a job in government. Now we are happy again."

"Excuse me," I said. "But are you by any chance an untouchable?"

"That is what they call us, men like Bannerjee," he answered. Then he smiled his broadest smile yet. "But you may touch me, please!"

So I did. And off he went into the railway-station to catch the last train back to Patna.

Back at the Ajatsatru Hotel Leslie was glad to see me back safe and sound. I ate a vegetable curry and went over to the station to post a card, passing a well-fed cow that was picking its way amongst the people squatting in the station-hall. Then I retired to my room. There was a notice on the door on which twenty-four 'rules and bye-laws' were written, and the first rule of all was, 'Copies of rules are put in every apartment and the Customers are supposed to have read and understood them.'

So be it.

6

The Enlightenment – Bodh-Gaya

After crossing the river Siddhartha remained in the forest, now deserted by his five disciples who considered that he had weakened his resolve when he broke his fast. He was provided with more grass by a grasscutter, or some say it was the same grass as he had used to cross the river. He spread it under a peepul-tree, and seated in the meditation pose he strove to reach the inner truth of human existence.

Siddhartha resolved not to move until he had achieved his aim, and even the animals and birds kept quiet. But whilst he tried to meditate his mind came under attack from Mara, the great tempter and harbinger of death. Mara is often represented as a fierce-faced demon with flaming hair. Yet he is in the background, being too repulsive in himself to tempt. In the foreground are his sons and daughters—pride and the lust for power, discontent, craving for sex, desire.

Siddhartha warded off Mara's arrows of desire and discontent. Now fully composed, he passed through the four watches of the night in four degrees of trance, each one leading to a higher state of consciousness. Finally, as dawn broke he reached the state of all knowing and became a Buddha. We are told that the earth moved, the sun shone brightly and at the same time rain fell softly out of a clear sky.

Flower-blossoms also fell from the sky around the seated Buddha, and fruits fell from the trees out of their due season.

The peepul-tree under which Siddhartha Gautama was sitting when he became a Buddha became known later as the Bodhi-tree, the Tree of Enlightenment, or Bo-tree for short. It is a type of fig-tree with light-green leaves of a very distinctive shape, known to botanical science as the *ficus religiosa*, and its descendant still stands, alive and well, on that very spot.

I went down to Bodh-Gaya again to see this tree and all the buildings and their surrounding gardens that have grown up in connection with it. Chief of the buildings is the Mahabodhi, which is not a stupa but a temple, sometimes loosely called a vihara, which for many years was in the possession of a group of Shiva devotees and is of great antiquity, having a tower 180 feet high in the form of a truncated pyramid. On top of the tower stands a model stupa, bell shaped in the Burmese style, with a finial of umbrellas forming the hti.

Leaving my motor-rickshaw amongst the souvenir-stalls I walked back a short distance along the outer wall of the temple precincts and turned right to reach the entrance. It was not difficult to find. The grey tower and even the four smaller towers could be clearly seen above the trees that make a garden of their surroundings, and at the gateway there was none of the hustle and toing and froing that one usually associates with Hindu temples.

The Mahabodhi of today was built in the sixth century. So it could not have been more than a hundred years old when Hiuen Tsiang saw it in the middle of the seventh century and described it in a way that does not altogether accord with the appearance of the present building. This is hardly surprising since there have been a number of restorations since that time. There is an inscription in Burmese which records one early in the fourteenth century. Apparently it was not a judicious one, since when further restoration was proposed in 1877 a

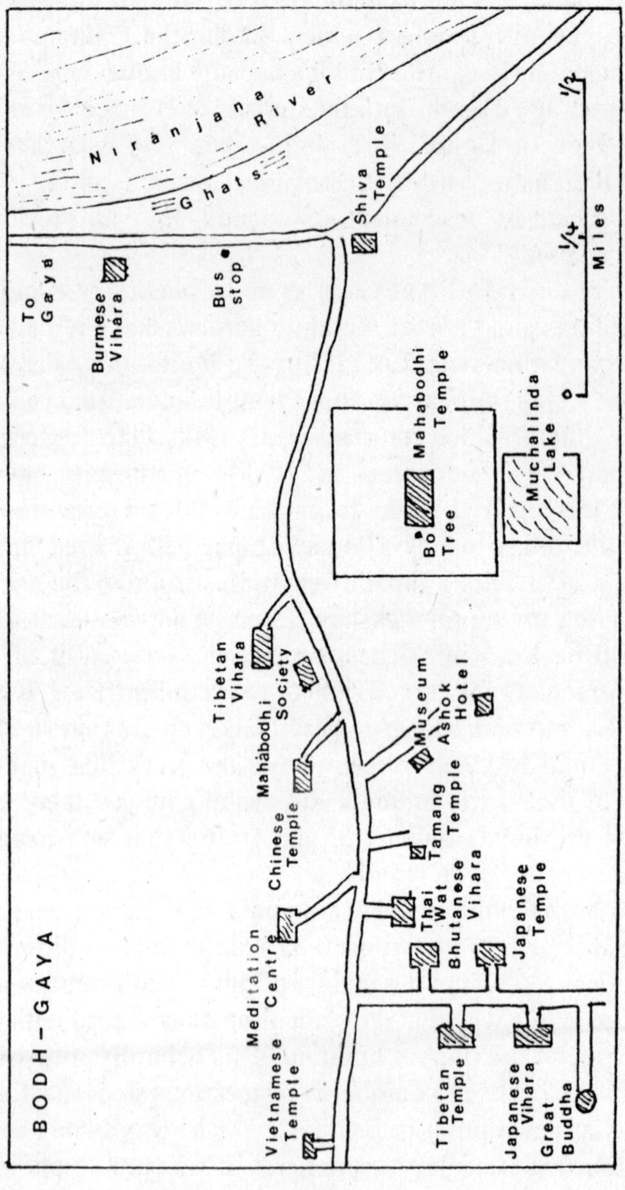
BODH-GAYA
Niranjana River
Ghats
Shiva Temple
To Gaya
Burmese Vihára
Bus stop
Mahabodhi Temple
Bo Tree
Muchalinda Lake
1/4
1/2
0
Miles
Tibetan Vihara
Mahabodhi Society
Museum
Ashok Hotel
Chinese Temple
Tamang Temple
Thai Wat
Bhutanese Vihara
Japanese Temple
Meditation Centre
Vietnamese Temple
Tibetan Temple
Japanese Vihara
Great Buddha

certain Dr Rajendrala Mitra inspected the building and declared that 'The Burmese carried out demolitions and excavations which in a manner swept away most of the old landmarks'.

Not only had the remains of the vaulted gateway in front of the temple been completely demolished, but also the stone pavilion over the footprint of the Buddha had been removed. The foundations of the older buildings that Hiuen Tsiang had noticed, had been cannibalised to provide bricks, and the wall round the Bodhi-tree had been partly relocated. Furthermore a large area round the temple had been levelled and enclosed in a new wall.

This sounds like a damning indictment. But one has to remember that by the time Sir Alexander Cunningham, then Director of the Archaeological Survey of India, had decided on a new restoration the temple had passed through many vicissitudes. He did not reject the active participation of the Burmese again, welcoming their subscriptions, when the new work was put in hand nearly eight hundred years later.

There was a temple there as early as the second century CE at the time of the Scythian kings, and there must have been some sort of religious centre there, described as a vihara or monastic settlement, much earlier than that, when Ashoka was setting up monuments at all the Buddhist holy places. Nor do we know what repairs King Ashokabala undertook just before the Moslem conquest in the twelfth century. By that time the temple had been taken into the Hindu fold, since already in the ninth century King Dharmapala had put a four-faced Shiva lingam there.

More repairs were undertaken to present a fine appearance for the Buddha Jayanti celebrations in 1956, and embellishments are still being added, making it one of the most attractive, beautifully kept and peaceful shrines in all India. The Thais and Burmese are applying squares of gold leaf wherever they can.

A temple guide wanted to show me the seven particular spots that a pilgrim should visit around the temple. But after leaving my shoes at the gate and receiving a number in exchange for them I preferred to walk alone down the steps and proceed straight to the great tree, which I had already seen beside the tower from outside the perimeter wall.

This was no problem. A marble ambulatory, kept scrupulously clean by sweepers with grass brooms, surrounds the temple, and people were walking on it in the proper clockwise direction, some murmuring the syllable OM over and over again, some muttering mantras in low tones and others simply stepping out in silence. Some of them were wearing the yellow robe, others fingering rosaries and dressed in the casual shirt and jeans of peripatetic westerners. There were big, robust people from Tibet striding heartily along, and there was a slim, slight Japanese lady in a yellow sun-hat.

I went along with them between the stone railing and the wall of the temple, turned the south-western corner and came face to face with the stone and brass railing round the tree. It was festooned with Buddhist flags and white pennants, many of them with Burmese writing on them. The large, spreading tree, some eighty feet high, emerged from the stone pavement, and between the tree and the wall of the tower there was a flat platform of red sandstone about three feet high and not quite square, which is called the Vajrasana, the Diamond Throne.

There is a large golden statue of the Buddha on this plinth, backing the west wall of the temple. It is a seated image, calling the earth to witness. For this is the Bodhi Pallanka, the Place of the Enlightenment, which the Buddha attained in the year 589 BCE at the age of thirty-five at the end of the night of the full moon of Baisakh, the spring month which Theravada Buddhists call Wesak.

One has only to look through the brass railings to see not only the Vajrasana, which replaces the grass on which the Buddha was seated, but also the artificial lotus blossoms and other flowers with which it is strewn. And if one is Indian one is inclined to do puja to the two black stone circles which are placed on the southern side of the enclosure. On one of them there are two footprints, and on the other there is a wheel, which represents the Wheel of the Law. On the opposite side, one finds a Tibetan monk reading from the scriptures, making use of a new book in the old style, that is to say with pages in board covers taken out of a cloth wrapping.

In fact there are now two peepul-trees. During one of the restorations of the temple the old Bodhi-tree became uprooted, and two saplings were taken from it and planted in different places, the one that I was looking at between the ambulatory and the back wall of the temple, and the other thirty feet to the west outside the railing of the ambulatory. Much earlier a sapling had been taken to Sri Lanka by Ashoka's son, Mahendra, the Apostle of Ceylon, and the descendant of that tree also thrives at Anuradhapura in the centre of the island.

Around the ambulatory there is a continuous marble bench under the perimeter railing, and I sat on this bench for a long time meditating about the significance of what had taken place under the Bodhi-tree. In the slightest breeze the leaves of the tree shivered like those of an aspen, and there was another light noise too. Purple berries were dropping off it and hitting the pavement with tiny plops. Eventually the inevitable happened. Some of them dropped on my own head.

I picked up some of these berries from the ground. They were no bigger than blackcurrants. Yet they had the distinctive taste and seeds of figs, proving that the botanical classification of the tree is not at fault. I even collected some of the berries that had dried off, and kept them in an empty film-capsule. Somehow I felt that it would be good to look at them in the years to come and remember where they came from, even to grow some some trees from them.

On the northern side of the temple, as well as the continuation of the long bench, I found a platform raised about three feet above the pavement and wide enough to walk on. It stretched for about sixty feet, far enough to have nineteen stone circles carved on it to resemble lotus blossoms. It is called the Chankramana, the Cloister Walk, where the Buddha paced up and down in meditation for the whole of the third week after his enlightenment. Some remains of stumps of pillars indicate that it was once a true cloister with a roof over it. Now it is open to the sky, another of the seven spots to be visited.

There is time too to look at the railing that surrounds the ambulatory. Like the rest of the temple it has had a chequered history. There are four parallel stone rails supported by pillars at intervals of eight feet. But they are not all homogeneous. The older sections, which are made of sandstone, have been dated to as early as the Sunga period in the second century BCE. Other parts, carved out of coarse granite, belong to the classical age of the Gupta period between the fourth and the sixth centuries CE.

Not unnaturally, with a gap of more than five hundred years, there are striking differences between the two. On the earlier railings, some of which are in the museum, traditional scenes are carved, such as the purchase for the Buddha of the Jetavana Grove at Shravasti. On the other hand the later ones are embellished with purely decorative motifs such as real and mythical beasts, men and women, and rosettes. There are griffins and centaurs, and along the top there are mermaids with their arms in the mouths of those legendary crocodiles with elephants' ears called makaras.

Twenty-three of the pillars were found by the conservationist Viceroy, Lord Curzon, in the residence of the Hindu superintendent of the temple. He was persuaded to return them to their proper places. So now there is a complete railing with eighty-five pillars round three sides of the temple and part of the front. Although force majeure had driven the Mahant to return his pillars to the site, it has to be said that subsequently six pillars were removed to the museum in Calcutta and the Victoria and Albert museum in London.

The outer walls of the temple are also of great interest. They look as if they are built of dark-grey stone, but in fact the material is brick. A feature of the tower is the rows of niches, arched over in imitation of the corbelled entrances to Buddhist caves. They were obviously intended for images but most remain empty. On the walls such niches are being filled up to such an extent that the lowest course of the temple looks completely new in parts. There are new statues carved out of the traditional grey schist, many of them of seated Buddhas in the different mudras such as the teaching pose, the earth is witness or the freedom from fear. I saw pilgrims applying gold leaf to those of them that were within their reach.

Between the temple and the gateway, half-way up the steps, there is another of the seven sites. This is where the Buddha spent the fifth week of meditation after his enlightenment, and where he said to a Brahmin, 'Only by one's deeds and not by one's birth does one become a Brahmin.' Reference is made here to another tree. But there is no tree, simply a stone pillar topped by a golden seated Buddha.

There is a special tree, however, on the southern side of the temple. It is called the Rajayanta Forest tree, and here the Buddha spent the seventh week of meditation after his enlightenment. At the end of this week two merchants, Tapussa and Bhallika, offered him rice-cakes and honey, and became the first people to join his order with the memorable words *Buddham saranam gacchami, Dhammam saranam gacchami*—I take refuge in the Buddha, I take refuge in the Doctrine.

Beyond this tree, which was shedding its berries like the Bodhi-tree, I walked down a path through the perimeter wall to an ancient ghat that was constructed in 1882 by one Cosain

Beepat Gir. The ghat leads down to a lotus-covered lake. It is a square tank with a statue in the middle of it of a great cobra sheltering the Buddha with its hood.

One would like to think that this is where the Buddha spent the sixth week after his enlightenment. According to the legend he was caught at that time in a thunderstorm, and the snake arose and kept the rain off him. Looking at it another way it can be said that the king of the Nagas, the ancient spirits of lakes and waters, approved of him and was protecting him. But the statue is modern and so, comparatively speaking, is the lake or tank, although it is almost choked up with the leaves of the lotuses, few of which were in bloom when I saw them, whereas the real, or supposedly real, Muchalinda lake is pointed out nearly a mile away and is no longer a lake, just a muddy pool.

On leaving the lake I had been to the locations of the third, the fifth, the sixth and the seventh week after the enlightenment. To find the place of the second week I had to walk up a hillock to the right of the entrance-gate. Here I found a small replica in white of the great tower, with a black image of the Buddha inside it and blue pennants outside. This is known as the Animesa Locana stupa.

It is hardly a stupa in the strict sense of the word. But it does mark the spot where the Buddha spent the second week after his enlightenment. The name means ‘the place of the unwinking gaze’ and the tradition is that he sat here gazing at the Bodhi-tree in gratitude for the shelter it had afforded him during his progress towards Samma Sambodhi, the supreme wisdom. Of course, if the temple had existed at that time it would have obstructed his view.

There remained the site of the fourth week to be found, and I am not certain that I found it. But I think it must have been marked by the stupa, a real one this time, to the west of the Bodhi-tree just outside the stone railing. It is not a large stupa, not much more than a man’s height, and it is built up in small terraces with Buddha images of various colours on them, in blue, white, yellow, grey and gold. Amongst these small images there are even tinier ones only a finger's length in height. They are of different colours because it is said that, whilst the Buddha was meditating, blue, yellow and orange rays shone from his body.

All these sites of the seven weeks are within a few steps of each other, and probably their exact locations are immaterial. They are simply symbolic of the weeks of progress in contemplation of the truth that the Buddha made whilst he remained in the forest of Uruvilva. That was before there was any stupa or vihara there, only the trees and the little longitudinally striped chipmunks and the birds. The trees still dapple the paths within the compound with their shade and overhang the many smaller stupas that are scattered here and there. It is a pleasant place to walk even if one is not contemplating the higher philosophy, and when one actually goes inside the vihara it is into a more austere world.

The great image is seated on a plinth with its back to the west wall. The original figure is said to have been over one thousand five hundred years old. But the one there today is very new indeed, and there is no means of telling how much it resembles the first one. Fully draped except for the right arm and shoulder, it looks all gleaming gold in the theatre lighting of alternating red and white electric-light bulbs, and the halo behind the head is divided into red, white, orange, yellow and blue segments, which are the colours of the Buddhist flag.

But not long ago the halo was white, the robe yellow and those parts of the body that could be seen were the natural brown colour of northern Indians, giving it a dignified yet humbler and less overpoweringly regal appearance. It looks as if the right hand is in the 'earth is witness' gesture, which the Buddha made whilst repelling the attacks of Mara. But it is hard to tell, as both hands are covered by the robe and the long white scarf spread over the forearms.

I saw flowers and fruits in vases and bowls in front of the main statue and the subsidiary images. For there is no animal sacrifice. The kindly fruits of the earth, as at a harvest festival, are sufficient offerings. In the old days the bodily relics of the Buddha were shown here once a year with due ceremony. Hiuen Tsiang describes them. There were fragments of bone looking like round pearls, bright and glistening and of a reddish white colour. There were also little pieces of flesh no bigger than a bean and shining red. The whole collection could have been less than a handful, which explains why so many places could claim to have parts of the *sharir*, or body, of the Buddha in their stupas. The original eight parts were subdivided and redistributed, specifically by Ashoka and possibly also by other potentates.

The Mahabodhi has now been taken over pretty well completely by the Buddhists, and the Shivaites are not to be seen there except at a shrine in the grounds. Yet if it really was built in the sixth century it must be about the oldest active temple in the whole country. To those who are accustomed to associate Buddhism with the hemispherical stupas of Sri Lanka and Myanmar, and with the pagodas of Nepal and China, it may seem strange to find a Buddhist temple of the typical Indian and Hindu kind. The tower could well be one of the great gateways of a South Indian temple or, crowned by its circular *kalasa* in the shape of an amalaka fruit, one of the temple towers at Bhubaneshwar in Orissa. Although there are architectural differences it may well have been the model for many such buildings and is a reminder that, however far the faith has spread, Buddhism was purely Indian in origin.

Fergusson, the great historian of Indian architecture, maintained that the Mahabodhi was 'anomalous and unlike anything else we find in India either before or afterwards.' He added that it was 'probably the parent of many nine-storeyed towers found beyond the Himalayas both in China and elsewhere.' But to the layman's eye it looks like the parent of many a temple-tower in India too,

I saw some devotees at the Mahabodhi. Two were extending themselves at full length prone on the ground, Tibetan style, in front of the temple. One had a board on which to throw himself, polished by innumerable prostrations, and the other had pads on his knees and hands to protect them from the marble pavement. Two bhikshus were meditating on their mats amongst the fallen berries by the stupa of the fourth week, which my little guidebook calls the Ratnagraha chaitya.

But the person who fascinated me most was the unkempt Tibetan lady who was sitting opposite the Diamond Throne and talking incessantly to no one in particular, using the English language in the urge to be understood by the world at large. Each time I passed her on my circumambulations of the temple she called out to me, "Come!" Three times I did not stop, afraid to be caught up in her endless, repetitive jabber. But the fourth time she called,"Englishman. You Englishman come!"

I stopped, surprised. "You know I'm English?" I said.

"You English know our people. I saw you one time Hong Kong. That time you young."

"You too."

"I was in the Gurkha school there. Teacher."

"You're not Tibetan then. Nepalese."

"Tibet. Nepal. All our people are Tibet. You know my name?"

I was about to say that I didn't. But she went on jabbering without giving me a chance. "My name Wangdi Lama. Nice name you think? Nice time Hong Kong also. My home very nice too. You don't think so?"

I was just going to remind the lady that I did not know where her home was when again she gave me no chance.

Indeed, for the next quarter of an hour there was never the slightest hope of interrupting her.

"My home very far up in the mountains. Maybe too far for you. Too cold too. You cannot breathe there and maybe you die. But we lived there. Happy too. Yes, very very happy. The air so clean too. No cars, buses. Hong Kong, you know, plenty smoke from cars. Our place all pure." She pronounced it 'pewer'. "Pewer also with Lord Buddha. Tara pewer also. In school holidays I go home. Go home! Go home! I went home. Very long way. First Pokhara. Then walking, walking. First Baglung. then Dhorpatan. Then Tarakot, Phoksumdo, Shey. Always north to Bhot, what you call Tibet. Namgompa, Dzong, Lar."

I wanted to say, Enough! But she rattled on. "I walk there many times. No trouble. My brother was leader. All the people said so. That was why he did the things he did. We thought Wal Sa would protect us. The Wal Sa in the cave by the lake. It is Buddha. Many heads and arms but still Buddha. Destroy evil.

"But my brother died. He had to. The Chinese came. Why did the Chinese come? I ask you, Why? We had done no harm. They said we were part of Tibet. So they had to come. Even that was not true. Since our fathers and grandfathers we have been in Nepal. Nobody troubled us. Even Katmandu. We never saw anybody from Katmandu. That was our life. My brother, Tschering, said the Chinese are coming. Yes, they were coming. There are Buddha people in China, but these were not so. They were nothing. They wanted our mountains. What for? Maybe someone tell them about the precious stones on Wal Sa. They want the stones, so they want our mountains. But Pasang and his people always took the precious stones. Only little by little. Selling them. India, Singapore, Hong Kong. Only little by little. No harm. We all knew that. Then these men come—two, three Chinese—and look. And we know, they come, others come too later. Not in peace. Soldiers, uniforms, guns, like that. So Tschering said, We cannot let them come. But how? They are many with guns. We are few. Is it the Wal Sa? Can that do anything? Maybe, he say.

"The Wal Sa is in the gompa, and the gompa is by the lake. But in the lake is another Wal Sa. This one not gold, stone. But you cannot, you could not see it. Why not? Because the lake was too full of water. And why? Because one time many years ago there was a slip. The mountain slipped, and the mountain-slip blocked the lake. So the water could not get out, and the water got higher and higher."

The conclusion was obvious, and I wanted to say so to Wangdi Lama. But again she careered on with her tale.

"That is where the Chinese will come, Tschering said. Up that valley from Bhot, from Tibet. I know that valley. It is very deep, very steep, very dry. Only little little water running down. Wal Sa will help us, Tschering said. He get all the people. Men, women, all people. We go to the lake, to the side where is the slip. The lake is very full. The water is near the top of the slip.

"Pasang said, You cannot do this. Do what? Do this. We want to see again the Wal Sa in the lake, my brother said. We must do it. But Tschering's idea was about the Chinese. He heard. We heard the pipes, the what you say, the bugles. They are coming. What for? They must not come. So. First the bugles very faint. Then louder. We worked on the slip. First small stones. Then bigger. Rocks. Ice too. We threw them all down into the valley. Then the bugles louder, the rocks bigger.

"Then we see them down below. They are coming up. Brown uniforms, brown like the valley. Brown cockroaches. Dry earth all around them. We dig out the rocks on the slip. The water starts to move. Little by little it moves. It is not enough. We hear shoot. One man shoot deer. No one shoot deer before in our mountains. They too tame. Chinese want eat. So they stop. Night-time. We work all night on the slip. Morning again the bugles. The work is not enough. Tschering, my brother, go down. He dig under one big rock. We call him, Come back! He stay. Come back, come back, Tschering! He call, Push the rock. Water little more. Little by little more, more. Come back, Tschering! No answer. Suddenly the rock moves. It go down, crash down. Water rushes after it. Water rush and roar. Rocks go down with water. More, more. Rocks, stones, earth, ice, everything go. Water roar more and more. Fill all the valley. No man escape. All dead. All Chinese dead. Float down in the water. And Tschering..."

"Tschering?"

"Tschering dead too. We jump back, save ourselves. Too late for Tschering. Water in the lake go down. Now we can see the stone Wal Sa. No one of us saw it before. It was not the same. It was one Buddha like here in India. Just one head, two arms like you. Smile on face. Why to smile, people dead? Still smile. People say, Tschering's idea wrong. To kill wrong. But Chinese did not come again, only our Tibet people running from their homes. They came. Many, many. We tried to help them. Then I went back to Hong Kong. Then finish there. Then come here for Buddha. Our people here, I stay with them. Cannot forget. One time no trouble. Someone like Krishna, O.K. Someone like Buddha, O.K. Someone like Jesus, O.K. Someone like Mahomet, that O.K. too. All can be peace in Lord Buddha."

It had grown late as I listened to this tortured tale, and it seemed strange to hear the Moslem call to prayer loudly proclaimed in this most Buddhist place. Yet it was to the sound of Allah-o-Akbar, God is Great, that I examined the stalls outside the Tibetan hostel, built in 1952, where I might have stayed if I had not settled down in Leslie's care at the Ajatsatru Hotel in Gaya.

Statuettes in the rough grey granite, much like those in the smaller niches of the Mahabodhi temple, were for sale at very reasonable prices and beautifully carved. The earth is witness, the meditation pose, the freedom from fear with haloed head, they were doubtless production line products, and yet the skill had not been lost. Even the tiny Buddhas a thumb-nail high had features and gestures clearly delineated.

It was too late to go further. So back I went to Gaya, past kine decorated for the Diwali festival and to the sound of fireworks. On the journey I thought of the Bodhi-tree, and of the other trees that are full of significance in the Buddha story, and I thought too of the snake with its many heads forming a canopy over the Buddha in the lake. For the tree-spirits, which are the woodland dryads, and the serpent-spirits, known as the Nagas, are never far away.

Next day I went to the museum in Bodh-Gaya, where it was possible to see parts of the earlier stone railing from the Sunga period that had not been relocated in the temple precincts. They were arranged in a square in the courtyard of the museum around a crowned Buddha in the earth-touching pose. Inside, there were more pieces of railings and black granite statues from the site. Like the museums at Nalanda and Vaishali, this is one of the Archaeological Department's official museums, and I was amused by a list of rules posted at the entrance. For instance No 3 of the 'important guidelines for visitors' states:

> Visitors are not permitted to pluck flowers, making noise, talking loudly, singing songs, playing tape-recorders and transistor radio, smoking, spitting, arranging meeting and picnic etc inside the museum campus.

I did none of these things, and the obliging custodian directed me to the other sites of Bodh-Gaya, to the modern temples in Buddhist Temple Street, the Meditation Centre and the Great Buddha statue. They were convincing proof, if proof were needed, of how much progress Buddhism has made in recent years in the land of its birth. For many countries have contributed to the whole, all with the same objective of establishing a presence in the place where the Buddha achieved enlightenment.

The first one that I saw, a little way to the left of the main road, was the Tamang temple. It was a pleasant, small building with white walls framed in red pillars and etherial Buddhas and Bodhisattvas painted over and round the yellow doorway. The Tamangs are Nepalese people who have spilled over into the Darjeeling district of India, and the inscription on the facade says, 'Duidal Jyangchub Choiling Monastery Tamang Buddhist Association H.O. Darjeeling - Bodhgaya 1992'.

Below this inscription and over the entrance-porch I saw a peepul-leaf faced by two deer, all done in yellow, and beside the temple there was an equally new stupa dedicated to the memory of the head monk:

> Erected for the welfare of the many by Ven Lama Urgen Kalsang Moktan head monk Tamang Buddhist Association and sanctify (*sic*) puja performed on 7.2.92. He passed away on 9.2.92. Tamang Buddhist Association devotionally remembers him for ever.

Thus the Tamangs, many of whom are to be found in the army as Gurkha soldiers, honour the man who died, according to the inscription, only two days after the consecration of the temple.

But not all the temples are quite as new as that, though they have all been put up in recent years. The Thai temple, for instance, which one reaches next, was completed in 1957 as the notice in the chaitya hall tells us:

> In the year 2500 BE (1957) the year that marked 25 centuries of Lord Buddha, the Government of H.M. the King of Thailand, including all the Thai Buddhists, at the hearted (*sic*) request of His Excellency, Shri Jawarhalal Nehru, the beloved Prime Minister of India, faithfully established

> the Thai Monastery in commemoration of Gotama the Buddha, the world peace-lover, at Bodh-Gaya where his enlightenment had been substantiated and wherefrom his doctrine had been brought to be realized and propagated to the world far and wide.
>
> | | |
> |---|---|
> | Expenditures for construction | 5,776,866.72 Tcs. |
> | | 1,753.00 Rs. |
> | Additional expenditure | 2,950,500 Tcs. |

This was all written in English with the same thing in Thai above and in Hindi below. The Tcs. refer, of course, to Siamese Ticals.

The Thai temple is built in the national style with rising, flying finials on the gables of the roof and two fearsome doorkeepers, one on either side of the entrance at the top of the steps. Inside it I found a display of educational posters with descriptions in Thai and captions in English stuck on to them, many of which had fallen off. I was able to explain the pictures to a local man dressed in a white dhoti, a brown long-tailed shirt and a grey woolly cap, who had taken it into his head to make the round of the temples as I was doing.

"This," I said, "is the old city of Ayodhya, named after the one in India in Uttar Pradesh. These are old Thai Buddha statues. This is the city plan of Bangkok. This is Wat Arun, The Temple of Dawn in Bangkok. This temple we're in now is the Wat Thai Buddhagaya under the patronage of the Royal Thai Government. And this," I went on reading the notice on the windowsill near the doorway, which was written in English and Hindi, 'says, Good luck is always with you, if you pay attention to it.'

What could this mean? I wondered, as I turned left into Buddhist Temple Street with my Bihari companion. The next notice said, 'Welcome to Royal Bhutanese Monastery'. And there, not far from the gate, was a typical pagoda of the Himalayas with three roofs, each half the size of the one below, and lavish, colourful carving on the roof-beams and in the deep eaves.

Originally the painted squares under the roof would have been the ends of wooden beams. But in the new age all this traditional wood-carving, such as one might have expected to find on the wooden parts of viharas before they were torched by the invaders, has been reproduced in concrete. The makaras of the finials are moulded in plaster, as are the two deer facing the leaf of the Bodhi-tree which, like those on the Tamang temple stand above the entrance. Not quite as new as the Tamang temple, the Bhutanese temple is still only nine years older. The inscription on the foundation stone is as follows:

> This stone was laid by His Excellency, Dr. A.R. Kiowai, Governor of Bihar, on the site consecrated by His Holiness the 60th Rje Mkhan-Po of Bhutan on the 22nd day of the ninth month of the Water Hog year in the 16th Cycle corresponding to 28th October 1983.

Inside the temple I found the main seated Buddha image draped in the maroon cloth which is the usual colour of the homespun of the Tibetan Himalayas. The begging-bowl was in his hands, and a silk scarf hung down below it. There were more white scarves draped on side statues, where a notice warned us that 'Touching of wall statues, spreading out legs and sleeping in the temple is prohibited'.

There was a similar notice in the Japanese temple, which was the next one on the left. 'Please be careful and silence', it said. 'Don't try to sleep here.' I saw that the notice was in English and Hindi but not in Japanese. Perhaps Japanese people would not dream of sleeping in the temple and would feel insulted if they were reminded not to. The more important notice was in all three languages and was entitled:

Slogan

Brothers and sisters of the world, let us tread the path of righteousness shown by Lord Buddha the all compassionate one to attain universal peace and happiness.

Most Ven. Nenkai Inada, President

This, the Indosan Nipponji temple, as one would expect of the Japanese, is the genuine article. The building has only one roof, with upward curving corners and deep eaves. But the beams of the roof and the pillars of the walls really are of wood, and of beautifully stained and polished wood at that. The ceiling is divided into squares by laths of wood, and each square contains a motif such as a crane, a lotus or a chrysanthemum.

The Buddha story is painted on the walls—Maya holding the sal-tree to give birth and the Buddha already standing up; Siddhartha seeing the old man, the sick man and the dead man; Siddhartha galloping away from the palace; starving near to death; receiving the rice-pudding from Sujata. It was a truly lovely place in the clean-cut Japanese way. I sat on the polished floor, naturally with my legs tucked under me and not stretched out. I really would have enjoyed a sleep in that peaceful haven.

In the temple compound I saw an enormous bell, every bit of five feet high, which was called the Bell of Peace. For sounding the bell there was a massive thick rod, six feet long and suspended on chains. It was supposed to be rung between 6 a.m. and 12 noon. But it was in fact silent. A notice in English and Hindi though not in Japanese said, 'To get on it is strictly prohibited'.

The Japanese have their benefactions here, and the Komyo medical centre offers free treatment to those who come to it. But the thing for which the Japanese are most noted in Bodh-Gaya, and clearly intend to be noted, is the great image of the Buddha at the far end of Buddhist Temple Street.

This Great Buddha, seated with hands in lap and grey head against the sky, reminded me of the open-air Buddha at Kamakura near Tokyo. But the Kamakura Buddha, about which Rudyard Kipling wrote one of his most thought-provoking poems, is only 35 feet high, although it was for a long time the second largest in the whole country. The taste for the gigantesque has led the Daijokyu sect of Nagoya to commission one nearly twice that height. The notice by the gateway tells the story:

> The Great Buddha (Daibutsu in Japanese) stands on this holy land of Bodhgaya, the place Buddha attained Enlightenment 2533 years ago. As a symbol of peace and happiness the Daijokyu sect of Nagoya has erected this statue in Dhyana Mudra (Meditation pose) seated on a lotus in the open air. The statue is a patch-work of blocks of Pink Chunar sandstone. The golden curl on the forehead is made of heavy bronze with gold plating. The statue has been designed by the famous sculptor-artist of the South—Shri Ganpathy Sathpathy, statue modelled by Shri Rishikesh Dasgupta of Calcutta and the construction of this statue undertaken by Messrs Thakur and Sons of Chunar, U.P. The Unveiling Ceremony of this statue undertaken by His Holiness the Dalai Lama on the 18th November 1989.
>
> Completion time 4 years. Height of statue 64 ft., of lotus 6 ft., of pedestal 10 ft.
>
> The Great Buddha Statue Management Committee - Bodh Gaya.

You approach the Daibutsu up an avenue of stone lanterns each with a different inscription in Japanese on it, which would be lit by oil-lamps or candles on special occasions. With each step forward the figure looms even higher until, when one reaches the railings round the ten-foot plinth one is craning one's neck backwards to look up at the head with its circular 'third eye', the *urna*, which is described as a curl on the noticeboard. Each hand, one placed palm upwards on the other, is ten feet long, and the length of the ears with their elongated lobes must be nearly five feet. On either side of the Buddha are his two special disciples, Shariputra and Maudgalyayana, who themselves became perfected beings called *Arhats*. They are much smaller, having become liberated from the cycle of rebirth under the Buddha's instruction and not by themselves alone.

I walked away from the Great Buddha casting backward glances at it and thinking of Kipling's poem and its beginning:

Oh ye who tread the Narrow Way
By Tophet-flare to Judgement Day
Be gentle when the 'heathen' pray
To Buddha at Kamakura!

To him the Way, the Law, Apart,
Whom Maya held beneath her heart,
Ananda's Lord the Bodhisat,
The Buddha of Kamakura.

It was not Kamakura, but it might have been the Buddha at Kamakura writ large. I could not think beyond that. The sun was hot and I was very thirsty.

Freshly pressed orange-juice at the stall outside the gate was the answer to my needs. Truly the shack was fly-infested, truly the dogs foraging under the bench I was sitting on got in my way, and truly the goats trying to get at the waste pulp of the oranges were a nuisance. But it was a wonderfully refreshing drink, which gave me the strength to visit yet another temple.

This one, almost opposite the Japanese Indosan temple, was also a very new building, opened as late as 1988. Seeing it I was bound to think of the persecution of the faith. For this was the Tibetan temple, similar in some ways to the Bhutanese temple, but with verandahs on two storeys around the chaitya hall. The notice, in English only, proclaims the 'Karma Tharjay Chkhorling Kagyupa Vajrayana Buddhist Monastery inaugurated by His Excellency R. Venkataraman, the President of India, for His Eminence Berce Khyentse Rinpoche, December 23rd 1988'.

Although the temple belongs to the Vajrayana sect of Buddhism, whose symbol is a thunderbolt, the image is a seated Buddha in human form wearing the saffron robe, which is in the tradition of the Hinayana, the Buddhism of the Lesser Way of Sri Lanka and Myanmar. The Buddha is both calling the earth to witness and holding the black begging-bowl, and he is sitting in front of a complicated reredos of trailing plants and supernatural beings.

The walls here, like the walls of the Japanese temple, have the Buddha story painted on them, which I found more intelligible than the symbols behind the Buddha. Here Siddhartha is very much the noble prince. One sees him practising archery in the court of the palace; one sees his wedding; one sees him out in his chariot passing the old, the sick and the dead; one sees him offered rice-pudding by Sujata, tempted by two very attractive young ladies, meditating in the forest in the company of a monkey and an elephant, teaching the monks, reclining as he passes away into Parinirvana.

There is another Japanese temple, the Daijokyo, which was the predecessor of the Great Buddha and was opened in 1983 by the President of India, who was then Shri Giani Zail Singh. Associated with it is a vocational training centre for boys and girls, which was opened two years later. There is also a Chinese temple, which was built in the nineteen-thirties in the days before Communism, and is therefore easily the oldest of the new foundations. In addition, not far from this temple there is a site for yet another one originating from a country that was created for Muslims. The plot has been set aside for a Bangla Desh Buddhist Pilgrimage Centre sponsored by the Bangladesh Bouddha Kristi Prachar Sangha, which shows an unusual link between Buddhism and Christianity.

And so the building continues. There is now a project to construct a large image of Maitreya, the Buddha yet to be, and this has been developed by the Foundation for the Preservation of the Mahayana Tradition which, like the Vajrayana, follows Tibetan ways. For Tibetan Buddhism, suppressed and persecuted by the Chinese invaders in its native land, has now burst out into the rest of the world under the leadership of the Dalai Lama. Buddhism has gone a long way since Kipling wrote:

Buddh-Gaya's ruins pit the hill,
And beef-fed zealots threaten ill
To Buddha at Kamakura.

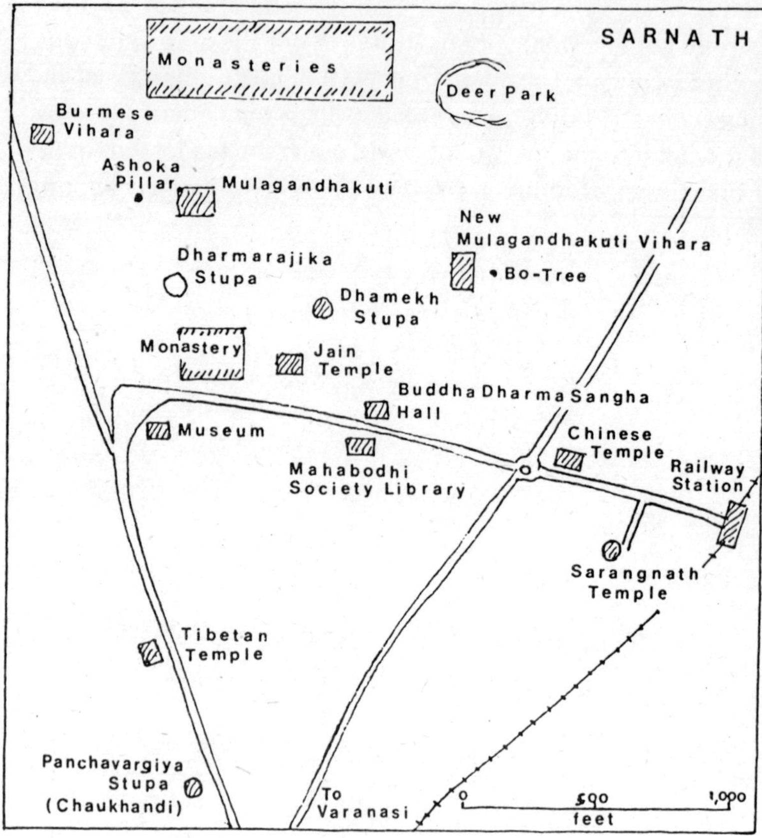
SARNATH
Monasteries
Deer Park
Burmese Vihara
Ashoka Pillar
Mulagandhakuti
New Mulagandhakuti Vihara
Dharmarajika Stupa
Bo-Tree
Dhamekh Stupa
Monastery
Jain Temple
Buddha Dharma Sangha Hall
Museum
Chinese Temple
Railway Station
Mahabodhi Society Library
Sarangnath Temple
Tibetan Temple
Panchavargiya Stupa (Chaukhandi)
To Varanasi
0 500 1,000
feet

7

The Wheel of the Law – Sarnath

After the seven weeks spent in the neighbourhood of the Bodhi-tree Siddhartha Gautama, who must now be regarded as a fully enlightened Buddha, considered what to do next. His two earlier gurus, Alara Kalama and Uddraka Ramaputra, had died. But the five disciples from Kapilavastu, who had left him when he gave up extreme austerities, had gone to Varanasi and were staying at Isipatana some five miles from the city in a deer-park that had been set aside for ascetics and sannyasis.

The Buddha also went to Varanasi, which was then called Kashi, and from there to the Deer Park, where he found the five men who had been his followers. They laughed about him, calling him their pleasure-loving friend who had given up fasting, and when he met up with them they just called him Gautama. For that he rebuked them, telling them that an Arhat ought not to be addressed simply by his family name.

In fact Gautama now came to be regarded as the Tathagata, in other words he who has come, a Buddha come to earth. He preached to the five sceptics in the Deer Park and won them over. He explained the noble eightfold path that he had come to formulate during his months of meditation, and the four great truths, the understanding of which leads to self-realisation.

This was the First Sermon, during which he converted the ascetic five—Mahanumna, Vashpa, Ashvajit, Bhadrajit and he of the Kaudinya family—and set the Wheel of the Law in motion, the *Dharma Chakra* which was to lead hundreds, then thousands, then millions to the principles of his religion, which is the *Dharma* or *Dhamma*.

As for me, I took leave of Leslie, wishing him luck on his marathon cycle journey and went to Gaya Junction early in the morning to catch the Doon Express. The booking-clerk was not yet in his office, and apart from ants and assorted flies a rat was scampering about amongst his papers. But come he did, and he sold me a first-class ticket for Varanasi Junction, Rs. 193 for 221 Km. Then my porter took me to the right section of the platform for my class of coach and I waited. At 6 a.m. the train came gently in. It was not easy to find a place. The overnight passengers from Calcutta were still stretched out on the seats and disinclined to move. It needed drive to displace them, and fortunately my porter had enough to carve me out sufficient room for the six hours of slow and sleepy travel.

> Please do not consume alcoholic beverages in compartment in consideration for other passengers

No indeed. In any case I had none. Those passengers in dhotis were sitting cross-legged on the bench-seats whilst those in trousers kept their shoes on and their legs down. A woman climbed down from one of the upper berths with her little boy and tried to freshen up. She had a jewel in the form of an isoceles triangle stuck to her forehead, and he had the signs of the zodiac drawn on his tee-shirt with the cryptic question, 'Do animals have horoscopes?'

I did not know the answer to that. At the next station there was a sign over the exit, in English only, which said, 'Suggestions and Complaints Book will be found in the Superintendent's Office'. I wondered what suggestion or complaint

I might make. Would it be that the train might go a little faster, or that there might be a compartment where one might consume alcoholic beverages, or even a compartment where one might be forbidden to smoke?

As we rumbled on along the line called the Grand Chord across the flat rice-fields, and crossed the wide Sone River, the inhabitants of the compartment fell silent, all loquacity gone. I turned to the Hindustan Times and read that an employee of the Forbesgunj Agricultural Produce Marketing Committee had been crushed to death under the wheels of a truck. I also read that the siege of the mosque in Srinagar, where a hair of the Prophet is kept, had been raised when the thirty-two activists had been persuaded to surrender their thirty hostages without bloodshed. There was also a piece about Indian Airlines and a plane with a wheel that fell off, and another that had jammed landing- flaps which caused such an excess consumption of fuel that it had to make an emergency landing in a field. It made me wonder whether to fly back to Delhi at the end of my pilgrimage or to try to get on a train.

The man sitting opposite me by the window lifted the glass a little, letting in a welcome puff of fresh air. But it was only to spit out the produce of his quid of twisted tobacco, which did double duty for him as snuff.

The station at Dehri-on-Sone was surprisingly large for such an unimportant place. But it was as nothing compared with the vast marshalling yards at Moghulsarai just outside Varanasi, where we lingered as if reluctant to leave those lines of rust-coloured box-cars, those heaving, panting shunting-engines, those rows of ancient wooden carriages and chains of tanker-wagons that looked as if they would be equally happy filled with water or petrol. It was the late breakfast stop. Tea and rice-cakes or samusas, fruit and nuts were bought on the platform. No wonder the mournful siren of the train sounded loud and long, and the departure was almost imperceptibly slow to give people time to scramble on and off. A cow kept up with the train for quite some seconds. Then the ticket-inspector entered our compartment. I showed him my ticket, another man produced a piece of paper, the other six passengers showed nothing.

Moghulsarai is where the Grand Chord via Gaya joins the main line from Calcutta to Delhi via Patna. Between that great acreage of railway land, on some corner of which Leslie had told me he was once robbed of all his possessions, and the city of Varanasi runs the great and holy Ganges, no wider than the Sone but flowing in a deeper and undivided stream. Its banks are higher than the banks of the Sone, and the railway bridge is higher too, giving a magnificent view of the bathing and cremation ghats ranged along the north-western side of the river. The Kashi bridge is of cantilever construction and is none other than the one which is the focal point of Kipling's story *The Bridge-builders* in which an unexpected flash-flood threatens to destroy the construction work and delay the opening of the bridge by His Excellency the Viceroy.

As for the city itself, only the back view was visible as we circled north of it through Varanasi City station to Varanasi Junction. From there I went to the familiar territory of the Hotel India with its Amber restaurant and Gup-Shup bar, offering 'Indian, Chinese and Continental catering', and its '24 hours 6 channel TV programme'.

There was no shortage of motor-rickshaw drivers offering to take me out to the Deer Park, though having seen the sombre little deer-park with its one lonely deer opposite the museum in Bodh-Gaya, I was not too keen to see another one. But Sarnath, said to be derived from the words Sarang Nath, an epithet of Shiva meaning Lord of the Deer, is now the name of the location which includes a whole complex of excavated and partly excavated sites as well as the little town that has grown up in association with them. A well known Jataka story shows how this came about.

In a previous incarnation the Buddha was a stag, the leader of a herd of deer at Isipatana where the King of Kashi used to go and hunt. The king killed so many deer that the stag went to him and remonstrated with him. In this way the animal got him to accede to his request that only one deer a day should be killed. After that the deer decided amongst themselves whose turn it would be to be killed each day.

One day the turn fell to a pregnant doe. She cried pitiably, lamenting the fact that the unborn twins in her womb would have to be sacrificed as well. So the stag decided to offer himself in her place and went to the king to tell him so. Of course the stag was a Bodhisattva, a Buddha who remains earthbound to help the world with his compassion, and the king was so moved by such an act of sacrifice on the part of an animal that he gave up hunting from that very moment and let the deer run free and unafraid.

Gopal, my driver, told me what I was going to see at Sarnath as he steered me in and out of the holes in the road and up and over the sleeping policemen, put-putting his way out of the straggling suburbs of Varanasi. But it was already afternoon, and I never did get to see the Deer Park that day as I found one of the most important monuments on the way. This was the Chaukhandi, which means the 'Square' and sounds an odd name for a stupa, since they are usually circular. However, this one is fairly late in time and is an exception to the rule. It was erected in the Gupta period, perhaps as late as the fourth century of our era, and for a long time it had a nickname, *Luri ka Koodan*, meaning 'Luri's Leap' because of a cowherd who had jumped to his death off the twenty-four foot tower that surmounts it.

This octagonal tower on top of the artificial hill is an irrelevance. As the Persian inscription on it tells us, it was erected by the local governor at the instance of the Emperor Akbar in 1588 to celebrate a visit made there by his father, Humayun, which gave him great pleasure although it only lasted for a day. No doubt, in order to build his tower the governor utilised some of the bricks of the stupa, which commemorates a much more ancient event. For it marks the spot where the ascetic five, the Panchavargiya Bhikshus, actually encountered the Buddha, having come out to meet him as he made his way towards the Deer Park. It is likely, therefore, that some sort of monument existed here even before the huge pile of brickwork, 74 feet high, was built up to dominate the surrounding countryside. The indefatigable Alexander Cunningham sunk a bore hole down from the tower of the Chaukhandi in 1835 and found nothing. Sir John Marshall had no better luck in 1904.

High though this stupa is, if Hiuen Tsiang is to be believed it was by no means the highest stupa in Sarnath in his day as he mentions one that was actually 300 feet high, which would have made it more than half as high again as the Mahabodhi tower at Bodh-Gaya. Today it is hard to visualise what these mighty works must have looked like in their glorious days.

Not far from the Panchavargiya Stupa I found the Tibetan temple, and it was impossible not to linger there in view of the notice painted beside the gateway, which describes the sufferings of the Tibetan people under the Chinese Communist regime. Placed behind one of the two plaster guard-dogs which watch over the entrance, this sign makes a poignant plea to fight to free Tibet. It lists the miseries heaped upon the Tibetans, and refers to Tibet's historic role as a buffer state between India and China, which has now been destroyed.

Within the courtyard of the temple, which was founded in 1955, the theme is taken up again under the heading *Genocide in Tibet.* It is stated that more than 1.2 million Tibetans have been killed in the Chinese occupation, more than 6,000 monasteries destroyed, thousands of Tibetans imprisoned and many Tibetans arrested and killed for demonstrating against the Chinese occupation. The notice says that the Chinese already outnumber the Tibetans in Tibet, 7.5

million Chinese to 6 million Tibetans. Furthermore the Chinese are using Tibet for dumping nuclear waste, whilst the Dalai Lama has been in exile since 1959.

Outside the temple there is a row of prayer-wheels, which are typical of Himalayan and Tibetan Buddhism, and inside it there is a huge golden Buddha in the 'earth is witness' pose. The walls are dark green with hundreds of Buddhas painted on them in maroon and pale yellow. Some precious tangkas, painted on silk, hang above the Buddhas, and in front of the main image there is a smaller one of Rinpoche Tsong Khapa of the Gelupa or yellow-hat sect.

It was plain to see that India has been good to the Tibetan Buddhists not only in the hills, where their refugee-camps have grown into small towns of a much more permanent nature, but also here in the plains. Opposite the temple, on the right of the road to Sarnath, stands the Tibetan College. Here every effort is made to preserve and continue the study of Tibetan language and culture. Indeed, anyone who wishes to know more about the plight of the Tibetans since the Chinese occupation is urged to write to or contact the Department of Information and International Relations, Central Tibetan Administration, Ganchen Kyishong, Dharmsala 176219 Himalaya Pradesh, India.

Thus the afternoon passed, so that it was not until next day that Gopal drove me all the way to the entrance of the Sarnath archaeological site. Even then I might not have got much further. For the museum is close to the entrance, and in the museum is the most famous piece of sculpture in all India. Also to be seen there are a number of other fine large pieces and many precious, portable objects that were found on site.

The world-famous sculpture is the capital of an Ashokan pillar fashioned in the form of four lions standing back to back on a drum which has wheels and animals carved on it. The wheels have twenty-four spokes, each spoke representing an item in the Doctrine of the Buddha. The beasts are the lion, the horse, the elephant and the bull, standing for the four cardinal points of the compass, respectively north, south, east and west. Anyone who buys Indian postage-stamps, uses Indian banknotes or reads Indian official correspondence is familiar with that quartet of polished stone lions. For ever since India was granted independence a picture of this capital has formed the official emblem of the government. Yet the pillar was only discovered as recently as 1905 during the very productive Oertal excavations. The whole piece stands on a circular pedestal with fluted petals carved in an elongated S bend, which are described not very convincingly as a lotus flower. The lotus, emerging pristine white out of a muddy pool, symbolises purity.

Apart from its beautiful and commanding appearance, the pillar is also interesting on account of its Brahmi inscription, in which Ashoka urges monks and nuns to avoid schism in the Sangha, which is the Order of the Buddhists. How far the divisions of Buddhism, which we see today, had advanced by that time we do not know. But clearly there already were variations on the Theravada, the regime of the Elders, otherwise the exhortation would have been pointless.

In addition to the huge red sandstone Buddha in the teaching mode with its enormous halo, nearly ten feet high, I found two low reliefs from the later Gupta period which were extremely interesting from my point of view. One of them enumerates the eight places the Buddhist pilgrim should visit, and the other depicts the happenings at each place which make them pilgrim centres. A short pilgrimage would take in the Birth at Lumbini, the Enlightenment at Bodh-Gaya, the First Sermon at Sarnath and the Decease at Kushinagara. But a longer pilgrimage would also include Kapilavastu, where the Buddha-to-be lived, Shravasti where he converted the bloodthirsty Angulimala, Vaishali where he spent his last rainy season, and Pava where he ate some supposed mushrooms in order not to disappoint his well-meaning host and was poisoned by them. I was to visit all these places in due course.

But now Sarnath. To begin with the beggar-girls upset me, especially those with babies on their arms. They were racists, clearly going for the white man in preference to the brown, and I was caught between compassion and detachment, both good Buddhist virtues. If they had been nuns in saffron robes compassion or the merit of giving alms might have won. As it happened it was only a degree of detachment that allowed me to go about in peace.

There were many stupas there. Some were large, some small. One was right outside the confines of the site and completely ignored, one was being rebuilt. It was the one under reconstruction that I encountered first. This was the Dharmarajika Stupa, which with a diameter of over forty-four feet must have been one of the largest before it was reduced almost to ground level. Its nickname for a long time was the Jagat Singh Stupa because at the end of the eighteenth century Jagat Singh, who was the Dewan, or Prime Minister, of the Raja of Varanasi of the day, demolished it in order to get a supply of cheap bricks. In the following century treasure-hunters completed the attack on the sacred pile.

How high the rebuilding will go remains to be seen. When I saw the men and women at work under the eye of a superior type of foreman the first circle had been completed. It was a brick wall some five feet high with an ambulatory encircled by another brick wall. This brought the stupa up to approximately the present ground-level, and work was going ahead on brick terracing above and within the base circle. The foreman did not welcome observation of too close a nature. So I looked on the other side of the path at a monastery courtyard, which is called Monastery V on the on-site plan. According to Dr Jairman Singh, author of *Sarnath Past and Present*, there are only four monasteries there. But no doubt he is discounting the smaller monastic courts out of the seven that have been identified as such.

I then went on to view the building that is called the Main Shrine or Main Temple. It made a change from stupas, as it is a rectangular building about 55 feet in length and nearly square, with the remains of immensely thick walls going up to about eighteen feet. Stone was included in the building as we see it today. But the original temple, which appears to have been constructed at the time of Ashoka, was rebuilt a number of times. As it continued in use until the eleventh century, a period of about 1,300 years, it must have had a very long life as a place of active worship. Of course it must have had an image of the Buddha in it, and it is called the Mulagandha Kuti vihara, the 'Original Scented Hut' because it is on the spot where the Buddha spent his first rainy season in Sarnath. His disciples had built a thatched hut for him, and there he spent three months in fasting and meditation, some say leaving behind the fragrance commemorated in the vihara's name, Or perhaps it had been built of sandalwood and had its own fragrance thereby.

The nearby Ashoka pillar links up neatly with the vihara. Pieces of the broken sandstone shaft of the lion capital, which is in the museum, have been assembled. But together they make up less than a third of the probable height of the whole pillar, and consequently they are not very impressive.

On the other hand the really outstanding monument within the area of the antiquities is the Dhamekh Stupa, which is not a mound but a circular tower with an immense amount of stonework on the lower section and an equally large amount of brickwork above the stone. 93 feet in diameter, the stone part rises to a height of about 45 feet, and the brick takes the tower sixty feet higher, though the diameter of the upper section is somewhat less. It is clear that this tower bears witness to a late flowering of Buddhism in India, since a seventh century inscription was found inside it when General

Cunningham first investigated it. It was not unusual to envelop an old stupa in a new skin thus enlarging it, sometimes more than once, and that is probably what happened in this case.

This is certainly the stupa that attracts the most attention from today's pilgrims. On the lower courses of the stone drum it is still possible to see flowers, birds, human beings and geometrical patterns carved in low relief, and enthusiastic visitors have stuck gold leaf on some of the carvings that are within reach. Patches of the stone have also been blackened by the smoke of candles, thus upsetting the Archaeological Department, which has stuck up a notice saying, 'Do not light candles etc around the stupa'. Furthermore a sign points to the 'candlestand', which is a three-tiered, curved terrace on the outer side of the circular ambulatory.

The significance of this stupa lies in its name *Damekh*, which appears to be a shortened form of *Dharmachakra*, meaning the Wheel of the Law or Doctrine. It is logical, therefore, to assume that it marks the spot where the Buddha preached his first sermon to the ascetic five, which is recorded in the Dharmachakra Pravartana Sutra, the Book of the turning of the Wheel of the Law. Yet other opinions have been held. The author of my little *Tourist Handbook to Sarnath-Varanasi* thinks that *Damekh* is a shortened version of the Sanskrit *Dharma Meksha*, which he somewhat infelicitously translates as 'Pandering of the Law'. On the other hand Dr Jairman Singh, in his more scholarly work, opines that this may well be the spot where the Buddha preached his second sermon, the full version of *Damekh* being *Dharmapadeshka*, signifying 'Preacher of the Dharma'.

The discovery of a clay votive-tablet referring to the monument as the Dhamaka Stupa appeared to settle the matter in favour of Dharmachakra. But if this stupa marked the place of the first sermon, what did the demolished stupa commemorate? The answer really came to light when Jagat Singh demolished it. His workmen found a stone urn about twenty-seven feet below the top of the sixty-foot mound, which contained a reliquary of green marble. Inside it was a part of one of the eight portions of the relics of the Buddha, which Ashoka had had removed from their original burial-place to be close to the spot where the Wheel of the Law had been set in motion by the First Sermon. Jagat Singh had the ashes scattered in the holy Ganges. But he presented the green casket, together with its other contents, to Jonathan Duncan, the British Resident in Varanasi at that time. He in turn passed it on in 1794 to the Bengal Asiatic Society in Calcutta. It then disappeared, and when General Cunningham asked to see it forty years later it could not be found. Nor has it been found to this day.

According to the archaeological evidence this stupa had already been rebuilt and enlarged six times when the present reconstruction was commenced. When it is suitably completed no doubt pilgrims will pay their respects here too, thus bringing it to life again after an interval of a thousand years.

After visiting the Dharmarajika and Dhamekh stupas I went further on beyond the archaeological compound to see the genuinely new temples in Sarnath. The original and most important of these is the Mahabodhi Society's own Mulagandha Kuti vihara. The tower of this building is a smaller, simplified version of the nine-storeyed tower of the Mahabodhi temple in Bodh-Gaya, and one may well ask how this relates to the old Mulagandha Kuti vihara in Sarnath. The answer is that the latter may well have also had a tower of this type. When Hiuen Tsiang visited it he noted that the tower of the now ruined temple was some sixty feet high, whilst the six-foot thickness of the remaining walls indicates that they were built to carry a heavy and lofty structure.

The Mahabodhi Society of Sarnath, which has done so much to promote the revival of Buddhism in India, is an offshoot of the Mahabodhi Society of Calcutta, which came into being in 1891. The Society managed to get enough donors to start building the modern Mulagandha Kuti in 1922, when the foundation stone was laid by Sir Harcourt Butler, uncle of the then Governor of Uttar Pradesh, which at that time was called the United Provinces. After that the vihara was nine years a-building under the energetic direction of the Venerable Anagarika Dharmapala, founder and general secretary of the society, and with the active and financial help of Mrs Elizabeth Foster of Honolulu.

Following tradition caskets containing valuable relics were enshrined in the vihara. Firstly, there is the reliquary found at Taxila during the Sir John Marshall excavations of 1913-14 in the small Buddhist chapel close to the Dharmarajika Stupa of the place. This reliquary contains a silver scroll engraved with an inscription dated the equivalent of 79 CE, which states that the relics are of the Blessed One, but does not state from which of the original eight portions they came. In any case they were considered important enough to be presented to the Mahabodhi Society by the Viceroy of India, the Earl of Willingdon in 1931. Secondly, there is the silver casket found in 1929 in a large stupa at Nagarjunikonda in Madras Province by A.H. Longhurst, then Superintendent of the Southern Circle of the Archaeological Survey of India. This reliquary was also presented to the society by the Viceroy in the following year, and was enshrined in the vihara.

`May all living beings be happy 2475 BE 1931 CE`

Thus concludes the account of the foundation of the vihara, which continues to be actively in use with people coming and going all the time. Outside, when I was there, popular music was blaring out of loudspeakers to stir up suitable enthusiasm for the local elections. But inside the vihara I found six persons dressed in black who were chanting in front of the Buddha image under the direction of a yellow-robed *bhikshu* from Taiwan.

As in so many of the modern Buddhist temples, the walls of the new Mulagandha Kuti are embellished with the scenes of incidents in the Buddha's life. Although they were executed by a Japanese artist, Kosetsu Nosu, and partly financed by the proceeds of his own sales, these paintings were donated principally by a British Buddhist, Mr B.L. Broughton in the year 1936. There were several scenes amongst them that I had not already seen. There was, of course, a picture of the Buddha's meeting with the five ascetics on his way to Sarnath. But there were also pictures of events that happened in places I was yet to see. There was the Buddha preaching to King Bimbisara in Rajagriha, and there was the Buddha taming and converting the wild criminal, Angulimala, near Shravasti.

This temple also has its Bodhi-tree, which is a transplant from the one at Anuradhapura in Sri Lanka, and in the grounds of the temple on the far side of the tree can be seen the Buddha and the five ascetics modelled more than life-size in plaster. They are in a grove beside a bell which was 'opened', as the notice puts it, in 1993 by the President of Sri Lanka and called the Indo-Sri Lanka Peace Bell. The large figures are more prominent than the bell, and so they should be, since the tree-studded lawns around the vihara are extensive, and in this way one's eyes are attracted to them from a distance, though they are far from being gigantesque like the Great Buddha at Bodh-Gaya.

All the monuments to the First Sermon—The Damekh Stupa, the Dharmarajika Stupa and the Mulagandha Kuti Vihara—are close to each other. So there is not much point in arguing about which precisely marks the spot where this great event took place. One has to imagine the old deer-park covering the whole area. Originally it would have been a king's hunting domain like the New Forest in England, looking rather different from the artificially laid out lawns and carefully planted trees that are usually called to mind by the word 'park'.

And indeed there is a much reduced deer-park there today, though one might prefer there not to be. As in the park at Bodh-Gaya, I could see but one forlorn deer in the compound with scarcely any pasture on the brown ground of baked mud, together with a token zoo featuring some guinea-pigs and storks for the children to look at. To me the lake on the other side of the little zoo looked equally sad, though it has its place in the Buddha story and was purposely planted with lotuses for the 2,500th anniversary of the Great Decease. Hiuen Tsiang called it a lake in which the water 'neither increases nor decreases' and in which the Tathagata used to bathe, wash his clothes and rinse his begging-bowl.

Of the other modern temples at Sarnath the oldest is the Burmese one, which was built in 1934 near a back entrance to the site close to the offices of the Archaeological Department. It has a gateway that was donated by the same good folk of Windermere, Rangoon as became responsible for the Sujata shrine in the village of Bakraur. The temple itself and the small monastic vihara attached to it owed their construction to two ladies also of Rangoon with the son of one and the daughter of the other. I spent some time here with the elderly watchman, whom at first I took to be an aged pilgrim resting on the bench outside the temple. He told me that one of the Buddha images was of sandalwood and had been presented by Thailand. The main statue, however, is of the distinctive Burmese alabaster-like marble and has a wall painting behind it of a forest tree and a deer, which are symbolic of the Deer-Park. For here too, we are told 'our Lord Buddha Gotama preached his first sermon 2523 years ago'.

Here I spoke to a boy, who said he did not go to school but helped his father to sell Benares silks in a nearby shop. As I sat over a clay cup of tea at the teahouse by the gate of the temple, he tried to persuade me to go with him to the shop. But Gopal was waiting at the handlebars of his auto-rickshaw and with him I went to visit the other places that were worth seeing.

I leaped across a puddle to get into the Chinese temple in Dharmapal Road, which 'was erected by Mr. Lee Choon Seng of Fukien, China and also of Singapore in 1939' and got an extension when 'the vegetable plot and mango-grove measuring eleven bighas had been purchased and donated to the temple by the Chief Abbot Rev. Teh Yu, Mr. Liang Shieh Yao and Mr. Liang Shieh Kuei in March 1982'. Also in Dharmapal Road I found the Mahabodhi Society library, which had been built in memory of Mrs Foster of Honolulu and houses a valuable collection of books related to Buddhism, including a complete set, in English, of the *Sacred Books of the East* edited by F. Max Müller. One was welcome to look around, as indeed one was welcome to go into the meeting-hall of the Buddha Dharma Sangha of the Society, in front of which stands a bust of its founder, Anagarika Dharmapala, who was born in Sri Lanka in 1864 and died at Sarnath in 1933.

But it was the search for the site of the Japanese temple, which was not yet built, that led me to the unknown stupa near the railway-station. Perhaps this was the one mentioned by Hiuen Tsiang that was 300 feet high, since I estimated its diameter at not less than 200 feet. It stretches the whole length of a tank, which has a lot of watercress in it and in which I saw women washing and boys swimming, and it still rises to a considerable height. Yet there is no mention of it in most of the guidebooks.

Probably the reason is that there is a Shiva temple with a white tower of the usual cigar shape on top of the mound. The temple is reached up a long flight of broad steps, and its name is highly significant. It is called the Sarangnath temple, in other words the temple of Shiva as Lord of the Deer, and indeed Shiva is often portrayed holding a deer in one of his hands. But the presence of the Hindu temple has precluded detailed investigation of the giant tumulus. So the rest is silence.

It would have been appropriate to come to Sarnath from Varanasi by train, walk out of the station under the archway, which is shaped like a Buddhist *toran* and embellished with a swastika, and come face to face with this mighty stupa a hundred yards or so away. But what one faces today is a huge mound with a big banyan-tree and a peepul-tree beside it, some acacias on it, and the steps leading up to the temple. Yet the bricks which held the stupa in place, running vertically rather than horizontally, can still be clearly seen. So it is strange that the only Shiva temple in Sarnath stands on the remains of the largest of the Buddhist stupas, which flourished when there were 1,500 or more monks in the monasteries there.

To visualise what Sarnath must have looked like in those days before the decline that culminated in the fire and slaughter brought when Qutub-ud-Din devastated Varanasi and the surrounding land in 1194, we have to think of places like the Shwe Dagon pagoda in Rangoon or the Swayambhunath Stupa in Katmandu. The white and gold of the great stupas could be seen from afar, like the towers of the cathedrals in the West, as the pilgrim made his way with his companions towards his goal. Above the great mounds were the *htis* of multiple mushroom rings which culminated in spires. The Main Shrine would also have had a tower on it, perhaps similar to the one at Bodh-Gaya and decorated with many Buddha statues and Buddhistic reliefs. The streets would be full of saffron-robed bhikshus with shaven heads, whose begging-bowls the pilgrims would fill. People would be walking clockwise round the stupas murmuring the mystic OM, others would visit the lotus lake, others the park containing the Vihara of Perfect Wisdom.

Nowadays new temples have been bravely built to take the place of the old, and are still being built. The peace of the

Raj was the ambience for the beginnings of a great revival of Buddhism in the ancient land, which increases day by day.

8

The Order of Monks – Rajagriha

Whilst the Buddha was at Sarnath he was approached early one morning by a young man of Varanasi named Yasa, who had tried all the luxuries of life and grown weary of them. The parallel with the Buddha's own experience is clear.

As the Buddha was explaining the four Noble Truths to the young man, the latter's father came looking for him and remained to listen to the great teacher. He was converted on the spot, becoming a lay follower of the Buddha with the words *Sangham saranam gacchami*, I take refuge in the Order. He thus became the first to use the triple formula of *Buddha*, *Dharma* and *Sangha*, the Buddha, the Doctrine and the Order, which is still current today as a confession of faith. His son, Yasa, eventually became a saint, one of the *arhats* that one sometimes sees represented over the doorways of temples.

At the end of the rainy season Gautama Buddha told the monks whom he had been instructing to go forth singly and spread the teaching of the Dharma. He himself returned to Uruvilva and taught there, delivering his message in a way that all could understand by starting with simple matters and gradually moving on to higher things. There he made many converts, particularly from a sect of yogis with matted hair, who worshipped fire and water.

From Uruvilva the Buddha went the relatively short distance to Rajagriha. He had already met King Bimbisara there in the days before his enlightenment, and he wanted to see him again. As soon as Shakyamuni Buddha arrived the king went to visit him and became, himself, a convert, cementing the relationship by inviting the Buddha and his followers to a meal on the following day, during which he served the Buddha himself. He also presented his own royal park to the Buddhist Order of monks for their own use. Lying just outside the city walls, it was called the Venuvana, the Bamboo Grove. Huts were erected in the Venuvana to shelter the monks during the next rainy season, and thus the first Buddhist monastery was created.

I went back to Gaya to get to Rajagriha, though it is possible to reach the place under its modern name, Rajgir, by train from Patna. In Gaya I asked Leslie how best to get there, and he introduced me to the owner of a sweet-shop on the corner next to the Ajatsatru Hotel.

I call it a sweet-shop, though the sweets were nothing like the wrapped and packaged sweets and chocolate one buys in the West. They were freshly made bites that it was possible to eat on the premises, and which people were in fact eating as they chatted like men talking over their drinks in a pub. White was the predominant colour—the white of rice, the white of milk and the white of refined sugar, mixed in different proportions to make various kinds of sweet balls, flavoured with mango or jaggery or pistachio. The metai-wallah was an amiable man, who hired out to me his own Maruti and his chauffeur to go with it for the day. It was a conveniently narrow vehicle with sliding-doors, and it had a swastika painted in red on the hub of the steering-wheel, and a garland of marigolds draped across the windscreen in honour of Lakshmi. Yet the driver, Mahmoud, was a Muslim.

First we had to cross the wide Phalgu river on a cantilever bridge built in the British time, under which some people were defecating on the sandy islands in the stream and others were washing clothes. Then we proceeded through the avenues of different trees that flanked the road—the acacias in yellow bloom, the carobs, the neems, the sal and the peepul. The ridges of sleeping policemen appeared across the road wherever two or three houses were gathered together, and so we went on by fits and starts across the plain, whilst isolated hills appeared on either side as we approached Rajgir.

It was forty miles to Rajgir. But first we had to pass through the cyclopean walls of Rajagriha, which had clearly been a much bigger and more important place than the modern Rajgir. From the South Gate, through which the road zigzagged on the first hill we had encountered since leaving Gaya, to the North Gate was over two miles. The small town of today, a mere village in comparison, is three miles beyond that.

Mahmoud was not as conversant with the sites of Rajgir as one might have liked him to be, and this was the reason why he first took me to a place that was not Buddhist at all but Jain. Perhaps he could have been excused for this, since the Jains and their naked saints have much in common with the Buddhists and have always lived harmoniously alongside them.

The Jains here near Rajgir have built a most elaborate cultural centre, in which the incidents in the lives of the saints and great men and women of the Jain story are displayed in detailed tableaux of modelled figures in rural or architectural settings. There are very many of these tableaux, and they seemed to me to be more suitable for children than for adults. For this reason and because they were not part of my pilgrimage, I did not linger over them. This surprised the ladies at the door, who were anxious to involve me in their philosophy and introduce me to their religion.

These ladies wore little white cloth pelmets over their noses and mouths lest they should inadvertently breathe in a

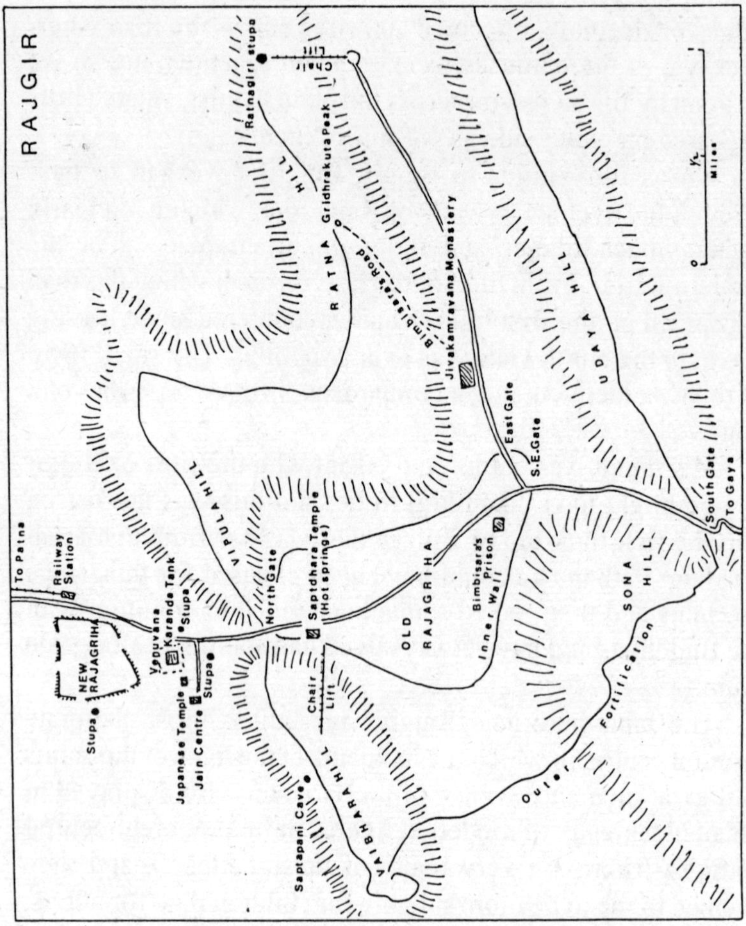
RAJGIR
To Patna
Railway Station
NEW RAJAGRIHA
Stupa
Venuvana
Karanda Tank
Stupa
Japanese Temple
Jain Centre
Stupa
VIPULA HILL
North Gate
Saptdhara Temple (Hot springs)
Chair Lift
Saptapani Cave
VAIBHARA HILL
OLD RAJAGRIHA
Bimbisara's Prison
Inner Wall
SONA HILL
Outer Fortification
South Gate
To Gaya
S.E. Gate
East Gate
UDAYA HILL
Jivakamravana Monastery
Bimbisara's Road
RATNA HILL
Gridhrakuta Peak
Ratnagiri stupa
Chair Lift
0
½
Miles

living creature such as a mosquito or a fly, and one of them told me about the modern development of the Jains of whom, she said, there were at least a crore, which is ten million. She told me about their foundations and their medical charities, and she urged me not to miss visiting the Jain temple in Leicester.

The visit to the Jains may have been irrelevant to my pilgrimage. But it proved to be a lucky diversion, since it was on the pathway outside their exhibition-hall that I met Swami Ananda Chaitanya Das, an eighteen year-old bhikshu from Kuala Lumpur, the capital of Malaysia, who became my guide from then on. Ananda had finished his morning duties as an assistant at the local medical centre, and having nothing special to do he took me to the nearby Japanese temple, which had a beautiful Buddha in the earth is witness pose in it, carved in Burmese alabaster. It was installed on May 16th 1992, and high above it, in a welter of ornamentation, there was a large photograph of the founder of the temple.

The Japanese temple is new, spacious and colourful. It is also on the way to the old Venuvana Park, which can be reached from it in a few minutes by a bridge across a little stream. There are still a few clumps of bamboo in the Bamboo Grove. But most of the space is occupied by the Karanda Tank, in which the Buddha used to bathe, and the trees and walkways that surround it. There is an image of the Buddha facing the lake, with a small Thai temple adjacent to it, and there used to be a small zoo there also, as the remains of an aviary suggest. Now, fortunately, the zoo is no longer in existence.

Maybe the wild-life that runs freely in the Venuvana has not changed much since ancient times. One of the sutras refers to the place where the squirrels used to feed. It was where Shariputra approached the Buddha one evening after coming out of a period of meditation. The Buddha asked him why he looked so bright and why his complexion was so clear. He replied that he had been experiencing emptiness and was now fully within it.

Ananda, which means the Joyful One, was not misnamed. His enthusiasm was immense, and he delighted in showing me round. His problem was that, being of Tamil extraction, the local Indians took him to be one of their nationality instead of allowing him the distinction of being a foreigner from overseas. This problem reached a point of crisis when we went to the hot springs, which gush out of Mount Vaibhara. The hot waters have become public baths. But they are under the supervision, as it were, of the Shivaite temple that has been built around them. We were invited to approach the entrance to the temple sanctuary to view the image inside it. When we demurred, the pujaris heaped scorn on Ananda but not on me, which made him extremely annoyed.

It may have been for this reason that he made his next remark. At the foot of the temple steps we found a nearly naked sun-blackened man, who looked as emaciated as the starving Buddha must have been. He was crawling about on the ground, and I gave him some coins. Ananda simply laughed cheerfully and said, "It is his karma."

Up behind the white buildings of the Shiva temple and the hot-water baths lies the Saptaparni cave. This cave is where some authorities say that the first Buddhist Council was held shortly after Gautama Buddha's death. If that is so, most of the five hundred delegates must have gathered outside, since the cave is too small to have accommodated that number. There is now a kind of ski-lift to take you up to it, making things easy for the modern pilgrim wilting in the heat of the day.

Between the temple-steps and the foot of the chair-lift a policeman with a large stick was pacing about amongst the food and souvenir-stalls. Ananda did not like him. "He makes the shop-people afraid," he said.

"How?" I asked.

"They have to pay him respect."

With that equivocal answer still in my ears we went back to the Maruti, and retraced the road into old Rajagriha through the North Gate so that we could get to the other particular spots that had been frequented by Siddhartha Gautama. The old city had been built on fairly flat land. But it was almost completely surrounded by the hills that must have been its main defence. In the middle, inside an inner wall, was Bimbisara's palace. Outside the East Gate of the inner wall were the Buddha's special places.

There was not much left of the first site that we reached. But the bottoms of walls, which had lain under the ground before being excavated, clearly showed that there had been a built-up area there, which could have been a small monastic complex. This was the Jivakamravana, which had originally been a grove of mango-trees. Jivaka was King Bimbisara's physician, said to be a son of one of the town's courtesans. He had studied medicine in Taxila and made a name for himself with some striking cures. So the king made him responsible for the health of Gautama Buddha and the members of the Order as well as for his own. In this way Jivaka met the Buddha with the result that he joined the Order as a lay member. Since the Buddha often went to the mango-grove, Jivaka presented it to the Sangha, and that is how a monastery came to be established there.

The hills rise up steeply behind the open square of the Jivakamravana, well-wooded on the lower slopes and more craggy and bushy higher up. On top of the highest peak a white pimple was visible, and that is what we headed for next. There was another chair-lift to make it easy for us. But we had to wait for it to start up again after the midday break, and it was then that Ananda told me some more about his life-style as a bhikshu.

He rose, he said, at 2.30 a.m., recited mantras and had breakfast at nine o'clock. After that he would go and serve in the hospital, and in the afternoon he would study under his guru, particularly Sanskrit texts. He would eat only once more and go to bed about 9 p.m. At the hospital they did a good number of operations on cataracts. But they were short of funds. One such eye operation might cost Rs. 2,000. It seemed a goodly sum to him, but is actually the equivalent of only £50, which would not go far in the British national health service.

Although I was quite willing to pay for both of us to go up the mountain and back on the chair-lift, Ananda had a strong objection to me parting with my money. He told me the man in the ticket-office was a friend of the monks, who had done him some service, and thus he was able to get his tickets free. The least I could do in return was to make a contribution through him to the medical charity he was associated with. He said he had taken medicines to the monks in Tibet and had been given a hard time there by the Chinese overlords, who had arrested him on suspicion of being a spy. He was due to make another visit there when the winter was over for the same humanitarian cause. If he was nervous about it, he did not show it. He simply said cheerfully that it was his mission.

Ananda told me that we were entitled to jump the queue when the chair-lift finally started up. I could not understand why. But it meant that we were amongst the first to heave ourselves onto the moving chairs, taking care to avoid those that had already been broken in the short time that the lift had been in operation. Thus we were raised effortlessly up the mountain with our legs dangling above the rocks and trees. Women who were gathering firewood below us did not bother to look up as we passed.

At the top it was time for tea at the refreshment-stall beside the track leading to the summit. Or one could have a cold drink out of the refrigerator which stood on a wooden platform under the trees. But Ananda would have neither, sitting patiently whilst I drank. The white pimple that I had first seen from the Jivakamravana had become enormous. It was a large stupa, and its beautifully clean lines made it shine against the sky. There were golden Buddhas facing the four points of the compass from the fuller's-white hemisphere, and the great mound was surmounted by the traditional *hti* of mushroom rings diminishing in size up to the golden peepul-leaf above.

Except for the four Buddhas and the peepul-leaf, which must have been as big as a small bush, the whole thing was white, even including the lanterns and the guard-dogs that we passed as we went up the steps to circumambulate the stupa in the proper fashion. The view of the hills and plains from the mountain-top was also magnificent, and I was reminded that the name of the State of Bihar is actually a short form of 'vihara', so called because there were once so many Buddhist monasteries and temples within its borders. But to find out more about this particular stupa I had to go along the ridge of the mountain to a much smaller memorial stupa, which had been built in memory of the Most Ven. Nichidatsu Fujiguruji.

Born on 6th August 1885 at the foothills of Mt. Asoin Japan, joined the Nichiren Buddhist order at the age of 19, in 1903. He came to India and worked with Mahatma Gandhi in India's non-violent war of independence. Gandhiji gave him the name 'Guruji' and included Na Mu Myo Ho Ren Ge Kyo, the essence of Buddhism, in his prayers. It was his firm belief that this autra had the power to counter the threat of total annihilation of the world caused by the nuclear disarmament.

Guruji built 70 peace pagodas all over the world. The Rajagriha Shanti Stupa atop Ratnagiri Hill was completed in 1969.

As a pacifist and advocate of complete disarmament he made his life a vehicle for the spread of the message, peace and amity, and led many peace marches. In recognition of his services he was conferred Jawarhalal Nehru Award for International Understanding in 1979,

This great disciple of Lord Buddha and Nichiren Boddhisattva and much loved by Mahatma Gandhi, Most Ven. Fuji Guruji, entered nirvana on 9th Jan 1985 at Atami in Japan at the ripe age of 101.

The notice beside the stupa, which gives the above details about Fuji Guruji's life, is headed 'Na Mu Myo Ho Ren Ge Kyo'. This Japanese mantra means 'Honour to the Lotus sutra of the true Dharma' and was formulated by the Nichiren school in the 13th century. But the rest of it testifies to the universal use of English as the world language today. However, it does have some odd features. Firstly, the actual date of his arrival in India has been scored out. Secondly, I found it impossible to fathom what the word 'autra' might mean, unless it be a misprint for 'sutra'. Thirdly, it was hard to see how the 'total annihilation of the world' could be 'caused by nuclear disarmament'. And fourthly, if he was born in August 1885 and died in January 1985, he would have been 99 not 101, unless the traditional Chinese style of reckoning was used, in which case he could have been 100.

This was not for me to judge. But what I did pass judgement on was the Government of India tourist brochure on Bihar, which has a photograph of the Shanti, or Peace stupa in it and states that the stupa is on Vulture Peak. I had thought that I was being chair-lifted up Vulture Peak when, in fact, I was going up Ratnagiri, the 'Jewel hill'.

Yet Vulture Peak below, along the ridge of Mount Chattha, is the one that is renowned in the story of the Buddha, and the approach to it is through a gate beside the remains of the Jivakamravana monastery, The path up Gridhrakuta Hill, to give it its Indian name, is steep. But the pilgrim is helped by the stone staircase mentioned by Hiuen Tsiang, which is called Bimbisara's road. Archaeologists now believe that the big stones of which it is made were part of a very ancient fortification. But Buddhists are told that King Bimbisara had it built to make it easier for him to visit the Buddha on top of the hill.

There are still two small stupas alongside the road, which were investigated at the beginning of the century without producing anything of note. Higher up there are real steps, that were clearly cut as such, and at the top of the hill the remains of some large stone walls show that there must have been some quite substantial buildings up there. Indeed, though the portable items have been removed to the museum at Nalanda, the whole area is studded with the remains of old Buddhist monuments, which are in complete contrast with the blinding white new memorials on nearby Ratna Hill.

Gautama Buddha had a long life, and for many years he would come back to the Bamboo Grove, the Mango Grove and Vulture Peak at Rajagriha. In his later life his particular patron, King Bimbisara, was dead and his place had been taken by Ajatashatru. The Buddha's cousin, Devadatta, who had always been antagonistic to him, and had hated him ever since he had beaten him in their bridal contest, thought that this change of ruler would give him a better chance of supplanting his hated rival as head of the Order.

Three incidents are recorded, in which Devadatta tried to encompass the Buddha's death. In his first attempt he hired an assassin. After the assassin had done his work, he himself was to be killed by two men. These two men were to be killed by another four, the four by eight and the eight by sixteen men. He hoped that in the bloodbath of fifteen people after Gautama's death the core of the plot would never be unravelled.

The plot was foiled, as was another attempt on the Buddha's life by Devadatta, which is a favourite subject for sculptors and artists. He arranged to have a fierce bull-elephant, named Nalagiri, made drunk and let loose against the Buddha whilst he was on his begging round in one of the narrow streets of the city. But as the elephant came towards him, leaving no way for him to escape, it lowered its trunk, stopped and bowed down before him. Devadatta's third attempt on his cousin's life took place on Vulture Peak itself, He had a huge boulder rolled down the mountainside towards him as he was walking up Bimbisara Road. It only injured his foot. So perhaps it was a natural fall of a fragment of rock after all.

Vulture Peak yielded a wonderful stone Buddha in the teaching pose to the Nalanda museum. Under the stool on which he is sitting there are two deer facing a wheel, on which the spokes are very finely carved. But no ancient statues remain in situ.

However, there are many other places of Buddhist interest at Rajagriha. Ajatashatru, who converted to Buddhism after his youthful misdemeanours, managed to get one of the eight portions of the relics of the Buddha, for which he built a stupa. It is still a matter for debate as to which it was of the ruins that can be identified as stupas today. There are two stupas near the Bamboo Grove and there is another further north and to the west of the smaller Rajagriha that Ajatashatru had built outside the ring of hills. Fa Hien said that the latter was Ajatashatru's stupa. But Hiuen Tsiang, who visited Rajagriha over two hundred years later, said that this one had been built by Ashoka.

Of course they could both be right, as it was not uncommon to make a new stupa by building a new skin over an old one. The mound is now about thirty feet high. In the outer part of it were found a number of clay stupas not more than two inches high, in each of which there was a terracotta tablet inscribed with the Buddhist creed, 'Buddha has revealed the cause of all phenomena proceeding from a cause, as well as their suppression. So says the Great Sage.' 'Maha Shramana' were the words used for Great Sage, and the writing and language is of the eighth or ninth century, long after the time of Ashoka.

On the other hand, Hiuen Tsiang was told that the stupa to the east of the Bamboo Grove, and now close to the main road, was Ajatashatru's. Not much of this one is left apart from the stone base, and some stone pillars which most likely belong to a much later date.

Reading Fa Hien's account of his visit to Rajagriha, I thought once again how strange it is that we have to rely on the travel books of two Chinamen for reliable details about the places which were the goals of the Buddhist pilgrimage before they crumbled and decayed and were finally destroyed. When Fa Hien went to Rajagriha, the hill-girt city was already deserted. 'All is emptiness and desolation,' he writes. 'No man dwells in it.' However, although the capital of Magadha had been moved to Patna after Ajatashatru's reign, Fa Hien found quite a lot to see in both new and old Rajagriha, and what is more, he tells me what that mountain crag was which I had seen from the train and thought must be the Vulture Peak. He has been writing about Patna, and then he says:

> The travellers went on from this to the south-east for nine yojanas and came to a small solitary rocky hill, at the end of which was a building facing south—the place where the Buddha sat when Sakra, ruler of the Devas, brought the Deva musician, Panchasikha, to give pleasure to him by playing the lute. Sakra then asked the Buddha forty-two questions, tracing them with his finger one by one on the rock. The prints of his tracing are still there, and there is also a monastery.

A *yojana* is the distance an ox-cart might travel in a day, usually calculated at six or seven miles. So the nine *yojanas* would be something over fifty miles from Patna. The divine lutanist is often portrayed in Buddhist temples, nor does Fa Hien leave out the miraculous element that has adhered to the Buddha story. But first he describes New Rajagriha in the following words:

> There were two monasteries in it. Three hundred paces outside the west gate King Ajatashatru, having obtained one portion of the relics of the Buddha, built a stupa, high, large, grand and beautiful. Leaving the city by the south gate and proceeding south four li (about a mile) one enters a valley and comes to a circular space formed by five hills, which stand all around it and have the appearance of the outer wall of a city.
>
> Entering the valley and keeping along the mountains on the south-east, after ascending fifteen li (about four miles) the travellers came to Mount Gridhrakuta. Three li before you reach the top there is a cave in the rocks facing south, in which the Buddha sat in meditation. Thirty paces to the north-west there is another cave, where Ananda was meditating when the Deva Mara, having assumed the form of a vulture, landed in front of the cave and frightened the disciple. Then the Buddha, by his mysterious and supernatural power, made a cleft in the rock, put his hand through it and stroked Ananda's shoulder so that his fear immediately left him. The footprints of the bird and the cleft for the Buddha's hand are still there, and thence comes the name of Hill of the Cave of the Vulture.

That was Fa Hien's story, and that was how the Buddha's life was wedded with the natural landscape in the imagination. Pilgrims were told tales that would stick in their minds for the rest of their lives even if they came from distant lands. But Ananda, the modern bhikshu from Malaysia did not appear to be familiar with such lore. I took him in the car back to the place of the hot waters, and there I left him to walk back to his vihara. We thanked each other for a day well spent and parted without proposing any further attachment.

By the time I got back to the Ajatsatru Hotel it was dark. Leslie came up to me like a faithful wife to see how her husband has fared. But there was someone else in the Sujata restaurant too, apart from the groups of local young men high on masala spices and pepsi-cola. It was the fair-haired man I had seen sitting on the ghat and spoken to on my way back from Sujata's village.

"You still here?" I said.

"Why not?" he answered.

He wanted to catch the night train to Varanasi, and that was why he had come up from Bodh-Gaya in the early evening before dark. In fact it looked as though he was planning to visit the same places as I had seen.

"Where were you staying in Bodh-Gaya?" I asked. "Ashok Hotel?"

"No. Burmese vihara. It was more right for me."

"How so?"

"It's simple. You have nothing there. So you want nothing. You can meditate. And it's near the Bo-tree."

"You can meditate there too."

"I tried."

He told me his name. It was Mark Klugman. And very soon, after Leslie had got one of his waiters to bring us two Kingfisher beers, he began to tell me something about himself. He had grown up in the middle of the United States in that part which is often called the Bible belt, where the people believe that the word of God was first given to the world according to ancient Jewish history and legend.

"I began to wonder about that when I went to Vietnam," he said, "and Hong Kong after that. But I still went to church. It's Church of England in the cathedral there. Not all that different. Same old God of the Jews handing out rewards and punishments. But I guess now they don't talk about the punishments so much. It was the thing to do to go to that church. I was in business by then, trying to beat the Brits and the Chinese at their own game. Exporting yachts to the West Coast. Build them much cheaper in Hong Kong. Well too. Those Chinese are really great craftsmen. Sure you want to hear all this?"

"Sure I do," I said. But I think he would have carried on anyway.

"I was married by then. Got married in Vietnam. She was tall for a Vietnamese, but still a lot shorter than me. Sure I did love her. That wasn't a question. There wasn't any family. None she told me about. So there wasn't anyone to leave behind when I went back to the States. There was a little boy. My son. We called him Reuben. I guess that was my name for him. They don't call their kids Reuben in Vietnam. And he was my son. She said that was for sure."

I asked Mark Klugman if he had crossed the river and visited the Sujata shrine after I had talked to him at the ghat. He said he had, on the following day, and he had also gone on up to the cave.

"I had nothing to eat all that day," he said. "Maybe you could call it a kind of short fast. There's a fast somewhere in all of them—Buddhist, Moslem, Christian. Don't eat after midday. Don't eat before sundown. Don't eat meat. Don't eat at all."

"The Buddha gave up fasting."

"Sure. It didn't work." He was gazing straight ahead as he had been at the ghat. "I told you I was in Hong Kong," he went on. "Well, she didn't come at first. She was a nurse. Wanted him to grow up a real one hundred per cent American. We were in San Diego. Most of the time in Hong Kong I was on my own. Used to go sailing with an old Brit colonel who lived up on the Peak."

"So she was like a single mother."

"You could call it that. It wasn't what I wanted. We just visited. I'd go to the States on business. She'd come to Hong Kong in the school holidays. We had arguments. I didn't like her attitude to Rube."

"What's that mean?"

"Kept him like a pet poodle. Couldn't do anything on his own. Couldn't even say anything on his own. When they came to Hong Kong I tried to get him into things—swimming, sailing, getting out. He was ten by then. She wouldn't have it. Too delicate, she said. I'm a nurse. I ought to know. All that crap. One evening I came in and they were in the bedroom together. Voices quiet. She was just going on at him, not loud, quiet. Monotonous. Just going on and on. No answer from him. He was dead quiet. Just like she was some kind of hypnotist. When I opened the door, there they were. He was lying on the bed. She was sitting on it and looking, I don't know, kind of guilty. Next day was Sunday. But they stayed in. No sailing for Rube. The Colonel and I went out without him. In the evening she and I drove up to the Peak. You don't know the Peak."

"I do," I said.

"It was for the sunset. You can see a long way from up there, across the islands, into China."

"I know," I said.

"I had an Oldsmobile. Big car for Hong Kong streets. But I was used to that kind of car. There's an old house up on the Peak. Used to be the Governor's place. I parked near it on the edge of the hill. Then we got out to walk. Rube wasn't with us. You've got to understand that. He said he didn't want to come. That annoyed her. But he dug in, and we went out just the two of us. Had some eats at Repulse Bay. You could've said we were having a great time. I turned the car round to face downhill. Make it easy for leaving. Then we got out and walked over the grass to look at the view. Islands like a lot of ink blots. We were hand in hand when we went back to the car. I opened the door for her and slipped the lock on when I shut her in. Then I went round to the driver's side and let it out of gear. You understand I had my foot on the brake because I knew the handbrake would never hold her on its own. It was one of those dashboard brakes weak as hell. Then I jumped out. It sure did go. At the bottom of the first straight it shot off the curve and down into the bushes. I heard the bushes cracking and the crash."

"I don't think you ought to be telling me this," I said.

"Well I am telling you," he answered. "Because of what happened after that. I told you the Colonel lived on the Peak. So I went down to his house and told him what had happened. At first he thought I'd been the one in the accident. My clothes were torn and they had a lot of blood on them. Because I'd crashed down through the bushes to see what I could see. There wasn't a chance. Neck snapped. He called the ambulance, police, fire-brigade. Everything. Gave me half a bottle of brandy. Told me I was darned lucky. Poor old girl. And so on."

"And why tell me?"

"Because of what happened next," Mark Klugman went on. "I told the Colonel I hadn't been in the car. He said he was darned sorry. He didn't say it. But I knew he was thinking it. Did she kill herself? I said 'No'. So he said, 'It was a darned rotten accident'. I said 'No. I did it'. That was after we'd been up to the car with the ambulance and they'd taken the body away. He wasn't having it. Said I was in a state of shock. Have another shot of brandy. Lie down. Feel better in the morning. I told the police. They wouldn't listen either. Said there was no evidence."

"Uncorroborated confession," I said. "You didn't do it. Just imagined you did it," I added.

He turned and looked at me at last. "You're just like the rest of them," he said. "Sure I've thought about it till I was blue. When I went sailing with the Colonel again we went to an island I hadn't been to before. There was a temple on it. It was called the Temple of Vacuity. Vacuity means emptiness, the void. How can you have a temple of nothing? Then I thought it was my emptiness it was all about. It was like I'd fallen through a hole in life, like those dreams you have when you're falling down and down and going to hit bottom and be killed every second but you don't. I had to meet the emptiness and work with it. I still think I did it. But it doesn't matter now."

Mark was staring ahead again and had finished his tale. I noticed that he had not once given his deceased wife a name. Perhaps, I thought, she had no more substance than his crime.

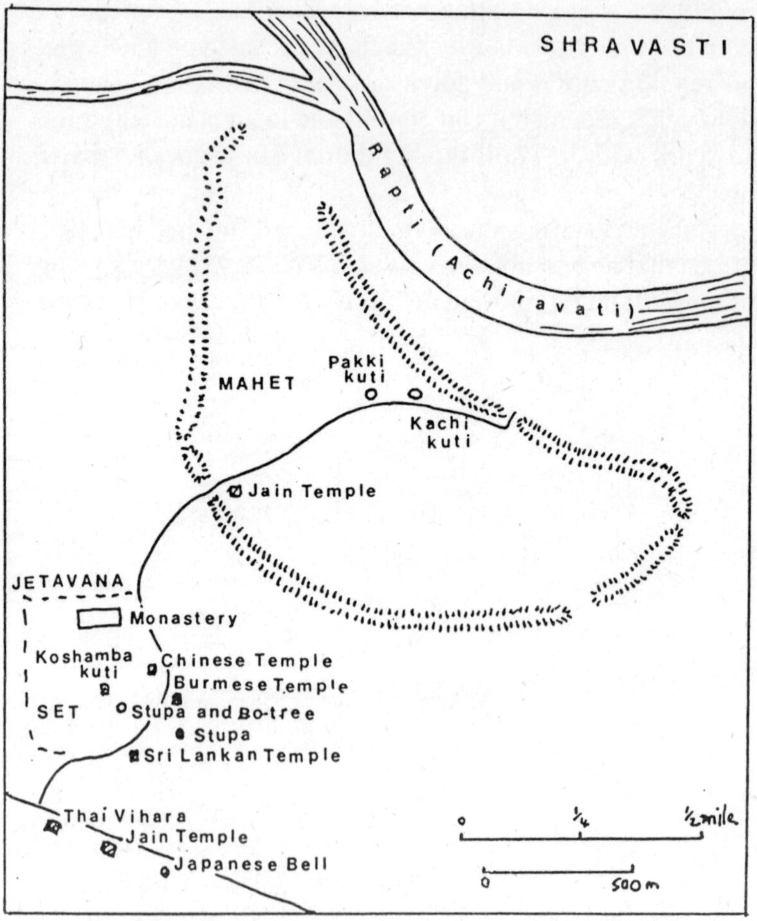
SHRAVASTI
Rapti (Achiravati)
MAHET
Pakki kuti
Kachi kuti
Jain Temple
JETAVANA
Monastery
Koshamba kuti
Chinese Temple
Burmese Temple
SET
Stupa and Bo-tree
Stupa
Sri Lankan Temple
Thai Vihara
Jain Temple
Japanese Bell
0 ¼ ½ mile
0 500 m

9

To Heaven and back – Shravasti

After he had spent a rainy season at Rajagriha, the Buddha went back to Kapilavastu to see his family. It was a journey of a little under four hundred miles, and it took him sixty days on foot. As a *shramana*, a wandering seeker after truth, the Tathagata stayed in the Nigrodha Grove under the banyan-trees outside the city, where others of his kind congregated.

King Shuddhodana was not amused, and neither was Siddhartha Gautama's wife, Yashodhara. She sent their son, Rahula to him to ask for his inheritance. It was an ironical gesture, which she must have regretted, for the boy was inducted into the Buddhist Order and handed over to one of Gautama's closest disciples for instruction. The disciple was Shariputra, one of the two *arhats* represented beside the Great Buddha at Bodh-Gaya.

Back in Rajagriha the Buddha made another important conversion in addition to the physician, Jivaka, who had given him the Mango Grove This was a man named Sudatta, and also called Anathapindada, or many say Anathapindika, 'Supplier of the Needy' because of his generosity. He was a banker, who lived in Shravasti, the capital of the kingdom of Koshala, and was visiting Rajagriha to see his brother-in-law, who lived there.

Anathapindada also pronounced the Three Refuges and joined the Sangha as a layman. He was so keen to have the Tathagata near him that he told him he would find a suitable place in Shravasti, which would become a retreat for him and his people during the rainy seasons. When he got back there he looked around for a suitable location, and found a park that looked to him to be just right for the Buddha's needs. But it was owned by one of the princes, a son of Prasenajit, King of Koshala, named Jeta. It is said, probably with some exaggeration, that Anathapindada, whose banking activities also included dealing in gold, was obliged to cover the whole park with gold coins in order to reach Prince Jeta's asking price.

The Buddha travelled to Shravasti mainly along the same road as he had followed to get to Kapilavastu, crossing the Ganges near Patna and carrying on through Vaishali, the Licchavi capital, and Kushinagara. On arrival he settled down in the park, which was known as the Jetavana. It was a shady place, with mango-trees like the Jivakamravana at Rajagriha, and there was a tank for bathing.

At some time during one of the Buddha's stays at Shravasti a remarkable event occurred. It was a miraculous event, and whether or not it is accepted as a physical or a psychological experience, it is firmly established in the Buddhist canon. He went up to heaven and back. The purpose of his visit was to preach the *Dharma* to the gods, and more particularly to his mother, Maya, who lived in the heaven of thirty-three abodes. The happening is the subject of many fine sculptures that have survived to the present day, which show the Buddha descending a ladder back to earth. He came to ground at Sankissa, which is seven miles from Farrukhabad not far from the ancient city of Kanauj.

But the event that is always known as the Miracle at Shravasti took place when the Buddha walked on air in a kind of levitation that has also been frequently portrayed. This miracle was performed for a purpose as well. There were six gurus resident in Shravasti who claimed to have miraculous powers, and they challenged the Tathagata to a contest of miracles. The Buddha won by rising up off the ground like a flying yogi and producing flames of fire from his shoulders and streams of water from his feet.

At the more mundane level, the Buddha was also staying at Shravasti when he went out to tame a famous and dreaded robber, who was nicknamed Angulimala, 'Finger necklace' because of his habit of stringing together the fingers of his victims and wearing them as necklaces. He was the son of a court Brahmin, and as such he enjoyed a certain amount of protection. But as he was the leader of a large gang of highwaymen, we may think of him in terms of the latter-day thugs. Ignoring warnings, the Buddha went out alone, found Angulimala, who was a well educated man, and engaged him in a conversation that has been preserved and recorded. The result was that the criminal was converted, joined the Order and returned with the Tathagata to the monastery that by then had been built in the Jetavana.

For many years Shravasti, far off the beaten track, was lost to view. Even as late as 1949 Murray, in the sixteenth edition of his famous handbook, recommended going there by elephant from Balrampur. In the second edition of the book, published in 1894, Shravasti was not mentioned at all though Baedeker, in the one and only edition of his Indien published in 1914, does refer to the site and the sculptures taken from it to the Lucknow museum.

Near the border of Nepal north-east of Lucknow, Shravasti is still remote, and although I did not get the chance of going there by elephant, I did manage to travel on a puffer-train. I had decided to catch a train at Gorakhpur which would take me to Gonda, and from there go north to Balrampur. But some problems arose which, at one stage, made me heartily wish that I had accepted Dirba's proposal to drive me there from Piprahawa.

I had grown to like Gorakhpur Junction and to respect the station staff there. It was a clean and tidy station, on which cows did not unduly get in the way. There was a tourist information-officer, who kindly saved me the trouble of getting my own railway-ticket, and the station stalls sold everything from magazines to peanuts. So when I reached the 13.15 for Gonda, which was already standing in the station, I was happy and optimistic. As usual, fearing to be crowded out, I was early. But this did not worry my porter, who climbed up on to the gangway between two coaches in order to get in and open up a first-class carriage for me from inside.

After that I was happy enough just sitting there. A man with a hammer came along and tapped the wheels. The Kushinagar Express came and went. A gentleman whose visiting card said, in the Devanagri script, 'Pee Es Pande', joined me and we engaged in conversation. The problem was then that 13.15 hrs. came and went, and nothing happened. Mr Pande, who was a teacher of economics at the Pharenda middle school, was anxious not to be delayed. So was I, as I was not keen to reach Gonda after dark.

Mr Pande's reason for anxiety was that, as well as being a schoolmaster, he was local agent for the Bharatiya Insurance Company, and he was on his way to a conference of insurance agents in Naini Tal up in the hills. There would be four hundred delegates, he said, and it was going to be cold. I looked at his card again. As an afterthought some words had been written in English, 'Member of the Zonal Managers Club for Agents'.

Time passed, and still there was no activity on our train. Mr Pande left his case in my care and went down the platform to seek information. He returned without any. Then he suddenly sprang into action. "There," he said. "We must go there." A train had slipped quietly into the platform on the other side of the tracks, and in a flash Mr Pande was off, leaping down on to the tracks and climbing up on to the other platform. Mesmerised by his agility I followed him.

But I was not so quick. He only had an attaché case, and a jersey against the cold of Naini Tal. I had a bag, which I threw down the offside of the carriage on to the oily tracks. Stumbling over the tracks and not knowing whether another train might sidle into the station along the same line at that very moment, I reached the other side. It was a high English-style platform, not at all like the low Continental ones, and in the absence of steps it really was a struggle to return to passenger level. But still, I managed it, and in a shambling sort of run followed Mr Pee Es Pande into the Kathgodam Mail. By the time I got into the train he had disappeared down the corridor, and I was on my own again. The conductor came along and told me that the air-conditioned coach, in which I found myself, was absolutely full and nothing could be done about it.

"Then I'll stand here by the door," I said.

"It is not permitted," he answered.

"I'm only going as far as Gonda," I replied.

He went away down the central corridor past passengers who were thickly spread on either side of it, and after a while, as always happens in India, something was arranged. A seat was found for me which would not be needed until the passengers wanted to stretch out and sleep again. No bakhshish was suggested or paid.

In India the mail trains are faster than the expresses. But this one was in no hurry. There was little to see through the steamed-up, air-conditioned window-panes, tinted blue against the glare of the sun, and it was after dark when the train reached Gonda. As there were no taxis in the station-yard, I asked my porter if he could find me a car to take me out to Balrampur. His response was to take me to a particular pedicab man, whom he knew, and I was pedalled off into the night.

My pedaller said he knew just the man for me, and I was not worried whilst he remained on the main road. But soon he plunged off it into a dark alley, past a family of goats and along a narrow lane. He accosted a man whose head was wrapped in a scarf, and spoke to him in low tones. The man grunted and waved him further on. I was thoroughly alarmed by now, shouted at him to turn round and told him to take me to the only hotel in Gonda, the International. It seemed a great distance, and when we got there, a red bulb over a door was the only thing that showed me what might be the entrance.

At the reception desk there were several men chatting, and I thought that they looked up at me oddly. I was told there was no room. When I insisted and pleaded with them, there was a pause. Then it was suggested that I should go up and look at a room first. A boy led me upstairs into a long corridor that was dimly lit with red lights. It suddenly occurred to me that I might be going to sleep in a brothel. But by that time I would have been ready to put my feet up anywhere. So I moved into a bare room that was quite clean but far from being attractive enough for any sort of assignations that I could imagine. Then I had my meal in the equally dimly lit restaurant downstairs and went back upstairs to meditate.

Next morning I spoke to the man at the reception-desk, who was one of the three that had been there the night before.

"Why didn't you want to give me a room last night?" I asked. "Didn't you like me?"

"It is not you," he answered. "It is the police. We must report arrival of all foreigners to police by 4 p.m."

"What if they arrive after four?"

He spread his hands. "That is the problem. But we could see you were in much need."

"Indeed I was," I said. "And now can you tell me how to get to Balrampur?"

He tried to get me a car. But he had no success. In all that city with a population of about two lakhs there was not a taxi to be had, and I still believe I was in the only hotel. No wonder all the guidebooks are silent about Gonda. There is simply nothing there—except for two hundred thousand people. We discussed the possibility of a bus. Their schedules were unknown.

"There is one thing," he said. "You will take the train."

So take the train I did. It was on the little narrow-gauge railway that I might have travelled on before from Naugarh, and the wooden carriages of the 8.50 express were occupied but not overcrowded. I had bought a second-class ticket for Rs. 7 (about 20p) as the clerk in the ticket-office had told me that there would be no first-class coaches. He was wrong. It was the opposite of what had happened at Patna. But it did not matter. As the valiant locomotive huffed and puffed and pulled the train bravely out of the platform on time, I travelled happily with a second-class ticket in a first-class coach.

As we chug-chugged and rattled briskly along I saw a considerable mound, with bushes and a tree on it, to the west of the line near Serampur. No doubt it was a stupa. But whether it had been recorded and investigated or not I did not know. After that we reached my goal in less than an hour, and naturally I got ready to get off the train at Balrampur. I would have done so if my fellow-passengers had not told me to carry on to the next station, Jaikhundi. This was sound advice. The City station is rarely the best one at which to alight. The Junction or the Cantonment is nearly always better. And so it was, though my guidebook had been recommending Gainjohwa for Shravasti, wherever that might be.

My pedicab man wanted to take me out to Shravasti there and then, which was an amazing gesture considering the distance he would have had to pedal. But I persuaded him to take me to the hotel which I had heard about from Durbe instead.

The Maya Hotel was a large and spacious bungalow, which had originally been the guest-house of the Raja of

Balrampur and was now run by a private company as a 'travotel'. My room was furnished in excellent Indian style with chairs that were low enough to be more suitable for sitting cross-legged than in the European manner and some hanging scrolls called *tangkas* on the walls, which had Buddhist motifs in a mixture of Indian and Chinese styles. There was also something that I thought I was never going to see again—a mosquito-net to enclose me on my bed at night.

The gardens in the grounds of the bungalow were being carefully tended by several gardeners who looked old enough to have been some of the raja's retainers, and the ornamental gateway was manned by a khaki-clad gatekeeper. In the centre of the garden, in front of the travotel,. there was a circular raised platform approachable up a flight of five steps, which looked as though at one time it must have been a bandstand. In front of this platform stood a Victorian gun, on the barrel of which could still clearly be seen the letters VR with the crown above, and the broad arrow of the Royal Ordnance factory with the words *Honi soit qui mal y pense* below.

All the buildings were whitewashed a pale cream colour, which formed a perfect backdrop to the enormous pinky-red bougainvillea that shaded the entrance porch. The verandahs were wide and had ceilings supported by black wooden beams, in the corners of which there were two or three large honeycombs hanging down for eighteen inches or more.

Opposite the wrought-iron gates there was the statue of a Buddha in yellow robes and in the 'freedom from fear' pose, seated under a baldaquin supported by four pillars. On the drum on which the Buddha was sitting two of the Three Refuges were written in the Hindi script—*Sangham saranam gacchami* and *Dhammam saranam gacchami*—and on the square on which the drum stood there were the words 'Buddha Park', also written in the Nagri script, which is used in Hindi. The park was just a common with a few cows and children on it, a peaceful place as was the hotel itself. It would have been good just to sit around there or chat to the gardeners and the gatekeeper. But the pilgrim is for ever on the move, and the manager of the Maya Hotel was more successful than the receptionist of the Intercontinental in Gonda had been. He soon found me a jeep to take me the ten miles along the Bairach road to Shravasti.

It was a straight single-lane road with brick verges, one of which was under repair. So we proceeded in erratic bursts, which my betel-chewing driver accepted without comment. It soon became clear that Shravasti is rapidly developing as a pilgrim tourist centre. Even before we reached the right-hand turning to the ancient site, we came across the Thai monastery, which was built in 1982, the large Japanese bell, the site for an 'Indian Buddhist temple' and the pure white Jain temple that was being built.

My driver did not stop. He did not look as though he was going to stop at all until I forced him to a halt outside the Sri Lankan temple, which was opposite the gate to the Jetavana. This Sri Lankaramaya was opened by His Excellency J. R. Jayawardene, President of Sri Lanka, in 1978. The attached monastic accommodation, the Nava Jetana Maha Vihara, which I took to mean the New Jetavana Great Monastery, was opened ten years later in 1988. The resident monk showed me the golden Buddha in the chaitya, and the mural scenes from the Buddha's life which had been paid for by pious donors. There was the temptation scene, and there especially was the Miracle at Shravasti with the Tathagata presenting a transfigured appearance. The information given at the door was that he had spent the third rainy season after his enlightenment at Shravasti, and thereafter twenty-four more, nineteen of them in the Jetavana opposite, which I now entered.

It was as I had hoped and half expected. Behind the women who had spread out their washing on the roadside to dry, the trees of the Jetavana gave ample shade, the bushes, lawns and flowers were beautifully trimmed and tended by the gardeners, and one was able to follow the many paths beside the excavations with ease.

On my map of Nepal and Uttar Pradesh, sheet number 631 based on the 1946 revision of the Survey of India, the antiquarian site is called Set Mahet and enclosed within a dyke. Set, now often called Sahet to rhyme with Mahet, is the southernmost of the two villages, in reality outside the old city wall indicated by the dyke, and Mahet, which has the city wall around it, is half a mile to the north close to an ox-bow lake formed out of the old course of the Rapti river, which was called the Achiravati in the Buddha's day. It is now clear that Set, or Sahet, was the location of a large complex of Buddhist viharas and stupas which grew up in and around the Jetavana, and that Mahet was the city of Shravasti, where the King of Koshala had his palace. The site was brought to light by General Cunningham in 1863. But systematic excavation has only been undertaken recently, some of it as recently as 1986.

How wonderful it would have been to go there in the General's day on one of the Raja of Balrampur's elephants. There would have been elephant-grass all round the ancient forest, which the elephant would push aside with her great legs. In the grass, here and there, would be piles of bricks and bits of wall which the mahout, a local man, would point out with his elephant-goad. One would get down from the howdah, not wearing shorts and sandals, of course, but in stout breeches with riding-boots, or puttees thick enough to thwart all but the most determined of snakes. Then one would prod about with a stout stick and dig a little, or rather cause someone to dig with the pointed spade provided by the elephant stable-boy, where the corner of a building or an unevenness in the ground gave rise to hopes of a find.

Certainly one would find something, even if it was only a terracotta votive tablet or a fragment of a stone cornice. And then a turbaned peasant, barefoot and dressed in a skimpy dhoti, would silently appear as if from nowhere with a statue of a standing Buddha in his hand in bronze so fossilised in verdigris that it would be hard to tell of what it had been made, or else a seated Buddha in stone, perfect except for one broken arm. The peasant would hand them to the Sahib, not for sale of course but out of the deepest respect, and the Sahib would take them and give the peasant, who was an elder of the village of Set, some money, not in payment for the relics but to help pay for a new village well to be dug or for a permanent roof to the village moot-hall or for a buffalo to replace his aged beast and pull his plough.

The first buildings that I came to in the Jetavana, which is now protected by the Archaeological Department, were the remains of two temples, numbered 11 and 12. They were typical, consisting of a central chamber and two side-rooms. Since the central chambers had ambulatories around them, we must assume that they contained images. At Temple and Monastery No 19 an inscribed plate of copper was discovered, which proved to be a charter of King Govindrachandra of Kanauj granting the revenues of certain villages around Shravasti to the monks of the Jetavana. The date of the charter is the equivalent of 1130, which is both an indication of how late in time the great monastery was in existence and a refutation of those who claim that Buddhism had decayed and practically disappeared in India centuries before the Moslem holocaust.

The buildings here, in fact, range over a long period from the sixth to the tenth century, and the charter is proof of the identifcation of Set with the Jeta park and Mahet with Shravasti. As well as the viharas there are, of course, many stupas of which only the foundations have survived. In Stupa 18 an inscribed relic-urn was found, and not far from it are to be seen the Double stupa and the Bo-tree in one and the same enclosure. As the Singhalese Chronicle relates, Anathapindada planted a sapling from the Bodhi-tree in Bodh-Gaya there. The original tree was recently replaced from the same authentic source and is now the object of some veneration, indicated by the flags on the protective railings and on those parts of the stupas that could be reached through the railings.

Temple No 3, up the main avenue a little to the north of the Bo-tree and facing east, marks the spot where the first permanent building was erected by Anathapindada for the Buddha's use. It is called the Koshamba Kuti, and a large image of the Buddha was found there, which was set up in the reign of King Bala of the Kushan dynasty. Hiuen Tsiang saw this image in the brick-built temple, and it is still possible to see the two brick terraces in front of the temple, called the Chankramana as at Bodh-Gaya, on which the Tathagata used to walk. The nearby Temple No 2 is called the Gandha Kuti, the Scented Hut, and is where Anathapindada built the Buddha's original living-quarters. There appear to have been wooden pillars supporting the roof.

There are the remains of many more temples and viharas in the Jeta park, including the Sundha Kuti and the Great Vihara, which is close to the northern entrance to the park and, in terms of the number of bricks remaining on site, must surely be the biggest of all the visible buildings. Fa Hien said that it stood seven storeys high. All these remains have been tidied up, cleaned up and, in some cases, built up in a way that would have disappointed the old-timers on their elephants.

But why do I write down these details of the Jetavana, which must already be recorded in the papers of the archaeological survey? The reason is that there is no guidebook to Shravasti that I know of. Even Dr Schumann, in his excellent and learned book *Der Historische Buddha* published in 1982, relied on an improvised sketch-map provided by 'a local tourist guide.' Strangely enough, more than ten years after the publication of that work I was given a duplicated copy of that very same map by an aged white-bearded man, who was clearly well known to to the official custodians of the ruins and who hurried up to me for that particular purpose. The longer than A4 sheet of paper was called *Philosophi of Sahet Mahet, Sravasthi, Distt Bairach. U.P. India* and it included the walled city of Shravasti, which I was now going to see.

There was no doubt about the walls. The cutting of the road through them has revealed plainly a rampart of earth that is still twenty feet high, though it has been weathered down and is partly obscured by bushes and trees. On some sections of the three-mile long wall the remains of a brick parapet can still be seen. Inside the wall the land is mainly forest,too cluttered with the building material of the ages to be cultivated. So far it has hardly been touched by the archaeologists, though traces have been found of occupation that dates back as far as the first millenium BCE, four or five hundred years before the time of the Buddha.

However, there are a number of prominent buildings that it is impossible to miss, and the first of these, just inside the wall on the right, is not Buddhist at all. It is a Jain temple, which marks the birthplace of the third of the Jain Thirtankaras, who are their saints. Here, as in Rajagriha, the Jains lived alongside the Buddhists and in reasonable harmony. Although their metaphysical systems were somewhat different, their ethics of asceticism were much the same. Quite a lot remains of this brick temple, including two high walls and a lofty dome. But it is not improved by people using the smooth and snake-free floor under the dome as a latrine.

After that I was glad to be driven to the middle of the forest, where there is a large, stupa-like brick building nicknamed the Pakki Kuti, meaning that it is a well-built construction in contrast with the Kachi Kuti, or roughly built building further on. This mound, which has a square base of buttressed brick walls some ten feet high, rises to an overall height of about thirty feet. It has a square hole in the middle of it, thirty feet by fifteen feet, which is lined with bricks. Possibly the hole contained an image and there were stone plaques on its walls. Furthermore there is a tunnel running right through it at ground level, along which I was invited to scramble. It is roughly cut and perhaps the work of treasure-seekers. But the central pit was clearly purpose built.

My own theory is that this pit, and the similar pit in the Kachi Kuti, originally contained a tree. Tree-worship was widespread in the Buddha's day, and specific trees are still accorded special honour in many parts of India to this day. For the Buddhist the peepul-tree had a particular significance as being the Tree of Enlightenment, and it is not unreasonable to imagine that these pits contained such trees grown from the seed of the authentic Bo-tree at Bodh-Gaya. The visitor would enter the pit through the tunnel and circumambulate the trunk of the tree.

It has been conjectured by some that the Pakki Kuti, the 'Fine Hut', was built by King Prasenajit for the Buddha as the Hall of the Doctrine, and indeed on top of it there is an apse-ended nave, not very big, which could have been a small hall. It has also been called the Angulimala stupa, inducing some people to call the broken tunnel running to the middle Angulimala's cave.

A couple of hundred yards away, the Kachi Kuti or 'Rough Hut' is the one that really ought to be called pukka. The pit in the middle of this stupa is bigger, and wall plaques done in high relief, portraying the life of the Buddha, were found on its interior walls. It is altogether larger, and the brick outworks are more convincing as buttresses than the earth-breaks on the Pakki Kuti. So it is thought to be the Sudatta, alias Anathapindada stupa mentioned by the Chinese pilgrims.

These buildings stand out even above the trees. You can clamber up to the top of them and look across the green treetops wondering what lies below still waiting to be discovered. Though the hills are too far away to be seen, there is a glimpse of the Rapti river. We are told that the towns were built beside such rivers for waterborne communication and commerce—Shravasti on the Rapti, Kapilavastu on the Banganga, and Bodh-Gaya on the Niranjana. If so the rivers have changed much down the ages. Nowadays they are swift torrents when in spate and a maze of shallow streams in the dry season. They carry no water-transport to speak of, and are fordable in many places.

There were other visitors to the Angulimala stupa when I was there. A whole family had somehow crammed itself into an ekka gari, drawn by one long-suffering horse. They climbed over the ruins calling out to each other, and I left them to it. My pan-chewing, red-lipped driver thought that this was the signal for a quick dash home. But I made him stop again, this time at the Burmese temple, which is to the east of the Jetavana and one of the oldest of the new temples at Shravasti.

This temple was founded in 1930 during the British time and consequently had to be registered under Government of India Act No. 21 of 1880. A white building, which stands at the top of two flights of steps, it is already showing signs of maturity with the sharp angles of new construction weathered away. On the first floor I found women making mattresses for sale. Then the one and only monk appeared, gave me tea served in the Chinese way, and offered me sweets. Up on the second storey I peered into the chaitya hall and saw the Buddha image carved in the translucent greeny grey marble of the Burmese hills.

Beyond the Burmese temple there is a ring of trees and undergrowth on a modest elevation, which my *Philosophi* plan calls a stupa. And surely it is right. There, surrounded by rice-fields, is another stupa waiting to be investigated, another tumulus containing unknown relics.

Opposite the Burmese temple, on the other side of the road, the seven-storeyed Chinese pagoda rises above the trees. It is the home of the Shravasti branch of the Mahabodhi Society of India, and it has a vihara attached to it in which some monks live. I found three boys there in three shades of robe from yellow to orange. They stood together for a photograph, one with his hands behind his back, one with his hands clasped together in front of him, and the third with one hand clutching his robe.

I also found Andrew Belcher there. He was sitting on the steps in front of the pagoda, and I would probably have missed him if the sudden squawk of a minah bird had not drawn my eyes in his direction. Anyway his appearance was far from striking. He was just a middle-aged man, grey at the temples and wearing red braces under the jacket of his cotton suit. But when he saw me looking at him, he responded with "Nice day! What's the hurry?"

I told him that the hurry was because my driver was dead keen to get back to Balrampur as soon as he decently could.

"Don't worry about that," he said. "You can go back with me."

And so I did, surprised that he was driving himself, as few foreigners, or Indians for that matter, do in India. He took the wheel of a blue Ambassador car, which he had hired in Lucknow. On the way back to the Maya Hotel we introduced ourselves and talked about our travel experiences, and in the hotel itself, at dinner in my room, he told me how he had become a Buddhist.

"I started off poor," he said, "got rich and then got poor again. That's happened to a lot of people. But with me it was different. It seemed as if it had to happen. It all started when I was a soldier in Hong Kong."

Hong Kong again! I thought, remembering Mark Klugman's story.

"That's where I met Fung," he went on. "It was in a place up on a hill called the Temple of a Thousand Buddhas. I don't know if there really were a thousand. But there were certainly hundreds of them in rows on shelves round the walls, and in the middle there were two big statues back to back, one of Buddha and the other they call Kwan-Yin, the merciful one. I was looking at that one when Fung came up to me.

"You can help me," he said. I asked him how, and he said he wanted someone to read and write English. He could speak it in a way, but he couldn't read or write it. I had nothing much to do after duty as I was living single in barracks. So I did help him. I was in the Pay Corps, see, so I could handle money.

Fung told me he'd been to the temple on Peng-Chau island and had his lot cast. He showed me the ticket he'd got, printed in red, and he took me there too. There were three figures in it, which he explained to me. On one side was the money-god, on the other the peach-blossom girl, and between them the god of the far north, of ice and snow. The money-god was riding a black tiger, and he killed his enemies by shooting pearls at them. When they hit anyone they exploded like plastic bombs. But in the end the peach-blossom girl made some arrows out of peach-wood and killed him too."

"Sounds like a nature myth to me," I said.

"Yes," he said. "But Fung believed it. He came from nothing, you see. Actually I think he was an illegal immigrant smuggled in on a boat. But he did have some relatives in Hong Kong, or maybe they were just members of the same clan. What Fung's lot said was this: Once upon a time King—I forget his name—had many enemies. He went away from his country to a great mountain, climbed up the mountain and built a house there. Then the light of the Buddha shone down on him and filled his pockets with gold. He shot his enemies with arrows of gold and built many more temples and palaces.

"Of course Fung took it that he was going to do the same. And actually he did. One of his people had a little old house on the Peak. He got him to pull it down, raised some money and built a block of flats there. That was the start. Multiple mortgages. More money. He went on building. That was where I came in. He said I brought him luck, got me to buy myself out of the army and run the English side of his office. There was a property boom. He could have sold his flats at a profit and retired rich. But he wouldn't do that. When I told him to sell up and give me my cut, he quoted that king and his lot. He went into office-blocks and hotels. I worked harder than ever in the office.

"Fair enough. Fung treated me like a brother, and I didn't lack anything. He felt he could trust me more than one of his own kind. It was strange. He wasn't cunning but he always succeeded. You're name's John, I once said. John Fung. That's a Christian name. How come you believe all this business of the King and the Peach-blossom girl and the Buddha? He just laughed. 'That was missionaries,' he said. 'Many ways to the truth.'

"After ten years Fung wanted to go and cast his lot again, and he asked me to go with him. So we went. His wife was sick and his children were at school. So his family didn't go with us. But the real reason, he told me, was that they thought it was all a lot of rubbish. I told him it was a lot of rubbish too. I went with him but I didn't go inside. When he came out, his head was deep in his shoulders and he was thinking hard. I told him he'd been a fool to go in because it had upset him. All he said was that the truth can't upset. So I asked him what his lot said, and this is it: King what's-his-name fell sick and died. He left many monuments and the people worshipped his memory.

"So then he asked me how much ready money we had invested, and I told him. He said he was going to build just one more thing and finish. 'What's that?' I said. 'You'll see,' he said. He got a Feng Shui man to choose an auspicious place on the hills behind Kowloon, and then he began to build. It was going to be a pagoda of ten thousand Buddhas with nine storeys rising up to the sky. I objected. I said it was a waste of money and would ruin the company. He said, 'I am the company!' And that was that.

"He started building. As it got higher, he got happier. His wife died, and he had her buried in a vault cut into the hill beside it. The funeral just seemed to make him happier. When the pagoda was finished, he paid off his debts and built a little house on the hill by the vault, and went and lived there in a suit of blue cotton pyjamas and a pair of slippers. I went up there to see him and told him he might have listened to my advice. But he just pointed across the bay at the skyscrapers. 'There are my monuments,' he said. 'Now I am ready.'

"Ready to die, he meant, and he really was. 'But you're not sick,' I said. 'No, but I soon will be,' he said. 'Be patient. I've seen the Buddha lights on Tai Mo Shan.'

"So that was it. Well, I hadn't been a fool. I'd branched out on my own account. But somehow after John Fung pulled out all the confidence went with him. My businesses went bad. My wife got fed up and went to Australia. All I had left were rents from refugees in a mortgaged block of flats in Shamshuipo. I went to see Fung again, and I found him lying on a bed in the open air on the flat roof at the back of his house. He could hardly get up to greet me. 'You see,' he said. 'Very sick. Cannot stand!' And he smiled from ear to ear. He wouldn't have a doctor or a telephone. 'No telephone, no worry!' he said, and I told him I wished I could say, No worry, because I was broke and my wife had left me.

"Then he made me really angry. 'Better,' he said. 'Remember Peach-blossom shot the great man riding a tiger.' I wanted to shake the old fool to bits I was so angry. Then he said, 'Look!' He pointed at the top of Tai Mo Shan, the mountain to the west of us. The sun was going down behind it and outlining it in black, and round the edges of the black the last of the sun seemed to be dancing in an orange haze.

"'Look! Look!' he says. 'The lanterns of the Buddha!' Then I grabbed him and shook him and shouted at him. 'It's only the sun going down, you fool!' I said. 'What's so good about that?' And then I dropped him onto the bed. He fell awkwardly and rolled off the bed on to his back on the floor. 'It is good,' he said. 'Buddha good. King what's-his-name good. You good. Peach-blossom good.' Then he died, and I thought I'd better scarper before there were any awkward questions."

"And that's how you became a Buddhist?"

"After a lot of hard thinking, yes. I'd had a dream that kept coming back night after night. I was on one end of a seesaw, and someone was thumping down on the other end and shooting me up into the sky. But I never could make out who or what it was that was shooting me up like a rocket. But when I got into thinking and talking and studying about Buddha, that dream stopped."

10

The Superman – Vaishali

Doubtless Sudatta Anathapindada hoped that Shakyamuni Buddha would remain at Shravasti in the Jetavana. Nevertheless, although the Buddha went back there many times later, he returned to Rajagriha for the next monsoon season, which he intended to spend in the Venuvana. But in the Licchavi republic north of the Ganges the rains did not come. There was famine and cholera in the land. The elders of Vaishali, their capital city, sent a deputation to beseech King Bimbisara to persuade the Buddha to go there and help them.

Thus only three years after the Enlightenment there is a new Buddha, a Buddha who is thought to be capable of working wonders, a superman actually called that—*Mahapurusha*. The new Buddha went north with some of his followers, including one of the early faithfuls, a cousin named Ananda, and after five days they crossed the Ganges. We are told that immediately the heavens opened and rain fell.

At Vaishali the grateful citizens accommodated the group in a forest called the Mahavana, the Great Grove. The Buddha himself stayed in a building called the Gabled Hall, leaving Ananda to deal with the cholera epidemic. Whether it was the spell cast by the recounting of the Ratna, or Jewel sutra that was the effective cause, or whether it was the clean water brought by the rain, the cholera ceased and health and happiness were restored.

In the following year at Vaishali the first Buddhist nun was accepted. Thus the Women's Order of bhikshunis began against, it must be said, the initial reluctance of Gautama Buddha. The first nun was his own step-mother, Pajapati, now advanced in years, who had begged to be allowed to join the Sangha during the Buddha's return visit to Kapilavastu. At their meeting in the Banyan Grove he refused. Whereupon she cut off her hair and donned the yellow robe, presenting a kind of fait accompli when she caught up with him at Vaishali. Her advocate in persuading the Buddha to change his mind was Ananda.

Much later the Buddha passed through Vaishali with the faithful Ananda and other disciples on his last journey to the north from Rajagriha. When they reached Vaishali, instead of staying in the Great Grove provided by the citizens, they went to another grove, the Amrapalivana, which belonged to an elderly courtesan named Amrapali, the Mango girl. Next morning, at a grand breakfast, she presented the grove to the Sangha before they moved on.

Another tale is told of the Buddha in Vaishali at that time. He was sitting under a tree beside the Markata Tank when Mara, the tempter, appeared to him again. Mara reminded him of what he had said to him immediately after his enlightenment. He had told him that he had achieved his aim and should now be ready to enter Nirvana, and the Tathagata had replied that he would not enter Nirvana until he had alleviated peoples' suffering and saved them from the evils of their ignorance. Mara, as the herald of death, told the Buddha that he had now done that too and should now be ready to leave the world. In his answer the Buddha, who was now eighty years old, told Mara not to be impatient. He would only have to wait another three months.

It was the last time the Buddha was to be in Vaishali. After having gone into the city for alms, he returned to where he was staying and looked back at Vaishali with an elephant look, that is to say turning completely round to view it for the last time.

But Vaishali played its part again in the annals of Buddhism when it was host to the Second Buddhist Council. This was held a century after the first one, which met at the Saptaparni cave in Rajagriha shortly after his death. Seven hundred of the Thera, the Buddhist elders, met at Vaishali to hammer out the Buddhist canon, which was then preserved in an oral tradition. Eight months were spent reciting the canon and ensuring that it was not getting altered or corrupted.

However, there were some delegates who wanted Buddhism to embrace a wider metaphysical field and called themselves the Maha Sangha, the Great Order. This was the beginning of the schism between the Lesser Way of the Elders, the Hinayana of Sri Lanka and South-East Asia, and the Great Way, the Mahayana, which spread to Tibet and China.

I visited Vaishali from the Chanikya Hotel in Patna. It was no great distance, and my driver, Moti Lal, thought he knew the way. But first we had to practically traverse the city from west to east in order to get to the long road bridge over the Ganges, where a small toll had to be paid. It was forty miles, most of it along some amazingly narrow roads which were really no more than village streets. Green hands of bananas were growing to ripeness on all sides, and groves of mango, neem and acacia trees gave the countryside almost a forested appearance. First we headed north on the main road to Nepal. But at Hajipur we had to turn left and rattle our way through Lalgunj and over innumerable sleeping policemen to get to our destination.

Moti Lal did not like the delays. "We are hopeless," he kept saying. "Hopeless! In your country it is not like this?"

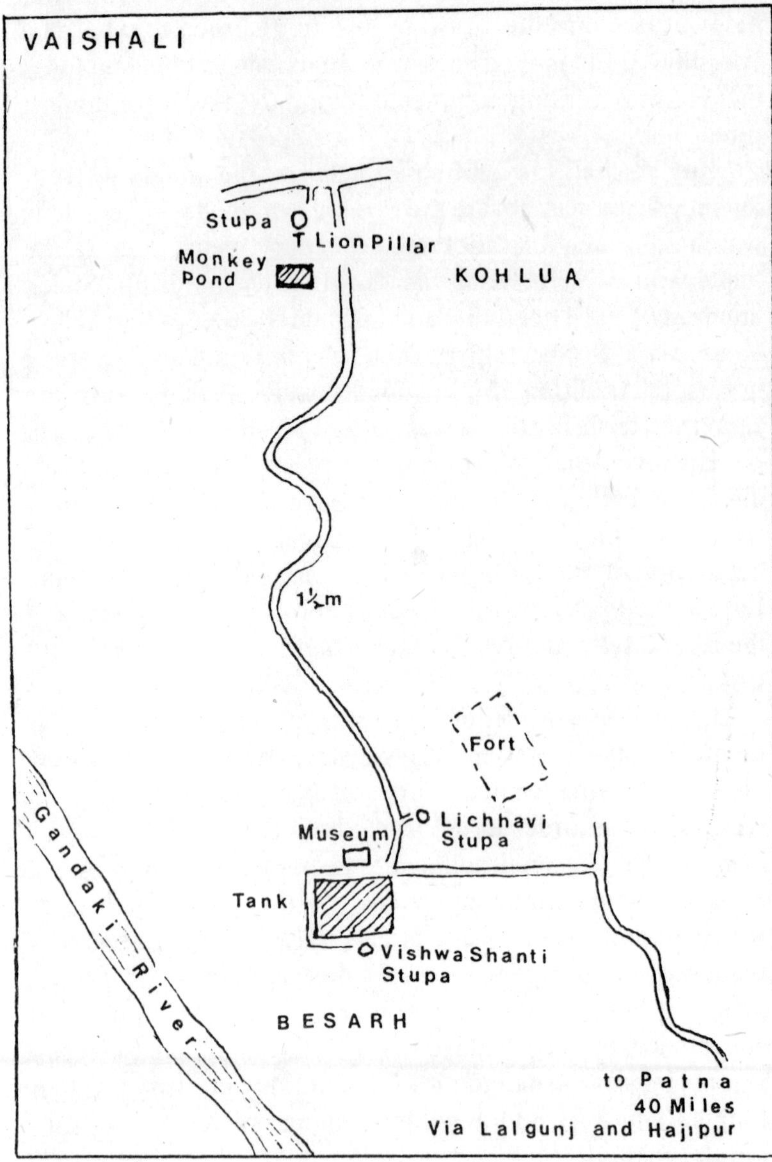
VAISHALI
Stupa
Lion Pillar
Monkey Pond
KOHLUA
1½ m
Fort
Lichhavi Stupa
Museum
Tank
Vishwa Shanti Stupa
BESARH
Gandaki River
to Patna
40 Miles
Via Lalgunj and Hajipur

"Not quite like this," I agreed.

"So. We are hopeless. You think we are hopeless?" He pronounced 'hopeless' with a curious upward lilt like that of a petulant duchess.

"Not quite hopeless," I answered cautiously.

It took an hour and a half to get there, and it was only when we had nearly reached our goal that the road straightened out and we found ourselves on a tree-lined lane raised up on a causeway above the fields. At the end of this lane there was a large tank with water-buffaloes in it. Little naked boys were playing on the great black beasts and diving off them into the water, whilst even smaller little girls were driving even bigger buffaloes alongside the tank.

The office and museum of the antiquities of Vaishali stand beside this tank, and the curator was there to show me around. There was quite a lot to see. Amongst other things there was a small relief of Amrapali, the dancing-girl who gave up her profession when she learnt about the Buddha and became a nun. It was executed in the traditional three-bends posture. But the features looked to me to be remarkably unfeminine, perhaps recalling Amrapali's age when she became a convert. However, the most striking exhibits in the museum are from nearby Kolhua. There is a crowned Buddha in black schist from as late as the ninth or tenth century, and another in the same earth-touching pose that has lost its head and is dated even later to the eleventh century.

Yet the stupa that stands close to the museum is a very old one and so worn away that nothing of it remains above ground level. It stands in lawns and gardens, which are beautifully maintained by the Archaeological Department's gardeners, and it is considered to be so significant that a great dome-like roof of corrugated aluminium, itself the shape of a stupa, has been built over it to protect the scanty remains from the elements.

To the untutored eye there is little to protect. There are simply a few muddy bricks in a circular pattern rising to a height of a couple of feet and weathered down with the wear and tear of ages. Even the relic casket, which was found inside the original mud stupa, only contained ashes mixed with mud. But the fact remains that the first stupa here was probably built by the Licchavis immediately after the Great Decease to contain and commemorate their share of the ashes of the Buddha.

So the stupa must have been built in the fifth century BCE, perhaps simply of mud. Subsequently it was enlarged three times, firstly in the time of Ashoka, then in the first century BCE and subsequently in the first century CE.

Other finds in the stupa included a punch-marked copper coin, two glass beads,a conch shell and a small, thin piece of gold. It is said that it was built in the same place as the vihara in which the Buddha used to reside when he stayed in Vaishali.

Once again I moved from the old to the new. On the other side of the tank there was a large stupa under construction, and judging from the noticeboard inside the barbed wire that protected the building-plot, it was going to be a replica of what the old stupa may have looked like before it crumbled away. It was to be called the Vishwa Shanti stupa, and as at so many other Buddhist sites Japanese piety was responsible for the project. When it is completed it will surely attract pilgrims. But I was the only one that day.

Moti Lal had not thought this work in progress was worth a visit. But he could hardly refuse to drive me a mere mile and a half to Kolhua, which is the other site of ancient Vaishali and in many ways the principal one. Feeling our way along narrow tracks on the bunds between the rice-fields, and scattering village people out of our way, we came to a brick stupa which, in contrast to the one close to the museum, stands high above its surroundings. Nor is it only the stupa that is important. Beside the stupa there in an Ashoka pillar, crowned by a lion, which faces it.

Looking at the complete stupa today one would not think that it had been excavated. But apparently a casket was found inside it in 1958. Here too there is a tank, and between the tank and the stupa there are circles of brick, which were once the foundations of smaller stupas. The tank is called the Monkey Pond because there is a legend that a monkey offered the Buddha water from it, which miraculously turned into honey. The story is depicted on the frieze below the headless Buddha in the museum. Another version of the story is that the monkey offered the Buddha honey and then fell into the pond and was drowned, after which he was reborn as a god.

The departmental watchman insisted that the stupa was in honour of Ananda, the Buddha s cousin and closest disciple, and not of Gautama Buddha himself. This was not verified by the written information, which I found at the site and which I reproduce here just as it was on the noticeboard.

Pillar and Stupa, Kolhua

Kolhua formed a part of the ancient Vaishali. The site is represented by a monolithic inscribed pillar surmounted by a seated lion capital on the top and the remains of a bricks built stupa. Limited excavation between the pillar and the stupa has revealed that the stupa was built in three times. The site seemed to have gained importance during second phase. Besides miniature stupas of different plan and dimensions were also found around the stupa. The excavation has brought to light the details of the stupa. The pillar is assignable to Mauriyan period. The important find from the site include a beautiful stucco head of Lord Buddha, terracottas, inscribed plaques, a figure of standing Buddha, broken piece of relic casket, beads of terracotta and semi-precious stone etc.

But the statement that it is the Ananda stupa could be true, or rather half-true, since Fa Hien tells us he saw a stupa built over half Ananda's body. It happened that not long after the Buddha's death his close companion was ready to die too, and he left Rajagriha for Vaishali because he wanted his Parinirvana to take place there. But this did not suit King Ajatashatru, who set out in pursuit of him and caught him up as he was starting to cross the Ganges. At the same moment a deputation of the Licchavis arrived to welcome Ananda on the other side of the river. To resolve the dilemma Ananda expired in the middle of the river in such a fiery ecstasy that he cremated himself, leaving half his remains to one side and half to the other.

The watchman invited me into his living quarters, which were in a shack perched on the edge of the excavations. When I was reluctant to enter, he went into the shack himself and came out again with a pail full of objects moulded in clay. They included the Mango-girl, Amrapali, and although many of them looked hardly dry after the modelling, he seemed to think he could pass them off as antiquities. The village children were following us around, so I asked them what they thought. They grinned. "Yes, he makes them," they said. Whereupon the watchman angrily shouted at them to be gone.

Hiuen Tsiang, in his *Records of the Western World* refers to the lion pillar at Vaishali, to the stupa beside it, to the monkey pond, and to much else, little of which can be seen today. He says that the circumference of the city was sixty to seventy *li*, or more than ten miles. So it could easily have embraced both the antiquities near the museum and those less than two miles away at Kolhua. He found few people living there, even in the inner sanctum of the old royal precincts. But he discovered far more stupas than I did. There was a stupa where Shariputra became an *arhat*, which was situated to the north-west of the relic stupa. There was another stupa on the site of the Mango-girl's house, which commemorated the Nirvana of the Buddha's step-mother; another where the Buddha gazed for the last time at the city with the elephant look before walking towards Kushinagara to die; another marking the location of the Mango Grove; and yet another where the Buddha announced his impending death to his followers.

There was also the Vimalakirti stupa, where the Buddha delivered a sermon called the Vimalakirti sutra and was offered precious parasols. It is not surprising that Hiuen Tsiang should have lingered at this spot, since from the fourth century onwards this sutra was extremely popular in China and was translated no less than seven times into Chinese. Its central figure is a pious and wealthy layman, who had such a deep insight into the nature of things and the emptiness of reality that he was able to defeat in argument even the greatest Arhats.

These stupas were clearly visible in Hiuen Tsiang's day. But they must have varied in construction and need not necessarily have been of great size. So it is not surprising that they cannot be located today. Yet more stupas are mentioned, which were quite peripheral to the life in this world of Shakyamuni Buddha. One marked the spot where a thousand sons had looked on their father and mother.

This stupa commemorated one of the Jataka stories. It was the tale of a Rishi who lived a solitary life in the wilds and fathered a child on a roe-deer. The girl was of great beauty. But she had the hoofs of a deer instead of human feet, and wherever she trod she left the impression of a lotus flower on the ground. King Brahmadatta saw her and took her to his heart. In due course she conceived and gave birth to a lotus-flower with a thousand petals, and on each petal a boy was seated.

The other women of the court jealously said that the lotus-flower was an unlucky omen and threw it away into the river, down which it floated in a box, until it was retrieved downstream from the Ganges by the King of Ujiyana. Out of the box sprang a thousand well-nourished and strong young men, whom the king eagerly impressed into his army to attack Vaishali.

The thousand young men surrounded the city of Vaishali and were about to launch an attack when the deer-girl appeared on the city wall and told them that she was their mother. To convince them of the truth of her words she squeezed her two breasts and produced a thousand jets of milk, which miraculously fell into their mouths. In this way they were convinced and returned to their parents, whilst the people rested in peace.

The Buddhist element in this story was demonstrated by the presence of another stupa nearby, which commemorated the place where the Buddha used to walk to take exercise, and where he explained that the thousand youths were really the thousand Buddhas of our eon, the Bhadra Kalpa.

Hiuen Tsiang places the stupa containing half the remains of Ananda to the east of this spot. So, if this is correct, the stupa facing the lion pillar could not have been shown as the Ananda stupa in his day. Indeed, there were so many stupas at Vaishali that it would not be surprising if the provenance and significance of some of them had got misplaced. Most of them have now disappeared, though it is not impossible that they will be rediscovered by religious archaeologists in much the same way as old sites in the Holy Land have been retrieved by Christian researchers.

It was hard for me to visualise what all these stupas must have looked like in the old days. They could hardly have been in open country as most of the old Indian stupas are today. Many of them would have been in amongst the city streets or the focus of town squares, continually passed and repassed by the citizens. Others might have stood in their own grounds in association with viharas. There would certainly have been a more urban ambience than that of the paddy-fields and mango-groves which surround those of them that we can make out nowadays.

Yet by the time of Hiuen Tsiang's visit the city, for some unknown reason, had collapsed. He saw many more stupas than I was able to see. He says that, 'Both within and without the city of Vaishali, and all round it, the sacred vestiges are so numerous that it would be difficult to recount them all' But, 'At every step, commanding sites and old foundations are seen, which the succession of seasons and lapse of years have entirely destroyed. The forests are uprooted; the shallow lakes are dried up and stinking; nought but offensive remnants of decay can be recorded.'

These comments are similar to the remarks that Hiuen Tsiang makes about other key sites that he visits, such as Kapilavastu and Kushinagara. So it is not so much Buddhism that has decayed but the whole polity in which Buddhism flourished. We are not told the reason for this desolation and disintegration. It could hardly have been the collapse of the Gupta empire since, two hundred years earlier, Fa Hien had much the same to say about Kapilavastu, Kushinagara and Bodh-Gaya. It may have been that some regions supporting large populations simply became exhausted or stricken by pestilence, and urban centres had to grow elsewhere. Buddhism died in these places not because it was ousted by Hinduism but because there was simply nobody there to support the Sangha. In fact, when Hiuen Tsiang visited India another emperor, named Harsha, was on the throne in the North. He was a great philanthropist and perfectly sympathetic to Buddhism, which was still flourishing in many places.

Driving back to Patna with Moti Lal I thought about these things. At Lalgunj he stopped to buy fruit from the roadside vendors, and it seemed to me that the brick and wood buildings behind them had probably not changed much since the Buddha's day. It was the pepsi-cola and cigarette advertisements, and the phut-phutting, rattling motor traffic in the streets that made the difference.

"HOPELESS!" screeched Moti Lal as we bumped into and out of our thousandth pothole. Out in the open on the long Ganges bridge he nursed his car forward in intermittent surges, driving up to thirty miles an hour or so and then freewheeling down to near walking speed in order to economise on petrol. Lorries laden with bananas thundered past us, and in this way we trundled back to the Chanikya Hotel.

The cricketers were there no more. But there was a man in the foyer who could easily have been one of them. He was wearing a navy-blue blazer with some kind of a crest emblazoned in gold on its pocket, and light khaki trousers with suede desert boots. A small man, dark by European standards, he had a little black almost Hitler moustache. When I came into the hotel, he was asking the receptionist some questions about how to get to Rajgir and Gaya, though anyone looking less like a Buddhist pilgrim it was hard to imagine.

"I am not knowing," the receptionist was saying. "You may take one car, or you may ask at the station for taking one train. There may also be one bus."

"The train's alright," I said, "if you don't mind a crowd."

And thus it was that I introduced myself to Major Forswyke of the Gurkha Rifles.

"Yes, I want to see the Buddhist holy places," he told me later. "I was always vaguely interested in Buddhism, though most of the men in the regiment were Hindus. But it was a dog that really showed me the way. I was stationed in Bangkok. Not a real soldiering job. Liaison stuff. My wife was with me. She was a great animal-lover. Always had a dog. Sometimes two or three. Not proper guard-dogs. Little terrier types. Take them wherever she went. Actually carting them about the world wasn't that easy. She only had one by the time we got to Thailand.

"This job of mine meant going to a lot of diplomatic parties and all that rubbish, and Alice wouldn't go unless she could take the dog with her. She was a very determined person. So most times she did take the dog. It was just understood that the RSPCA lady could have her dog with her.

"As far as I could see there wasn't a lot different in our marriage from anyone else's. Cooling off a bit. Kids away at school back home. But after a bit I did begin to think there was something funny going on. Alice was out a lot. Animal welfare naturally. I was busy with paper work in the office and chatting people up. Suddenly it got a lot cooler, and I was sure there was something up. But I couldn't make out who or what.

"Then we went to another diplomatic do. Indian, I think it was. Curried eggs and coca-cola. And of course Suki, the dog, went too. As soon as we got inside Suki made a beeline for a chap in the centre of the room. Jumped up at him barking her head off. Then I knew it was him. German chap named Bacher in one of the aid groups, not good looking at all.

"After that came the voices. I don't mean just thinking voices. I mean real voices. Actually it was just one voice. It shouted at me. Could come any time. Do something. Kill them. Shoot them. They're making a monkey out of you. It didn't make sense. Why should I care? Nowadays people jump in and out of holes like rabbits and nobody cares. But the voice wouldn't let me go. Not a sergeant-major's voice, just nagging. It was hard. What could I do? I went down to Bacher's house and did a recce. Suki heard me and started barking."

"Yes, but what's all this got to do with Buddhism?" I said.

"I'll tell you," he answered. "I wanted to set fire to that house. 'Burn it!' the voice said. How could I burn it? Shoot them! Not so easy either. I wasn't armed then. Run them down! How? Bomb them! That was possible. Bacher had one of those old-style bungalows on the clongs. Mosquito-ridden place but easy to creep up to from the river. That's what I did. Made myself a Molotov cocktail and went by boat. The trouble was the dog."

"How's that?"

"The idea was to creep up to a window, light the cocktail and chuck it in. The house was an old wooden building. Would've gone up like a box of matches. That's just what I was going to do. But Suki barked again."

"And so?"

"It proved that they were there. I could recognise Suki's bark anywhere. But I had nothing against the dog. Why incinerate the dog as well? I did chuck the cocktail. But not into the house. I threw it in the garden. There was an almighty explosion, but nothing caught fire. Too damp for that. They came rushing out, dog first. Dog came up to me. The other two stood still pop-eyed. The dog stopped. Didn't jump up. Just stared at me. Big brown eyes. No blinking. Suddenly I thought about those stupas you see in Nepal with the eyes staring at you and the question-mark between them. That's when I really started trying to live by the Buddha."

"Maybe the dog was a Bodhisattva," I said.

"Maybe," he answered.

11

The Great Decease – Pava and Kushinagara

The last ten years of the Buddha's life were not the peaceful retirement a seventy-year old man might hope for. But he was certainly much respected, and he was a well-known holy man who was much in demand for the ceremonial inaugurations of palaces and moot-halls. It may be that his very popularity stirred up jealousies.

The Buddha's cousin Devadatta, who was Ananda's brother, openly urged him to hand over the Order to him. Devadatta was implicated in Ajatashatru's scheme to kill his father, King Bimbisara, and as we have seen he tried to kill the Buddha too when he refused to give up the leadership. When his attempts to murder the Buddha failed he moved to Gaya and founded his own Sangha, which still had some monks in it when Fa Hien went there a thousand years later. They paid their respects to the three previous Buddhas, but not to Shakyamuni.

Ajatashatru, although he had supported Devadatta, did in fact go to see the Buddha in the Mango Grove. He put a question to him, asking him what visible fruit there was in this life from the life of an ascetic, and he contrasted it with the lives of people such as elephant-drivers, charioteers, cooks, barbers, bath-attendants, potters, accountants and others, whose work was productive. It was a question that the king had previously put to six other rival teachers. The Buddha replied that the fruit was in communicating his higher knowledge to householders.

It is said that as a result of this meeting Ajatashatru pronounced the Three Refuges, repented of the murder of his father, and was accepted into the Buddhist fold. However, this did not stop him making war on the Licchavis and the republican federation to which they belonged.

It is clear from these and other events that the Buddha was involved in politics whether he liked it or not. The King of Koshala, successor to the Tathagata's friend, Prasenajit, made war against the Shakyas and laid waste to Kapilavastu, possibly at Tilaurakot, which was possibly replaced by Great Kapilavastu near Piprahawa. Nevertheless, in spite of the aggression against and destruction of his home city, the Buddha was to spend one more monsoon in Shravasti. Whilst he was there, he was told that his close disciple, Shariputra, had died near Rajagriha, and more alarmingly that Maudgalyayana, the other one of the pair, had been killed. Apparently he had been slaughtered by an assassin, who had been hired by the leaders of a rival school, thus paying the penalty for his success.

The Master returned to Rajagriha, and shortly afterwards he set out again with Ananda and a group of monks, heading north. They stopped at Vaishali to see the next rainy season through there. But the Buddha wanted to be left alone with Ananda, his staunch and loyal helper, to meditate. So he sent the monks away into the surrounding countryside. The Tathagata was now eighty years old and far from well. He talked to Ananda about the future of the Order. But he appointed no successor, saying that it was the *Dharma* itself that would be the island and the refuge of the faithful.

It seems that the Buddha wanted to return to Shravasti by slow stages in order to retire into one of the monasteries that were now established there, and await his death. So he and

Ananda set out with some followers on the familiar road to the north-west. The names of the staging-points on the way have been recorded in the Pali canon.

There were four villages and one town in which the Buddha tarried with Ananda and counselled the bhikshus who went along with him. There is no mention of the Great Gandaki river, which flows half a mile wide near Vaishali nowadays. The probable reason is that, in the Buddha's day this river did not run on the western side of Vaishali. The main stream would have been the river that is still called the Old Gandaki, which joins the Ganges well over a hundred miles downstream from the outfall of the Great Gandaki opposite Patna.

The sixth stage was Pava, a much bigger town which was the seventh place of the longer Buddhist pilgrimage. Here occurred the event which led to the Buddha's death before he reached his goal.

In this place a metalworker, upgraded by some to a goldsmith, named Chunda, wished to honour and please the Master. So he prepared a specially exotic meal for him, which has been the subject of much debate. It was called *sukara maddava* in the Sutra of the Great Decease, meaning 'pig delicacy', and so some commentators say that it must have been pork. I find this highly unlikely, as even a blacksmith would have known that *shramanas* such as the Buddha were normally vegetarians. More likely the fatal dish was something that pigs like, such as truffles, or more likely still some fungi that the blacksmith thought were edible truffles but were actually poisonous mushrooms.

The Buddha was suspicious of the delicacy and told his followers not to eat of it. But in a typical gesture he took some of it himself in order not to disappoint his host.

Pava, one of the principal towns of the Mallas, must have been a considerable place in antiquity. But it was lost to view for centuries, having been renamed by the Moslem conquerors, as was their wont. Cunningham tried to equate it, not very convincingly, with a place called Padrauna some fourteen miles north of Kushinagara, saying that the name could easily be reduced to Pawa. He is still followed in some publications, even as recently as 1994.

However, a dozen miles to the east of Kushinagara lies a town mainly inhabited by Moslem people, which is called Fajilnagar. In this town there are the considerable remains of an enormous stupa that would have been quite grand enough to enshrine the eighth part of the Buddha's bodily relics that was allotted to the Mallas of Pava.

I had returned to Gorakhpur to visit Kushinagara when I drove out to Fajilnagar with the good fortune of having the Burmese monk, the Venerable U. Nayaka, accompanying me. It was Sunday and the weekly market was in full swing. There was half a mile of booths set up on either side of a rough track, selling anything from foodstuffs to cloth or ironmongery. We made our way along this track, with the crowd of people reluctantly parting in front of us until U. Nayaka stopped the driver beside an even narrower alley going off to the left.

It was a cul-de-sac between two and three-storeyed houses, at the end of which there was a sign with somebody's washing draped over it to dry. On it the Archaeological Survey of India informed us cautiously that what lay ahead was the 'Ancient Mound, Fajilnagar'.

Ancient the mound certainly was. The asymmetrical and uneven surface, grass-covered, with two trees growing on top, showed that it had been partly cannibalised in the past, yet perhaps not quite so voraciously as one might have expected. The circle was still complete, some two hundred feet in diameter, whilst the height was more conjectural since the ground surface of the thick cluster of huts on the far side was considerably lower than the ground on which the houses were built on the near side. We thought that sixty or seventy feet was the approximate height.

The mound, which is actually the remains of a very large stupa, is surrounded on all sides by habitations except for one, where it abuts on to an overgrown plot containing grass-covered hummocks, which is said to be a Moslem cemetery, but where no gravestones can be seen above ground. It is also sad to have to relate that the mound is filthy. Whilst a family of mongooses has taken up residence on the southern side, finding cracks in the ancient brickwork that provide them with a den, the northern side is covered with faeces and obviously constantly used by the local people as a latrine.

So it was with some distaste that we left the mound and went down to the riverside, where another monument seems to confirm that this is indeed Pava. It commemorates the death of the last and historical of the great Jain teachers, Mahavira, who is said to have left this earthly life at Pava. Here, too, the ground around the memorial, on which some aspects of Mahavira's life are recorded, is covered with shit.

So we were not sorry to leave this uninspiring place and retrace our road. It was the road the Buddha must have trod, old and ailing. Although he felt very ill he insisted on walking slowly onwards. To outward appearances he was just a sick old man in dirty, soiled clothes, like the sick man and the old man who had first moved him to leave home and family. A follower of his old teacher, Alara Kalama, saw him and gave him and Ananda new robes.

Half-way to Kushinagara the party came to the Kakudha river. According to the legend it was here that oxen and their carts, fording the river, had stirred up the mud of the river-bed. But when the Buddha asked for a drink it became clear again. He bathed and lay down to rest beside the river.

As we saw, the river is still there, flowing throughout the year, a goodly stream about a hundred yards from bank to bank. On one side there was a group of little white Chhauti shrines and nothing else. The next river was the Hiranyavati, now called the Sonara. They waded across it and reached the

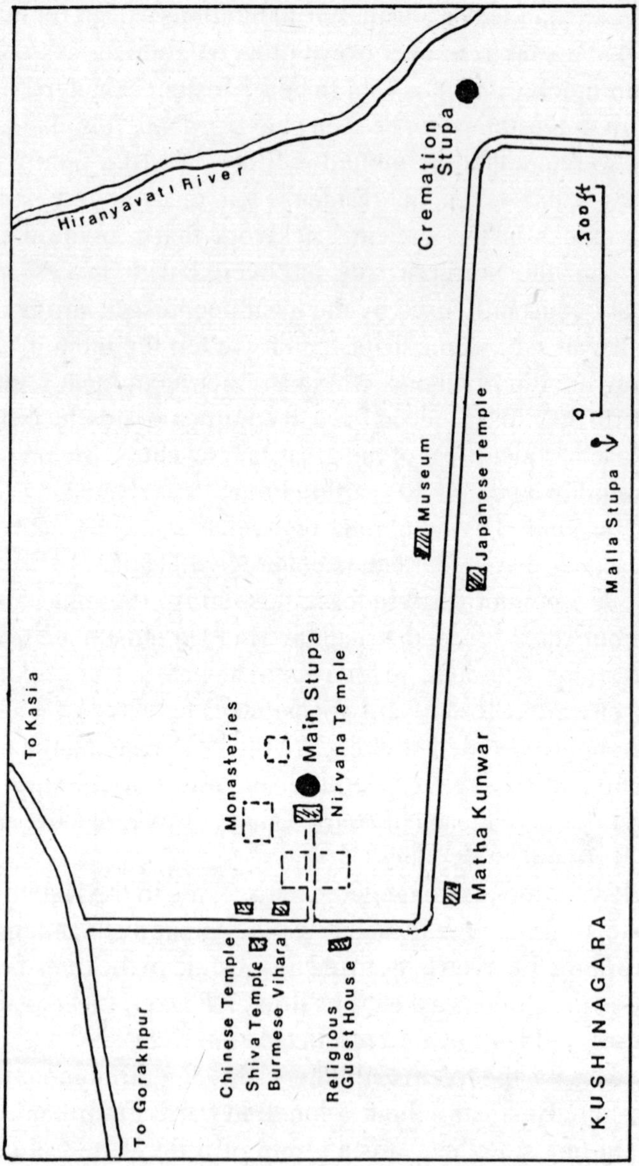
Hiranyavati River
Cremation Stupa
500 ft
Malla Stupa
Japanese Temple
Museum
To Kasia
Monasteries
Main Stupa
Nirvana Temple
Matha Kunwar
Chinese Temple
Shiva Temple
Burmese Vihara
Religious Guest House
To Gorakhpur
KUSHINAGARA

small town of Kushinagara on the other side, near which they rested under the sal-trees in the exercise-ground of the Mallas.

A number of local people came to see the Buddha, who was now famous after a ministry lasting forty-five years. One of them, named Subhadra, became the last person to be accepted into the Order by the Buddha himself, who told his people not to blame the poor smith for his death. That night, lying between two sal-trees, it appeared that he was meditating in a trance-like state. But in reality he lost consciousness never to regain it in this world, and slipped quietly away into *Parinirvana*, the full nirvana of liberation from the body.

I retraced the road to Pava for my visit to Kushinagara, which lies close to the small town of Kasia, thirty-four miles to the east of Gorakhpur. My old fixer, Sher Khan, who shares his name with the tiger in Kipling's *Jungle Book*, arranged for a car to take me there. Rather to my annoyance he decided at the last minute to come too. So off we went down the straight road past the Gurkha depot and the Gurkha war memorial, the Indian Air Force barracks and airfield, and a couple of elephants, out into the countryside.

It was mostly sugar in the surrounding fields, some of it laid across the road to be crushed by passing traffic. There was a patch of forest with monkeys in it, which hid the airfield from view, and every so often we came to a 'ripple' or a 'rumble' across the road, which heralded a level-crossing or a row of shop-booths in a kind of ribbon development too close to the asphalt highway for proper safety.

About eight miles short of Kushinagara we came to the Little Gandaki river, which I propose to equate with the Anoma of Buddhist lore. At this point it is little short of two hundred yards wide, though the stream itself does not often reach that breadth. A few boats were loading clayey mud from the banks to make building-blocks.

Soon after that we turned right off the main road under an archway welcoming us to Kushinagara and a short distance further on the first temples appeared. Sher Khan was all for not stopping. But I insisted, inviting him to take tea, and so we did, much to my good fortune. For at the tea-shop was the Ven. U. Nayaka, the Burmese monk who showed me Pava and who happily offered to show me round Kushinagara.

The first temple that we entered, on the right hand side of the road, appeared to be not to Buddha at all but to Shiva. Yet if it had not been for the snake across its body, the seated image could well have been that of a Buddha or one of the Jain saviours. Perhaps there was here an example of the Buddha being absorbed into the Hindu pantheon. There were even swastikas on the lintel of the door, with the syllable OM on either side of them, and under the image there were words of encouragement: 'He who drinks in the law lives happily with a serene mind; the sage rejoices always in the law as preached by the elect (aryas).'

"Not Buddhist," U. Nayaka said, with a hint of disapproval in his voice.

On the opposite side of the road stood the 'Theshuaglin Buddhist temple erected by Rev. Kuolen Bhikshuni of Hunan, China with donations from Chinese overseas 1948, 1956.' It was the first temple I had come across that had been founded by a nun, and it seemed appropriate that in the forecourt there should be a white statue of a female deity. I thought that it was Kwan Yin, the Chinese female version of Avalokiteshwar, the Bodhisattva of mercy and compassion. But U. Nayaka said that it represented Saraswati, the Hindu goddess of music and poetry and the creative sciences.

But that was only the beginning. We needed the driver again to take us down to the stupa that is known locally as the Ramabhar Tila, or 'hill' because it is close to the Ramabhar lake into which the Hiranyavati, the 'golden' river, now flows.

Traditionally this stupa marks the spot where the Buddha's body was cremated, and so it is often called the Angara

Stupa, or Stupa of the Ashes. But it should not be confused with the as yet unrediscovered Ashes Stupa seen by the Chinese pilgrims, that was built by the Moriyas of Pipphalavana to enshrine the ashes they received in lieu of bodily relics. So it has another name, the Mukutbandhana Stupa.

It is a large mound, with a diameter of more than a hundred feet, handsomely restored and standing in beautifully kept gardens that extend close to the bank of the river. Excavations carried out in 1964 revealed the bases of some subsidiary stupas and structural remains to the south that may well have belonged to an attached monastery. Some inscribed seals were found in nearby Kasia, which were dated to between the fourth and sixth centuries of our era. But no relics were found inside the main stupa.

Not long ago a Chinese monk lived in a banyan-tree on top of this stupa. But in the festival year of 1956 officers of the Archaeological Survey told him that both he and his tree had to go. They gave him a small house nearby, and subsequently he founded a small monastery across the road, which has a typically Burmese white alabaster statue of the Buddha in its shrine-room. There he died in 1973, blind and aged eighty-four.

Since the relics of the Buddha were divided amongst eight different peoples, it is not surprising that nothing was found in the Angara Stupa. On the other hand, one might have expected that the Mallas of Kushinagara, within whose territory the Buddha died, would have raised a monument to their portion in the very place of his cremation.

I went with U. Nayaka down to the tranquil Hiranyavarti river, called locally the Sonara, and beside it we found a whole forest of those little white Chhauti shrines with hibiscus blossoms on them on little earthen candle-holders, which had been lit up during the Diwali celebrations. Here he told me that there was, indeed, a place of vestigeal remains that are thought to be all that is left of the relic stupa of the Mallas of Kushinagara.

Returning up the road a short distance we stopped by the wall of a large new, blue-roofed Thai vihara on the left. A rough track led into the distance alongside the wall. U. Nayaka pointed out a clump of jungle with some banana-trees. "There," he said. It was not as far as it looked, perhaps half a mile, and in this flat land it had to be a man-made hillock.

But the jungle was thick with barbed creepers, the path to the top winding and uneven, and even at the top one could see nothing. However, on the far side it was possible to see a relatively bare section, in which some of the bricks of the broken down stupa were clearly visible.

Returning along the road to the place of the Buddha's decease we came to another new temple. This one had been constructed by the Japanese in the form of the ruined chaityas at Nalanda. There was a brick hemisphere with a hall inside it containing the image, which in this case was a Buddha in saffron robes.

The inscription says that 'In February 1975 we Japanese Buddhists paid homage to these holy villages, Kasia and Kusinagara. We were inspired by a genuine desire to return to the origin of Buddhism and projected construction of a sanctuary. Construction of the Buddhist Sanctuary reflects our sincere aspirations to embody humanity's ideal—stamping out war from the Earth. Feb. 1964.' *Arhats* done in black brushwork in the Japanese style flank the statue, and we are informed that this is also the home of the Atago Isshin Kyokai World Buddhist Culture Association and the Indo-Japan-Sri Lanka Buddhist Centre.

Opposite the Japanese temple there is a museum that is so new that at the time of my visit it was not yet open, and indeed one wonders what will be put in it as old artefacts discovered in the region are actually very few. But further down the road we were back amongst the things of ancient time. The building beside a small tank is quaintly called the 'Matha-Kuar Shrina' in the English language on the notice-board beside it. But surely Matha Kunwar is what is meant, possibly meaning the Dead Prince. It is an enormous seated Buddha, which was found years ago in a dilapidated state and restored to its pristine beauty by Burmese lovers of the Buddha in the 'Burmese year of religion 2470' which is 1926/27 in the Western way of reckoning.

The gilded statue, like those of the Jains, and unusually for a Buddha, is naked. It is in the 'earth is witness' pose, slim but not cadaverous in any way, with a smile of utter composure on the face. The Buddha sits on a stylised lotus, and in front of him there are little bowls for oil-lamps.

The Burmese also completely restored the main stupa at Kushinagara, which is located at the spot where the Buddha died. Appropriately called the Parinirvana Stupa, even now it is sixty feet high, and it was probably double that height when it was built, perhaps in the third century CE. The stupa was returned to its hemispherical shape in 1927 by the Burmese, who looked for relics at that time but did not find any. After that, it was split by a banyan-tree that was growing on it, and in 1968 it had to be encased in concrete, which has since that time gathered black streaks and some graffiti.

The nearby pavilion, which was built on the same great brick platform, is made of similiar concrete material. It was constructed for the festival year 1956 to decently house an immense reclining Buddha, which had been unearthed away back in 1876. The statue was in three parts when it was discovered in the ground, and again it was the Burmese who recovered it and put the three parts together. Inside the pavilion, which is called the Nibban, or Nirvana temple, the great image, which is nearly twenty feet long, had been draped in a costly red cloth covered with a golden silk pall.

It is not certain whether this is the same figure as the one that Hiuen Tsiang saw inside a great vihara built of bricks. But the dying Buddha lies on his right side like the other reclining Buddhas that I have seen in Sri Lanka, Myanmar and Thailand. Though the exposed parts of the Buddha's body are already golden, the Thais like to put gold leaf on it where they can.

The Parinirvana Stupa and the Nirvana temple are surrounded by the remains of buildings which have been excavated and tidied up in recent years. Ten of them, including the largest, are the remnants of monasteries, in which the ground-floor cells around a square can be clearly discerned. The rest of them are more higgledy piggledy and open to conjecture.

From there we went to Nayaka's own vihara, the Burmese monastery, or dharmsala, which was founded in 1902. It was donated by a gentleman named Kheez Arhi Baba and established by the monk, Chandramani, who in his old age had been the teacher of my guide and mentor. Nayaka rang the bronze bell for me, and told me he was fifty years old and had been a monk for over thirty of those years. Yet he was still a novice bhikshu with a way to go before reaching the full status of an elder. He eats but once a day, in the morning.

Finally Nayaka took me to the building called the Buddha Temple and Sri Birla Religious Guest House, which was built in 1942 with fourteen rooms to accommodate pilgrims. Here too, as in the first temple we visited, there are mottos:

> He is called a Brahmin who has shut out all worldly thoughts.
>
> He is called a Bhikku (Samana) who leads a life of rectitude.
>
> He is called a recluse (Pabbajita) who washes off his impurities.

There was nothing more of interest to see in the immediate vicinity. So I said farewell to the Venerable Nayaka and thanked him for his help. The ups and downs of Kushinagara still await clarification. The big stupas, of course, were already there when the Chinese pilgrims made their separate visits. But Fa Hien found the inhabitants few and far between, and later on Hiuen Tsiang found the place utterly deserted. Yet archaeological evidence shows that new monasteries were being built there up to the twelfth century, again refuting those who maintain that Buddhism had died out in India many years before the Moslem conquest.

It was in the religious guest-house that I met the lady Rohini. I do not know whether or not she was technically a bhikshuni. But she was certainly wearing the saffron robe. She even had a saffron-coloured tilak on her forehead, and what interested me in particular was that on the front of her robe she had a silver cross. She was not alone. Yet though she had with her a female companion, she was by far the more conspicuous and talkative of the two, being a large woman not far short of my own height and quite unafraid to speak to a stranger.

"You can rest here," she said, and she even brought a stool for me to sit on, though I would have been happy enough to sit cross-legged on the floor.

"You are dressed like a Buddhist nun," I said. "How is it that you wear a cross, which is the symbol of the Christians, on your chest?"

"Everything is possible," she answered, "as long as it is done in love. People say that Jesus was a Bodhisattva."

"Is that so?"

"How I came to know this is because my father was a police officer in Kashmir, and there was much trouble there. My mother died, you see. It did not suit her there. And I, of course, was the eldest daughter. So I looked after my father after that.

"Many times he had troubles. Some people said he was too soft. Some accused him of atrocities, not doing himself but letting others do it. He talked to me about it and said, What to do? I said he must apply for posting. But he would not leave his post. He was too proud. Ordinary criminals, we can do with them alright. If no criminals then no need for police. But this was political.

"We were Sikhs. No trouble about that. Sikhs have always been policemen. One day my father took me to a place in the city, in Srinagar. It was looked after by a Muslim. No trouble about that. This is what they say is the tomb of Jesus, he said. Nabi Isa. Prophet Isa they call him.

"Then we had to go to Ladakh. They call it part of Kashmir. But it is not. The people there are Buddhists. I learnt from them. And one day I went with my father to a monastery there. They call it Hemis monastery. And they said there is one book there which says that Jesus had an argument with his parents and went to Ladakh, and there he learnt Buddhism before he went back to his own country to teach the new dharma."

"I heard about that," I said.

"So we can believe in Lord Buddha and in Jesus too," she said. "My father died. An enemy shot him. And I was left alone. What to do?"

Sher Khan came across from the tea-shop to see what I was up to, and so I left the ladies in the guest-house and returned to Gorakhpur. He had seen me saluting the Buddhist images in the temples with the namaste sign, and he tried to make fun of it. "Why do that, Uncle?" he said slyly.

I was not amused. But I could go no further that day. So I let him take me into the Raj Hotel next to his travel office and carry my bag up to Room 23, which cost Rs. 60, or about £1.50, cash in advance to the man in his cubby-hole at the bottom of the stairs. There was no towel. So I went out to buy one for Rs. 25. There was no food either, and off I went into the town in the gathering cool of the evening to find the Bobina Hotel at the end of a long motor-rickshaw ride through the city streets.

There seemed to be no reason for building the Bobina in that part of the town, since it hardly looked the kind of place that would attract pilgrims going to visit the Gorakhnath temple. But there it was. There were no tables or chairs set out in the dining-room, since they had all been pushed back in anticipation of an 'event'. However, a table and a single chair were retrieved for me, and there I sat, an island in the spacious room, considering the menu and alone, until another island was created for two Italian visitors.

If they had not been speaking their own language, the two men could easily have passed for Indians. Indeed it is not for nothing that some Indians like to call themselves the Italians of the East, considering their animated speech and lively gesticulations. The waiter brought them a kind of coffee, which was called 'cappuccino' on the menu, and it was in discussing what the actual ingredients in their coffee-cups were that I got to talk to them.

They were both dressed in off-white shirts made of the local cotton, which gave them a similar appearance, though the one who spoke to me first was clearly the younger. They too were on the trail of the Buddha. They had been in Nepal where Buddhism, particularly of the tantric variety, still flourishes, and this was for them a kind of pilgrimage to the roots.

"At one time I was deep into drugs," the younger man said, speaking in his own language. "At the moments when my head was clear I shrugged my shoulders and told myself I was finished. I'd had my time and that was the end for me. Ordinary existence was not possible for me any more. It would be just without meaning. Sometimes I cursed the clever writers who told me it was the way to unlock the imagination. Sometimes I cursed the people who supplied the goods. But most times I just went on turning my arms into pin-cushions. I came East because I thought it would be easier. They were going to Afghanistan. Then it was Pakistan. Then Nepal. You could live on next to nothing, and it was no crime to be poor. People would not let you starve.

"But a funny thing happened. You know there are many temples in Nepal. They are kind of Buddhist. But not the Buddhist we know. Kind of Buddhist magic. People like me with nothing else to do got stoned and went in and out of them. Most times the watchman did not like it. But sometimes he was sleepy or had gone away to relieve himself and it was open.

"That was what happened at one near Bhadgaun. I was in there looking around and trying to put off taking my next fix, and someone else came in, snatched one of the small bronze statues out of its niche in the wall, and made off with it. I was transfixed. Even when I was starving I had never thought of doing that. Yet it was an easy way to make a quick profit if you could find an unscrupulous collector to buy it. Why not? They are still making them, often as good as before.

"This one was fourteen or fifteen centimetres high, just small enough to put in the pocket of an anorak. I had been looking at it before he came in. The Buddha was sitting cross-legged, and his mate was sitting on him with her legs wrapped round him. Both of them had crowns, and both of them had the third eye in the middle of the forehead.

"The man who stole it was gone in an instant. He went in and out as if he knew exactly what he had to do. And I was left there staring stupidly. I hadn't got the spark to go after him. And that was strange because actually I did know him. He was not hooked like I was. Or as poor as me. He got money from some kind of research grant to write about native customs.

"When the pujari came in I was still staring stupidly at the empty niche in the wall of the temple. And then I did the stupidest thing of all. I ran off. It did not take them long to find me. By then I was stoned again. Of course they did not find the image. They searched all round me. But they did not threaten. And then they went away. I could have told them who had got it. But that was no use. Marco would have hidden it or sold it by then.

"It preyed on me. The image was gone, but in my imagination it stayed with me. The two figures grew to enormous size. The dull copper colour changed to gold. They seemed to fill me and to fill the world. First it was the bodies embracing. Then it was the heads alone, gazing at each other. I went to Marco and begged him to show me the image so that I could look at it again. He denied all knowledge of it. I told him I had seen him take it. He said I must have been in the middle of one of my trips.

"And I really did think, then, that he might have been right. After all, I was not a reliable witness. Yet it was strange. Thinking about those two figures locked in love, I began to lose my craving for the needle. How many counsellors had I seen, how many rescue clinics had I been to back in Italy, and they had been no use at all. All drama. All fighting this and that. All clinging to this and that like shipwrecked sailors clinging to lifejackets.

"I started trying to meditate on those two serene figures. The Buddha is wisdom and the shakti is the perfection of insight. I saw what I had seen under the needle. The larger-than-life lovers, the magic floating through the air, the high towers of the magic city. I saw the demon figures with flaming hair, the animal masks, the heads multiplying and disappearing into the infinite, the dance of the skeletons. And then I discovered that they were already there in the Buddha figures of Tibet. The drugs had not created them. They were already there.

"So I learnt to meditate, and in the end I threw the needle away. I went to Marco and begged him again to tell me whether he still had the image. I told him why I wanted to see it, to see whether it was really the same as it had become in my imagination. He did show it to me. He had not sold it to anyone. It was his greed of the collector that had made him take it for himself. We went back to the temple together and put it back where it had been. The pujari saw us doing it and said nothing, only one word, *Hunchha!* So be it."

They were coming to arrange things for the event as the Italian finished his tale, and consequently we were eased out of the dining-room into the foyer of the hotel. It was an evening wedding-reception. Outside there were festoons of coloured electric-lights, and inside, the buffet tables were piled with coloured rice and curried vegetables, puratas, samusas, eggs, fruit and many-coloured sweets. As we were there, the host found it natural to invite us to join the feast,and I regretted that I had already eaten my dinner. The younger of the two Italians then introduced himself.

"My name is Luigi," he said simply, "and this is my friend, Marco."

Untypically for an Italian, Marco said nothing more than *Piacere*! And so I left them in their relative comfort, whilst I myself went out into the night to find a motor-rickshaw that would take me along the long, narrow, winding streets back to my own place.

12

The Aftermath – Nalanda

Often when the Buddha journeyed northwards from Rajagriha he would spend the first night after his departure at Nalanda, which is seven miles, or about one *yojana*, away. He usually stayed in the mango-grove given to the Congregation by a clothing manufacturer called Pravarika. Nalanda was also Shariputra's birthplace and the place where he died, becoming an *arhat* venerated by Buddhists world-wide. A stupa was erected by Ashoka in his memory, which was near the chaitya that carried his name. It was seen by the Chinese pilgrim, Fa Hien. But it has not been re-identified.

However, the events that link Nalanda with the Buddha's life are overshadowed by the renown of the place in later years as one of the great universities of India. Nalanda probably became a university, to which students would go from far and near, three or four hundred years after the Buddha's death, and it was certainly flourishing as such in the second century of our era, when Nagarjuna was a teacher there. It is to the Tibetan records that we have to turn for details, since Nagarjuna is revered as the sage of the Mahayana tradition that shaped Tibetan Buddhism.

Doubtless this seat of learning had its ups and downs. When Fa Hien passed through Nalanda in the fifth century, he said nothing about an educational establishment there. But

Hiuen Tsiang studied there for five years, and another Chinese scholar monk, I Ching, was there shortly afterwards for a considerable time. I Ching was particularly interested in learning about the Mahayana, or Great Way, and closely studied the Mahayana Sutra, which became one of the key texts in China as well as in Tibet.

The university is described in detail by I Ching as a monastery. It was, then, a monastic school, or a monastery that took students, as the monasteries still do in South-east Asia. The conduct of our own universities was not so very different in the days when both professors and students were expected to lead celibate lives and theology was still the queen of the sciences.

I Ching says that the name of the monastery was the Sri Nalanda Mahavihara, and he adds that all the monastery courts were very similar in appearance and layout. A hundred yards to the south of the monastery there was a stupa, more than a hundred feet high, on the spot where the Buddha used to stay during the three months of the rains. As at Sarnath, the Sanskrit name for this spot was the Mulagandha Kuti. Fifty yards to the east of this place there was a still higher stupa, which had in it an image of the Buddha in the *Dharmachakra Pravartana* mudra, turning the Wheel of the Doctrine. To the south-west of this stupa there was a very small chaitya about ten feet high. It was here that a Brahmin came to ask the Buddha questions, holding a bird in his hand. So it was called the Sparrow Stupa.

To the west of the Mulagandha Kuti stood a tree from which the Buddha was accustomed to take twigs with which to clean his teeth. To the west again of this there was an altar at which the novices received the rules of the monastery from their preceptors. The eastern side of this altar had a brickwork base inscribed with sacred Buddhist texts, and on it blooming lotuses were modelled in white lime. These lotuses stood out proud about two inches and were more than a foot in circumference. There were fourteen or fifteen of these flowers symbolising the traces of the lotus-like footprints of the Buddha.

I Ching relates how he tried to study a mysterious book called the *Dharani Pitaka*, which would enable one to ascend to heaven sitting on a vehicle drawn by a dragon, and there one would be able to order hundreds of gods about as one's slaves. But the desired objective could only be reached by performing and reciting the appropriate mystic gestures and formulae. It seems that here we are in the realms of tantric magic.

I Ching goes on to describe a monastery court. He says that usually it consisted of a number of monks' cells in rows of nine. The floor space of each cell was more than a hundred square feet and its window was in the back wall. The cells had high doorways without screens, so that one could clearly see the sides of the room from the outside. So there was no privacy amongst the monks, who liked to look into the cells at each other.

At each of the four corners of the monastery there was a big hall, built of brick. The main entrance to the court was in the west wall through a large porch, the roof of which rested on pillars. The walls of the porch were decorated with curious figures. Though the main door was not very big it was very strong, and it was closed every day at meal-time against intruders. The courtyard of the monastery was laid with bricks. Both floors and walls were thickly plastered and then polished to give the brickwork a mirror-like appearance.

Concerning the organisation of the monastery I Ching tells us that the oldest monk, irrespective of his learning or attainments, was ipso facto the superintendent. But there was also a Viharapala, a 'Protector of the Monastery' whose duty it was to circulate information regarding monastery affairs to the resident monks. If the monks had some business, they would assemble to discuss it. Then the Viharapala, with

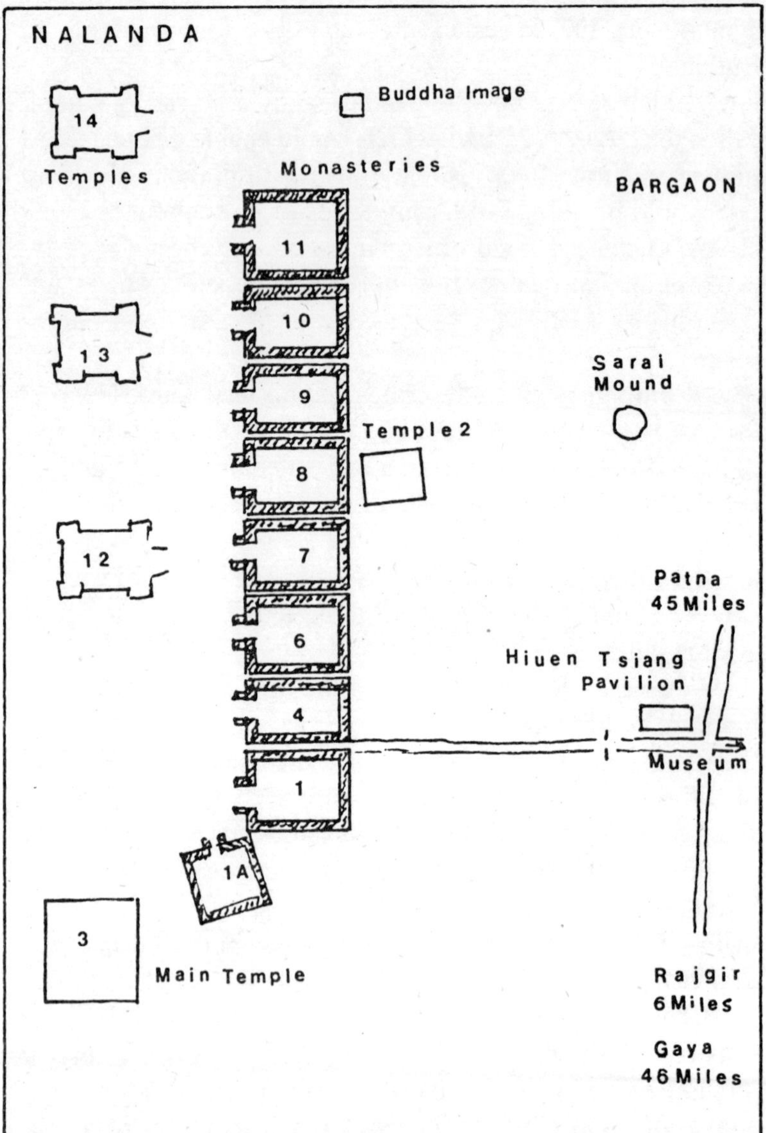
NALANDA
Buddha Image
14
Temples
Monasteries
BARGAON
11
10
13
Sarai Mound
9
Temple 2
8
12
7
Patna 45 Miles
6
Hiuen Tsiang Pavilion
4
Museum
1
1A
3
Main Temple
Rajgir 6 Miles
Gaya 46 Miles

folded hands, would report their decision to each monk singly, and if any monk objected to it, it would not be passed. Also no money could be spent without the consent of all the monks, and if a monk did anything without the consent of the other residents, he would have to leave the monastery.

There were ten different sects in the monasteries of Nalanda when I Ching was there, and he mentions that there had been as many as ninety-six different schools of thought, which he calls heretical. But he does not say why, or what the different sects were. He simply remarks that even within a monastery court there might be monks of different persuasions, and such monks could not study together.

I Ching says that there were seven monasteries at Nalanda. The archaeologists have uncovered eleven monastery sites, which were not necessarily all contemporaneous, though it is possible that the university continued to grow during subsequent centuries. For instance we know that in the middle of the ninth century the King of Sumatra endowed a college there. Then there is an inscription recording that Nalanda was rebuilt in the tenth century after a destructive fire, which indicates that it was still regarded as an important place of learning, though we do not know whether Buddhism was still the mainspring of the teaching by that time.

Yet the evidence suggests that Nalanda was still fulfilling its role as a seat of learning at the time of the Moslem invasion two centuries later. It was at the end of the twelfth century that the Turki warrior Bakhtiya Khilji delivered the mortal blow not only to Nalanda but also to the neighbouring monastery schools as well.

These great buildings with their high external walls looked uncomfortably like fortresses to the conquerors. Monasteries and stupas were torched, monks were slaughtered and monasteries burnt. The Moslem historian Minhaj states that Bakhtiya was curious to know what the great collections of books had been all about. But he could not find anyone who had read them. Those who could read them had either fled or been killed or were afraid to reveal their erudition. Thus it came about that the vast literature of Buddhism had to be painstakingly recovered from Sri Lanka, Burma, Tibet and China and in some cases translated back into its original Sanskrit.

I went to Nalanda in the same confectioner's car that I had used to visit Rajagriha. We passed a number of tourist buses on the way, and so it came as no surprise to me to find other visitors at the site. This did not worry me as the area of the antiquities is enormous, and the wonderful gardens with which they are surrounded make it a real pleasure to stroll about them. Fuchsias, poinsettias, hibiscus and acacia gave a profusion of colour to the verges,and it was diverting to watch gardeners topping two tall trees flanking the main entrance.

The monastery courts were much as I Ching had described them. Each one had twenty or thirty cells around a spacious quadrangle, with walls still standing or reconstructed to a height of about six feet. In some of them there remained a few vestiges of arches or stone lintels over doorways. Most of them are in a row facing west, as the Chinese pilgrim said, and opening on to an avenue, on the other side of which there is a row of large chaityas which once had huge Buddha images in them.

These image halls, often indiscriminately called stupas, chaityas, temples or even viharas, are approached up flights of steps. Inside them one gets the impression of being in a lofty cave, which was probably the intention of the architects. In one such cave you can see the interlocked legs of a colossal statue and some almost unrecognisable vestiges of paintings on the plaques under its pedestal.

But towering above them all is the building which is called the main temple. Its perimeter wall alone is nearly twenty feet high in places, and the facade of its great tower is the only surface which still has some Buddha reliefs and statues in its stone niches. This was surely a real stupa with a solid core. Steps go right to the top, and though a notice warns one not to risk the climb many people do.

It is difficult to assign a date to this stupa, since it was enlarged and modified perhaps as many as seven times. But the fact that the staircases, rising in three flights from the northern side are not a new addition for the convenience of tourists indicates that pilgrims and others were meant to go to the top, where there must have been a temple or monument on the flat surface of the summit. Surely this was the Mulagandha Kuti to the south of the monastic courtyards, which was mentioned by I Ching.

Little did the learned world realise that the village of Bargaun was located beside the ruins of Nalanda until Buchanan Hamilton went there early in the nineteenth century and found a goodly number of Buddhist images at the place. But later on, in the sixties of that century, Cunningham made the connection certain on the basis of the directions and distances given by the Chinese pilgrims and of some inscriptions found there.

However, the first systematic excavation of the site did not get under way until after the First World War. It continued for twenty years under the direction of the Department of Archaeology. The portable statues that were discovered there during this time were, of course, removed to museums to keep them safe from theft or wanton destruction.

Before going to the Nalanda museum myself I went northward down the main avenue between the viharas and the chaityas to the far end, where I could see another great mound, which was covered with grass. This stupa appeared to be outside the perimeter fence. So I ducked through the wire as many had clearly done before me. I was then confronted by a small boy, who took me aside to a modest building which contained a large standing Buddha in black stone with a few squares of gold leaf stuck on to it here and there.

It was the largest whole statue to be seen on the site, and yet it was not within the bounds. Presumably it had not been taken into the museum because it was in private ownership, and indeed it was not long before a man purporting to be the pujari came along to back up the boy's demand for money in return for the privilege of viewing the little temple and its image.

But the stupa still beckoned me. I had to go through the wire again, since it turned out to be inside the perimeter fence after all, in a kind of northern salient. I walked up the grassy slope beside the broken steps and into the cave. Here too there had been a large seated Buddha, and here too the massive stucco figure had been reduced to rubble.

Back in the main avenue workmen were carrying bricks, four on each head, to one of the chaitya staircases that was being rebuilt. The new bricks were exactly the same size as the old ones that had survived the centuries. Another workman was manicuring the grass with a small knife. At the entrance, which had scattered across it the green branches that had been lopped from the trees, it was time to rest in the shade. Four armed men were resting under the trees too, and I soon got talking to them. They were a squad of security police, each of them equipped with a rifle, and when I asked them if their work was really necessary they nodded vigorously in the Indian way, shaking their heads from side to side.

"There are many *badmarsh*," one of them said. "Even here in Bargaun there are criminals."

Indeed one of them insisted on accompanying me for my protection when I said I wanted to visit the most recently excavated stupa of them all. This is the Sarai Mound, not far from the main gate but remote from anyone except the badmarshes of Bargaun when one gets close up to it. Here, inside the cave, the image had altogether crumbled away, leaving only the pedestal on which it had once been and the plaques on the wall below the pedestal.

These plaques are the reason for the railing across the entrance to the cave and the locked gate. For paintwork can still be seen on them, which is fragile enough as it is without being fingered by thoughtless visitors. From the gate it is hard to see what subjects are portrayed on the frieze of paintings. But they will have been examined by the experts, who no doubt will report their findings.

One has to run the gauntlet of a line of beggar women to reach the museum, which is on the other side of the main road. But the ordeal is worthwhile, as it is possible to see there some of what one misses out in the open air. Apart from the black stone Buddha in the 'Turning of the Wheel of the Doctrine' pose I was interested to see some of the Tantric Bodhisattvas that people usually associate with Tibet, showing that here in India was the origin of the Vajrayana, the Way of the Thunderbolt, as well as the other Ways or, strictly translated, Vehicles.

There were also some curious terracotta pieces, one of them in the shape of a peepul-leaf with a mass of tiny stupas etched on it. The inscribed bricks could well have come from the altar that I Ching mentions, since they have written on them the formula which says, 'The Tathagata has revealed the causes of all phenomena which spring from a cause and also the means of their cessation. So says the great ascetic.'

The seal of Nalanda university in the museum reminded me that there still is a university faculty at Nalanda. In a revival of the old tradition, it is an institution for post-graduate research, which was set up by the Bihar state government in 1951 specifically for the study of Buddhist philosophy and literature. There is also a pavilion in the Chinese style, which is a memorial to Hiuen Tsiang, who did so much to keep the memory of Nalanda and its learning alive, as well as a facility for the faculty.

I Ching says that there were about 3,500 monks at Nalanda in his time. If they were all living in the eight monastery courts that he mentions, there must have been more than four hundred in each, which of course would not have been possible if there were only thirty cells. But the walls of the cells and of the monasteries are immensely thick. Obviously they supported several storeys.

In fact Hiuen Tsiang, who visited Nalanda before I Ching, states specifically that the monasteries had four storeys. So each monastic court might have housed about a hundred and twenty monks. Even so, this leaves us far short of the 3,500 monks of I Ching's time, still more of the 10,000 that Hiuen Tsiang said were there. So clearly the monks' accommodation must have spread considerably beyond the area that has so far been excavated.

In trying to visualise what these monasteries must have looked like at that time, we have to think of the many-storeyed monasteries of Ladakh, and of Tibet before the ruthless destruction of the 1950s during the Chinese so-called Cultural Revolution, which were doubtless built with those of the mother country in mind. Hiuen Tsiang makes it clear that the buildings of Nalanda made a tremendous impression on him. The 'soaring' and 'coloured' eaves of the monastery roofing, as he describes them remind one of the wats of Thailand.

'One gate,' Hiuen Tsiang says, 'opens into the great college in which there are eight other separate halls, standing inside the monastery. The richly adorned towers, and the fairy-like turrets, like pointed hilltops, are congregated together. The observatories seem to be lost in the morning mist, and the upper rooms tower above the clouds.'

'From the windows,' he continues in his description of the place translated by Samuel Beal, 'one may see how the winds and the clouds produce new forms, and above the soaring eaves the conjunctions of the sun and moon may be observed. All the outside courts, in which are the monks' cells, are of four storeys. The storeys have dragon projections and coloured eaves. The pearl-red pillars, carved and ornamented, the richly adorned balustrades, and the roofs covered with tiles that reflect the light in a thousand shades, these things add to the beauty of the scene.'

One source mentions that there were eighty-four monastic colleges at Nalanda. If there were a hundred and twenty monks in each, as I have surmised, this figure would produce Hiuen Tsiang's total of ten thousand almost exactly. But in the first half of the thirteenth century a Tibetan monk who visited Nalanda reported that there were only two inhabited colleges left, and there was only one teacher, aged ninety, who taught a Sanskrit class and lived in fear of the Moslem soldiery.

There were no books either. Yet such was the scope of Buddhist literature there in Hiuen Tsiang's time that no one monk could possibly study it all. There were, he says, a thousand monks who could explain twenty collections of sutras, five hundred who could expound thirty collections, and only ten who could lecture on fifty collections. There were no less than a hundred pulpits for lecturing on the sutras and shastras of the Mahayana, or Great Way, school, and students had to attend lectures promptly without losing an inch of shadow on the sundial.

The university had been founded seven hundred years before Hiuen Tsiang went there. It must therefore have been established in the first century BCE after, it is said, a nobleman had donated his garden for the purpose. Hiuen Tsiang was known as the Master of the Doctrine and greatly respected at Nalanda. So the dream that he had shortly before his departure and return to China was widely regarded as prophetic. He dreamt that all the rooms and courts of Nalanda monastery were deserted and foul. Water-buffaloes were tethered in the courts, and there were neither monks nor followers.

In his dream Hiuen Tsiang saw, on the top of a four-storeyed hall, a golden coloured man of grave and imposing countenance who said, 'I am the Bodhisattva Manjushri. Do you see that?' He looked and saw a fierce fire burning inside the monastery and consuming villages and towns. Then the golden figure said, 'You should go back soon, for after ten years Raja Shiladitya will be dead, and India will be laid waste and in rebellion. Wicked men will slaughter one another. Remember these words of mine' And after he had finished speaking he disappeared.

It was a fearsome portent. Perhaps those Mahayana followers of the Sky-Flower doctrine were not too perturbed. For they considered that all objective phenomena had no more reality than flowers in the sky. But Hiuen Tsiang took heed of his dream and departed. An indication of the size of the libraries of Buddhist literature in Hiuen Tsiang's time is given by the fact that, out of the Mahayana alone, he took 657 books back to China with him, loaded on to twenty horses. He also had a hundred and fifty fragments said to be of the flesh of the Buddha, but none of the bones. He was twenty-six when he went to India in the year 630 and he stayed there fifteen years. He spent the rest of his life as abbot of a monastery in China, translating into Chinese seventy-four of the books he had brought back with him, and lecturing on the Mahayana doctrine. He was eighty years old when he died, the same age as the Buddha.

Leaving the memorial to Hiuen Tsiang, I departed from Nalanda wondering whether any comparable centres of Buddhist studies exist today. Surely there is none so great. Yet one strange result of the persecution of Buddhism in Tibet, in China and in Mongolia is that the Mahayana has now emerged from its highland fastnesses and come back to the world below, generating increasing interest in the West as well as in the East.

It was quite appropriate that the person I met at Nalanda should have been a university professor. I had seen the yellow sun-hat at Bodh-Gaya, I had seen it again, as bright as a rising sun, on the top of the Mulagandha Kuti, and there it was again in the museum, a halo on the head of the little Japanese lady. I told her that, although I had seen her up there, I had not dared to go to the top of the great stupa myself, and she replied in excellent English that freedom from fear was what the Buddha had given her.

"You see," she said. "At one time I was a very fearful person. I told people I was so brave. But I only pretended. My heart was not strong. I blamed it on the bomb, because we lived near Hiroshima and I was in my mother's womb at that time. And each time my heart beat fast I thought I was going to die. I made my will. I arranged all the details of my own funeral. I called for the doctor, usually at night, to help me. But he said, Why are you afraid? I cannot find anything wrong. I cannot keep coming at night time. You say a coward dies a hundred times, a brave one only once. I died a hundred times, and still I was alive."

"I'm sorry," I said. "Or should I say I'm glad?"

We were standing by the seal of the University of Nalanda, which led the lady to remark that it was a very old university, but hers was very young. "It is in Shimizu-shi, Tokai University. I teach English there," she said. "My name is Akai."

We walked away from the museum together. Mrs Akai produced a wad of one rupee notes from her shoulder-bag, and gave one each to the beggar women as we passed them. I felt I had been improvident and thoughtless in not providing myself with the wherewithal. to do the same.

"Of course they are very helpful," she said. "So we can gain merit. We do not know why they beg. Many are widows. Some have no means to live. Some have nothing else to do anyway. So they give some service to people like me."

"And me too if I had thought ahead."

We had reached the Hiuen Tsiang pavilion, and under the ornamental eaves Mrs Akai continued her tale. "Of course we've always had the Buddhas in Japan," she said. We call them Butsu. But people forgot about them during the war time. Then it was all Shinto and Emperor and Country. And after the war, when I was growing up, it was all science and technology. So what was I to do? With all my dying fits my husband was getting tired of me. That was natural. There were not any children. Then I began to think that he was going to assault me and kill me.

"It was at night I had these thoughts. I was in one room and he was in another. And in the middle of the night I had such fear. I really believed it. I even phoned to call the police. My husband just stood there in his kimono. What could he do? If he tried to stop me, he would indeed assault me. Next day I knew nothing about it. It was not even a dream. Next time I called for the ambulance. When it came I refused to go to hospital. What could happen then? I left the house to live on my own. It was a small place, just one room. My husband said I slandered him. But I did not remember it. So I would not see him.

"In my little room there was still the fear. There was the panic and the dying. So I thought, What am I doing? I am living here in this little space like a nun. Maybe I should really be a nun. So I went to the Buddhist temple, which had been there many, many years, and we people at the university just thought of it as some kind of antiquity from the past. Still, it was open for anyone to enter. I went in. It was quite dark. But not so dark with some lights burning here and there.

"The Buddha was on a platform at the other end. Seated. Not so big. I think not stone or bronze, maybe plaster. Here in Nalanda the Buddhas were very big. This one was not so. But I had to stand there and look at it a long time. The right arm was raised, the palm of the hand facing. Do not fear. Pushing away fear. The face smiling. So long I looked. The outward eye and the inward eye. The outward eye looking at the Buddha, the inward eye looking at myself. My mind stopped racing. It slowed down. I lived again the nights of the terrors. But I looked at them from above and they did not terrify me.

Every day for a week I went to stand in front of that Buddha, not worshipping the statue, you know, but thinking of what the Buddha stands for and what he teaches. After that I did go in with the nuns for the university vacation. My mind was calmed there and my heart did not race. Well, I could not stay there for ever. But each year I go back, and each year the nightmare fades more. With the Buddha you cannot fear.

I offered Mrs Akai a lift back to Gaya. But she was going the other way, intending to catch the train from Rajgir down to Patna, and so we parted.

13

The Living Buddha

The great Buddhist stupas of India lie lifeless in deserted cities, into which only now a little life is being returned, mostly by the activities of Buddhists from overseas. The most that they can show is a hemisphere of restored brickwork and those few reliefs and effigies that have not been carried off to the museums.

But the last word is far from having been spoken about the times when Buddhism thrived as a normal part of everyday life in the land of its origin. As recently as 1994 a large bronze statue of the Buddha in meditation was dug out of the earth of Comilla on one of the old medieval monastery sites. It was found to be four feet high and five feet wide, and to weigh forty maunds, or nearly one and a half tons.

Comilla is today close to the eastern border of Bangla Desh, less than 150 miles as the crow flies from the frontier of the Union of Burma in the Chin hills. And it is in Burma that we can now see what many of those old Indian stupas must have looked like in their prime.

There is a tradition that Gautama Buddha himself visited Burma and left his footprints there, some of which appear to have been of superhuman size. But more prosaically Buddhism as an organised religion appears to have come to Burma, as it did to Sri Lanka, at the time of Emperor Ashoka.

At that time the Great Way was yet to be propagated, and it was the Narrow Way, the Buddhism of the Elders, or Thervada, that became established in Suvannabhumi, the Land of Gold.

The distance between the Tree of Enlightenment and Mandalay is only 750 miles in a direct line. So Burma is actually much closer to the source than that other stronghold of the original, undiluted faith—Sri Lanka. Indeed it is aptly said that to be a Burman is to be a Buddhist, that is to keep a faith unshaken by disasters, colonisation and misgovernment. Whereas in India the Buddhist monuments crumbled away and all but disappeared, in Burma the greatest of them have been preserved down the centuries and added to with loving care.

For a generation Burma, recently renamed Myanmar, stagnated behind a bamboo curtain set up by the socialist military junta which ruled that part of the land over which its writ ran. Naturally the local people came and went by many paths across the long frontiers with Thailand, China and India. But until 1994 there was only one official way of entering the country for foreigners, and that was by air or sea through Rangoon, now called Yangon.

Yet it is to Burma, the Golden Land, that we must turn to see what the great centres of Indian Buddhism may have looked like in the days when they were flourishing and when the countryside itself was Buddhist. One travels across the flat ricelands, divided into irrigated squares, and everywhere it is possible to see the white or gold finial and *hti* of a pagoda in the distance, probably in or beside a grove of trees, or nearer at hand the bell-shaped stupa itself is also visible with perhaps a line of hills in the distance or perhaps an endless continuation of the plain and the pagodas.

After some hours in the bus a more than usually large golden spire comes into view, and one knows that one is approaching a population centre of some note, where some particular relic is venerated or, at the very least, the pagoda has a noteworthy tradition. In such a centre you will find a hundred, two hundred and even three hundred foot high stupas such as Hiuen Tsiang mentions in his travels in the 'Western Land.' And the greatest of them all is the Shwe Dagon Pagoda, the Golden Stupa of Yangon, which rises nearly three hundred feet above a base that is itself on a 150 foot hill.

Just as the Indian stupas grew old or were damaged and had to be rebuilt and refurbished many times, so the Shwe Dagon has suffered and yet risen again each time greater and more glorious. After the English traveller, Ralph Fitch, had seen it in 1586, he wrote that 'it is the fairest place, as I suppose, that is in the world; it standeth very high, and there are four ways to it, which all along are set with trees of fruits, such wise that a man may go in the shade above two miles in length ...'

By that time the pagoda was already very old, dating back almost to the lifetime of the Buddha if the legend of its foundation is to be believed. Certainly it was flourishing in the eleventh century, when Anawrahta, the King of Pagan, visited it. By then it had been rebuilt a number of times, and it would be rebuilt again as acts of merit by successive kings.

Sometimes it was an earthquake that wrought havoc, sometimes unprincipled invaders. The whole of the upper part of the pagoda was thrown down by an earthquake in 1768, and it assumed its present form when King Hsinbyushin had the stupa rebuilt the following year. Such immediate and impressive response to disaster was not unusual. But when the British took Lower Burma in 1852, the pagoda was looted by the soldiery. It was then for its own safety placed under military protection for seventy-seven years until 1929, during which time a new golden umbrella, or *hti*, was provided by King Mindon of Upper Burma.

Since 1929 there have been two more earthquakes, and in 1931 a destructive fire wrought havoc amongst the pavilions on the northern side. Yet the Shwe Dagon looks as bright and beautiful today as if these setbacks and disasters had never occurred.

Who can doubt that the Dharmarajika Stupa at Sarnath, the Ananda Stupa at Vaishali and the Parinirvana Stupa at Kushinagara went through similar vicissitudes of destruction and reconstruction before they finally went down for ever. Just as at the Shwe Dagon there would have been avenues of approach to these stupas on all four sides, where the visitor would have been able to buy flowers and greenery to offer on the altars, or gold leaf to apply to the surfaces of the images. At the Shwe Dagon there is a long flight of steps, a covered way leading up the hill on which the pagoda stands. Here are the gladioli and the roses, the asters and the carnations, the marigolds and the frangipani, which the faithful place in front of the Buddha figures and which give a foretaste of the brilliant colours to come.

The southern staircase is a prolongation of a tree-set avenue such as Ralph Fitch saw, which brings the visitor from Yangon city. At the top of the stairs thirteen pictures tell the tale of the foundation of the pagoda and the reason for its existence. The story goes thus:

The Buddha was so impressed by the two brothers, Tapussa and Bhallika, who were the first to follow him after his Enlightenment, that he gave them eight of his hairs. Being merchants, they travelled, and they brought the hairs to Myanmar by sea. The hairs were then transported from the ship by elephant with due ceremony. But it was hard to decide where to deposit them. The problem was solved when, with the aid of some *nats*, the spirits of the extant religion, the hill was discovered within which a relic of each of the three previous Buddhas had been buried. This was the hill at Dagon, now called Yangon, alias Rangoon, on which the

Shwe Dagon pagoda stands. It therefore has the unique distinction of being the only stupa in the world in which relics of all the past four of the five once and future Buddhas of our era are enshrined.

It is said that, after the precious relics had been safely deposited, a slab of gold was placed on the relic chamber, over which a pagoda of gold was built. This gold pagoda was enclosed in a tin one, the tin pagoda in a copper one, the copper one in a lead one, the lead in marble, and the marble one in a pagoda or stupa of iron bricks.

This may have been all on a small scale, since we are told that when Emperor Ashoka wanted to find the stupa, it was hidden in the jungle and hard to locate. However, it was never completely lost to view like many of the Ashoka stupas in India.

So, at the top of the southern staircase one finds oneself facing the image of Kanakamuni Buddha, Konagamana in Pali. Our familiar Buddha, Gautama, is on the northern side. Kashyapa Buddha is to the west and Karakuchanda Buddha to the east. Thus all four, whose lives, or part of whose lives on earth are said, on the basis of scanty archaeological evidence and legend, to have been led in the Terai of Nepal between the River Rapti and the Himalayan foothills, are here assembled in gleaming golden bronze, each in his separate pavilion, in which people kneel, say their mantras, meditate and make their supplications. This is what makes the Shwe Dagon the greatest living Buddhist temple in South Asia and in the world.

The images sit with their backs to the great stupa itself, the first course of which is a square with rounded corners. Square bands rise in a series of narrow terraces. Then the squares become octagonal and the octagons give way to a circular bell. The bell turns into lotus petals, the lotus petals into a banana bud. From the base upwards all is golden.

It is hard to get far enough back on the main platform to fully admire the form and beauty of the stupa. But it is not hard to understand why, in times of lawlessness, it was prudent to place it under military protection. The total value of the gold and jewels which adorn it has been estimated to be not less than US $750 million at today's valuation.

The banana bud alone is covered with over 13,000 plates of gold, each one covering an area of thirty square centimetres. The great *hti* overhanging the banana bud weighs over a ton, even without the hanging bells and tin peepul-leaves that tinkle in the breeze. Admittedly it is hard to get to. But anyone with the nerve would find his choice there of over a thousand diamonds which stud the gold and silver plating. If he could get even higher, above the cone and the staff with its flag that turns in the wind like a weather-vane, he would reach the topmost point, which is a hollow golden orb studded with 4,351 diamonds weighing 1,800 carats between them, and tipped with a single seventy-six carat diamond.

One sees the *hti*, thc vane and the orb distantly, three hundred feet overhead. But near at hand are the little stupas that ring the lowest terrace, many with stone or stucco images of the Buddha in the earth is witness pose. In amongst them are small alabaster images which appeared, on the Sunday morning that I went there, to be as popular as the four Buddhas.

These statues represent the eight celestial bodies that rule the astrological scene, which are the sun and moon, the five planets of our solar system and a sixth, called Rahu, which is the hidden one that causes eclipses. Naturally, being Sunday, it was the sun, with its sign, the galon bird, that was attracting the greatest number of people. They were burning candles and sticks of incense, placing flowers in front of the white image and sprinkling water over it.

Just so one imagines the pagodas of India to have been—not only the now arid hulks of the main stupas but a whole world of stupas, large and small, of adoration halls, of astrology and divination, of coming and going, each person to his or her particular need.

There would also have been the many-roofed wooden pagodas, such as one finds in Nepal today, but which have disappeared long ago in India. Their counterparts at the Shwe Dagon are the many pavilions in the courtyard, which have up to nine tin roofs diminishing in size in pyramidal form to the top.

These pavilions are put to many uses. There might be a great bell in one of them or a wonder-working image in another. As in English cathedrals, history is enshrined here too. There is a monument with an account in four languages of the 1920 student revolt against British rule, and there is an inscription in three languages—Pali, Mon and Burmese—which tells the story of the Shwe Dagon.

That bright Sunday morning when I went there with my young student friend, Wunna, the pagoda was full of people, not all of them going round the stupa in the proper clockwise direction. Some stopped to muse at the place of their particular choice, some walked on happily, some knelt in the pavilions, some sat cross-legged in silent meditation on the quiet and secluded terraces of the Naungdaugyi Stupa, the small one that was built to house the hairs of the Buddha temporarily whilst the main stupa was being built. But those who reminded me most of what life beside the early stupas in India might have been like were in the south-eastern corner of the compound.

Here we came upon an authentic Bo-tree grown to spreading maturity, which had been propagated from a cutting brought back from the Tree of Enlightenment at Bodh Gaya. Under the Bo-tree there was a seated Buddha clothed in a saffron robe with a silvery tin baldaquin over his head, and in front of the Buddha a monk sat on a low dais decorated with the blue, yellow, red, white and orange of Buddhist flags.

The monk was preaching to a congregation of about fifty, who knelt on coconut matting or on the bare stone with their feet tucked behind them showing their soles to the sky. They listened, joined reverently and melodiously in the responses, and when the sermon was over they got up and walked away, leaving the Bo-tree rustling slightly in the breeze.

Wunna and I walked away too, under the palmyra palms at the entrance to the pagoda and into the city. That afternoon I caught the night train to Mandalay and visited the Kuthodaw Pagoda, where all the Buddhist literature in Pali may be read from the slabs of stone on which the Tripitaka have been carved. The 729 stelae are protected by the same number of small white pavilions, which are arranged in rows forming squares around the stupa, where the 730th stele relates how the work was done.

The Kuthodaw pagoda is considerably smaller than the Shwe Dagon, and its stupa is golden only from the bell upwards. It is comparatively modern, having been built in 1857 in the style of the Shwe Zigon Pagoda at Nyaung U down river from Mandalay. It is as if King Mindon saw the faith threatened by the British annexation of Lower Burma and built it as a declaration of faith. And well he did so. For very many of the palm-leaf manuscripts were destroyed in the Second World War, which was waged along the length of the land.

Yet the main characteristics of the Shwe Dagon are there—the bell-shaped stupa on octagonal and square terraces, the finial and *hti* above it, the staff and orb, the four adoration pavilions at each of the four points of the compass, the smaller stupas and Buddha images, the lion-like *chinthes* guarding the corners. In each of the pavilions a man was sitting beside a flat bronze bell shaped rather like an ambassador's hat, which he struck from time to time.

It has been calculated that it would take a man 450 days, reading for eight hours a day, to complete a reading of the whole Tripitaka on all 729 stelae. I could not even begin. So I walked up Mandalay hill to view the complex from above, and then I persuaded Win Tin, my driver, to take me across the Irrawaddy river, now called the Ayeyarwady, to Sagaing.

It was a hot afternoon, and the little Japanese pick-up hire vehicle with its feeble motor-cycle engine only just made it up the slope to the Ava bridge, which may have been why Win Tin was reluctant to go in the first place. It is the only bridge across the Irrawaddy in its entire length of over a thousand miles, and it could not have been better placed for this excursion, since Sagaing and its pagoda-studded hill lies at its western end.

There are indeed many stupas at Sagaing. But the one I have the sharpest memory of is the Soon U Pannya Shin Pagoda, not only because it took a long hard climb in the heat of the day to reach it, but also because I met Gerhardt there. Had I known it a taxi could have taken me up a road to the top of the hill. But the steep slope was beyond the powers of Win Tin's pick-up, and so with hardly a word he deposited me beside a formidable yellow *chinthe* with bright red lips and white teeth, three times his height, that stood guard at the foot of a long flight of steps.

The steps led steadily upwards within low walls, sheltered from the sun by a series of corrugated iron roofs and passing through wooded slopes. At intervals there were short flat stretches, where the walls widened to make room for stone benches for the weary, each one of which had been donated as a separate act of merit. On some of them people were sleeping with their feet up or lounging in their lungyis and hailing me sleepily as I toiled on. I was not surprised, since most Burmans sleep or rest in the afternoon having risen at daybreak.

I passed on the left a pagoda with many tin roofs, and on the right a ruined and abandoned one, which once had elegant doorways with flying finials but now had green ferns and bamboo growing on it right up to the topmost terrace.

This was in sharp contrast with the stupa at the top of the hill, which was being renovated even at the time of my visit. A sharp turn to the left through a small complex of tea-houses and souvenir shops brought me up on to the platform of the pagoda, from which there was a magnificent view of the Irrawaddy, the Ava bridge and the wooded hillside dotted with the white triangles that were distant stupas.

The Soon U Pannya Shin Stupa looked, in form and style, very like the Kuthodaw Pagoda to me, though I could not actually see the lower part of the bell. It was encased in a framework of bamboo, mostly covered with matting, which gave the craftsmen shade in which to work. I could hear the ting-ting of the masons' little hammers, no doubt tapping fresh gold-leaf on to the structure.

But inside the principal adoration pavilion everything was clear. There was a huge white alabaster image of the seated Buddha in a golden robe, with his right hand reaching to the ground and his left hand cradling a circle of ruby-red electric lights, which flashed intermittently round a core of emerald lights. The fillet round the head was golden, the lips were red, and the curled hair of the head, rising in the shape of a pyramid, was black. Black too were the eyebrows and the eyes, the latter being of particular significance since the Pannya Pagoda claims to have enshrined within its stupa, or some say within the rabbit, the two eyelids of Gautama Buddha. It happened thus:

During one of his journeys Gautama Buddha, together with his cousin and disciple, Ananda, came to this very peak on the heights of the Sagaing hills called Dhammika Nga Phu. It had already been frequently visited by the Buddha-to-be in a previous incarnation as a rabbit during the time of Kashyapa Buddha. So Gautama Buddha prophesied that a notable pagoda would be built there, in which his two eyelids would rest.

What happened was that King Tazishin Thiha Thu of Vijayapura felt unwell after chewing betel from the royal betel~cup, in which seven Buddha relics sent from Sri Lanka had been secretly hidden. The king ordered the royal goldsmith, Nga Sein Thin, to break the cup open. But only five of the seven relics were produced. The other two had been hidden in a hammer and an anvil.

The king ordered the arrest of the goldsmith, who absconded from Vijayapura to the other side of the river and hid in the home of a minister named Pannya. Since a bright light shone from the relics, the minister put them in a golden casket and ordered it to be placed on the Nga Phu peak, where there were already two pagodas.

Out of these two pagodas Pannya constructed one. The year was 1312 CE, and since he had built it without royal permission the new king, Ahtinkaya Sawyun, ordered him to be drowned. But thanks to the glory and influence of the relics he remained alive. Indeed, ten years later, in 1322, the king himself, with a multitude of people, crowned the stupa, hoisting the *hti* up some ninety feet to its proper place above the bell. In recent times the pagoda has been maintained by the Danaphyu Sayadaw of the Sagaing hills, from 1903 to 1957 by U Ariya Wun Tha and after that by his successor in the appointment, U Sandima Wun Tha.

This story can be read in English in the pagoda itself, and a charming bronze statue of a rabbit munching a carrot recalls the foundation legend. One may make one's donation here, or else on the other side of the Buddha image through a slot in the head of a very sturdy-looking frog.

I asked the temple attendant what was the significance of the frog.

"Now I know about the rabbit," I said. "But what about the frog?"

"The hill looks like a frog," he replied.

It was a surprising answer. I walked out of the main doorway to see what I could see about the shape of the hill, and only then did I realise that I could have motored up to the stupa, since an olive-green pick-up truck and a motorcycle were parked outside it. There too was Gerhardt, gazing at the view of another pagoda-studded hill with the many channels of the Irrawaddy behind it, and Mandalay in the distance on the other side of the river.

Although he was dressed like the Burmans in a purple lungyi with a shirt of check pattern over it, he was not a young man. In fact the little hair that was left to him was in bristles of grey and white that might just as well have been shaved off in the style of the pongyis, who are the bhikshus of Burma. But he had not yet reached that change in his life. He also had a distinguished air about him, which made one want to address him as Herr So and So. But he preferred to be called Gerhardt and he also wanted to talk.

Together we went back into the temple and had another look at the rabbit standing up on its hind legs like a hare with the carrot in its forefeet. "There's a story about this rabbit," I said. "It's the Rabbit in the Moon jataka."

"One day Saka, the king of the gods, wanted to test the Buddha-to-be. So he assumed the form of an old Brahmin, appeared in front of the rabbit and asked him for alms. The rabbit had nothing to give. So he offered his own body. Whereupon the bogus Brahmin lit a fire and the rabbit jumped into it. But the god intervened and he was unharmed. Saka then announced that in remembrance of the rabbit's great deed of merit, his likeness would appear from that time onwards on the face of the moon."

"No roast rabbit," said Gerhardt, whose English was quite good enough to follow the tale.

"Well, I suppose it's just a story," I said. "But what isn't?"

"I will tell you my story," said Gerhardt. "I could have been roasted too. For weeks I was getting daymares."

"Surely you mean nightmares," I said.

"No. These were daymares. They came to me during the day at any time, even in bright sunlight. And really I came here to forget it all. Here nothing like that could happen. I had cut my ties. But I carried it all around with me like my head was in a bubble. And all the time I was fighting someone who wasn't there."

We walked past the frog and out into a shaded cloister, from which our eyes turned to the golden stupa, gleaming and glittering in the afternoon sun.

"What were the daymares about?" I asked.

"It was like a court case," he answered. "An accuser and a defender."

"Which were you?"

"Sometimes one, sometimes the other. Mostly the defender. Because it wasn't me who brought the case in the first place, you understand."

"I don't understand," I said. "And what about the Buddha?"

"The Buddha taught me. The Diamond Sutra. Have you read it?

"I have. But I don't understand it yet."

"You never will," he said. "It's something you cannot understand in words."

"Anyway it doesn't belong here," I said. "It belongs to the Great Way."

"The Great Way or the Narrow Way. What does it matter? There is the Middle Way. There are no opposites. There is neither being nor not being."

"Is that what the Diamond Sutra taught you?"

"I still had the daymares. I said to myself over and over again what I thought I was going to say. Unprovoked accusations. Implacable malice. Paranoid delusions. Words like formulas."

"And who were you going to say this to? A judge? A jury?"

"That wasn't clear. Sometimes I was going to write a letter. Sometimes I was going to speak. I even wrote down what I was going to say so that I could learn my lines."

Gerhardt fell silent, and the tinkling taps of the masons' little hammers behind the coconut matting could be heard again. Then he began his tale. "I am not a young man, as you can see. And my wife was not young either. She was also sick, and I attended to her needs as best I could. Her greatest joy was to feed the birds in the garden and watch them bathing in the bird-bath. Her next love was for her dogs. I went along with that. She ate very little, got thinner and thinner and suffered from her heart. I tried my best. But the weaker she got in the body, the stronger was her spirit."

"A blessing."

"No. A curse. She began to have delusions. She called out the doctor so often that he gave up and refused to come any more. She called out the emergency night doctor instead, and he too could not find anything wrong with her except her damaged heart. Was it all a delusion: I thought so."

"Was what a delusion?"

"She accused me of wanting to kill her. In fact, I could have done that easily. She was so frail a tap with two fingers would have knocked her over. But she wrote to all the friends and relations telling them I was treating her badly and saying I was going off my head. Some of them believed it. Then she threw an egg at me. I pushed the egg away and knocked the egg-cup on to her arm. Then she showed the bruise to everyone. It was her proof. Then she waited till the middle of the night and called out doctors, nurses, ambulance-men, police and accused me to them of marital abuse. What could I do? I was the defendant, was I not? But they didn't ask me to say my piece. They just ignored me. I wanted to tell them it was all a delusion. I even had words for it. I called it paranoid schizophrenia. I thought that was something the doctors could understand. But they just took notes and didn't listen. 'Accuses her husband of assaulting her.' Then she got worse and asked me to take her to a nursing-home. I never saw her again."

"Do you want to see her?"

"We were married twenty years," Gerhardt answered. "It's a long time. I did want to see her. But she refused to see me. Once I did see her by chance when I took some letters to her. But she stared straight through me and said, 'You'll have to wait.' Well, I thought, she can't accuse me of assaulting her while she's in the nursing-home. Then she wrote me a letter saying she was staying in the nursing-home for three months and then she was coming back to the house. She planned to be there for three months—to get her strength back, she said. That was in October."

"It's November now," I said.

"How could we live together again? I was afraid the nightmare accusations would start up again as soon as she came back. That was when the daymares started. I didn't know what to do. How was I going to act? What was I going to say to defend myself? And that was how the real truth came to me. Someone told me she'd been seeing a lawyer and also planning to buy an apartment. It wasn't paranoid schizophrenia at all. She was simply trying to build up a case for a quick divorce."

"Three months."

"That was what the lawyer had told her, I guess."

"And he'd told her not to see you."

"That too."

"Well, why not?"

"And be branded a cruel husband? Hand over half my fortune to give the dogs' home? I came here to forget all that.

It was my first wife's country. She always talked about it with love. But we never came back here. It was difficult to do it in those times. But now I am here."

"But you don't forget."

"You cannot fight a ghost," he said.

"I don't know what you mean."

"After I had been here three weeks staying in the monasteries and visiting the pagodas I was still getting the daymares. Then I telephoned my daughter. She told me my wife had died the day after I left."

Gerhardt had said his piece and seemed relieved. He began to walk round the stupa in the proper clockwise direction and I went with him.

"So there was no delusion, no accuser, no defender. Just a plot and a story."

"Just a lot of words. What does the Diamond Sutra say? Words cannot express truth. That which words express is not truth."

Gerhardt and I walked together down the steps on the far side of the pagoda, and it was only after we had gone down two steep flights that I realised I had left my shoes at the top.

"I too," said Gerhardt.

"We'll have to go back up for them."

"You go back," he said. "I would say I would not be needing my shoes again."

So I struggled back up the steps, past the tea-houses and my shoes into the Pannya Pagoda for the last time. When I went down again Gerhardt had disappeared. Without waiting for me he must have gone on down to the monastery where he was staying. In any case, I never saw him again. For next day I went on another expedition that opened my eyes to what Sarnath and Nalanda and the other Indian Buddhist centres might have looked like before they crumbled into dust.

At Pagan a young man named Win, whose father was a mason doing restoration work on the pagodas, took me in a pony-trap to some of the five thousand pagodas that had been built there in the Middle Ages and were still in existence. Situated, like Mandalay, on the left bank of the Irrawaddy, Pagan was a thriving, populated region, the seat of many kings, before the Mongol hordes of Kublai Khan devastated the area in 1287.

But the pagodas, though abandoned and deserted, were not destroyed. They simply suffered the weathering of age, the destruction caused by earthquakes, and the looting of unscrupulous collectors. So it is possible, in Pagan, to see what those great images at Nalanda may have looked like before they were reduced to being the mere remnants of crossed legs, and how the Mulaghanda Kuti at Sarnath might have appeared before it became simply a pattern of thick walls one storey high. It is also possible to see the manner of making of those large and imposing statues.

In the Sulamani temple the four Buddhas are seated in the earth is witness pose, three times the height of a man, their bodies unclothed, the flesh coloured red except where the red surface has broken and fallen away. Even today, eight hundred years after they were installed there, fresh flowers are placed in front of them by those who frequent the temple. The Thandawgya image, a mile down the pony-track going back towards the river, shows clearly how they were made. For from this great statue, housed in its own building, which is now roofless and open to the elements, all the surface paint and stucco has been weathered away to reveal the core structure.

Nearly twenty feet high and consisting only of the trunk, head and arms of the Buddha, the image is made of greenish sandstone. But it is not one solid piece. It is built of sandstone blocks shaped like large bricks. In the same way many of the large images of Buddhas were built of real earthenware bricks, which were not so durable as the stone.

The Sulamani Temple also bears witness to the protection given to the Buddha by the snakes during his meditation on the road to Enlightenment. Two frescoes have survived in which intertwined serpents, the Nagas of the natural world, form a kind of canopy over him as at the Muchalinda lake in Bodh-Gaya. But many frescoes have been lost, as have many of the panels of the friezes illustrating jataka stories, which are on the terraces of some of the temples.

At the Ananda Temple, which is the crowning glory of Pagan with its golden sikra in the Indian style surmounted by a golden, circular stupa, the ten-foot thick walls bear witness to the architectural requirements of a heavy superstructure, such as must have existed at the Mulagandha Kuti in Sarnath.

This temple is not far short of two hundred feet high. In the heart of the building the four Buddhas, the same as those at the Shwe Dagon pagoda, are represented by standing images over thirty feet high on eight-foot high lotus plinths. At first sight the great golden figures, with their robes splayed out behind their long legs, look the same. But a careful inspection reveals different hand mudras and different degrees of dress.

At any rate the little woman who followed me round had no doubts as to which was which. She was smoking an enormous cheroot made of a roll of leaves that burned like dried palm-fronds, and she held a large lacquer bowl under it in case charred fragments fell off it and set light to her lungyi. As we reached each Buddha she gave me his name—Kakusanda, Konagama, Kassapa and Gautama. They are the Pali names as they are understood in Burma, in line with the Sri Lankan tradition.

Each of her cheeks had a peepul-leaf design in white transferred on to it.

"Look," she said. "Kakusanda. You see him smiling. Now come close and look. No more smiling. Now very hard."

It was true. But surely it was only an optical illusion. Thirty feet above our heads, the foreshortened view was indeed of a mighty and severe mentor, a master of minds. But the natural view was of the Buddha smile, kindly even if enigmatic.

As I left the Ananda temple I thought again of the Diamond Sutra. The words that Gautama Buddha spoke to Subhuti are written in that sutra, and amongst other things he said that 'at the end of the last five-hundred year period following the passing of the Tathagata, there will be self-controlled men, rooted in merit, coming to hear these teachings, who will be inspired with belief.'

We have now, after 2,500 years, reached that end and the prophecy has been fulfilled. As for me, I planted some of the berries from the Bo-tree at Bodh-Gaya in my home in Hampshire. Tended indoors with the greatest care, the best of them is now a sapling several feet high.

Further Reading

Abhinishkramana Sutra, *The Romantic Legend of Shakya Buddha*, tr. from Chinese by Samuel Beal, London, 1875, reprint Delhi, 1985.

Molly Emma Aitken (ed.), *Meeting the Buddha*, New York, 1995.

Alexander Cunningham, *The Ancient Geography of India*, London, 1871, reprint Delhi, 1990.

S. Dhammika, *Middle Land, Middle Way*, Kandy, 1992.

Fa Hien, *A Record of Buddhistic Kingdoms*, tr. from Chinese by James Legge, Oxford, 1886, reprint Islamabad undated.

Daisaku Ikeda, *The Living Buddha*, Tokyo, 1973, tr. Burton Watson, New York, 1976.

H.W. Schumann, *The Historical Buddha*, 1982, tr. M. O'C. Walshe, London, 1989.

Si-Yu-Ki, *Buddhist Records of the Western World*, tr. from Chinese by Samuel Beal, London, 1884, reprint Delhi, 1981.

Tarthang Tulku, *Holy Places of the Buddha*, ed. Elizabeth Cook, Berkeley, 1994.

Index

BUDDHIST TRADITION SERIES

General Editor : ERNST STEINKELLNER
Joint General Editor : ALEXANDER VON ROSPATT
Founder Editor : Late ALEX WAYMAN

ISBN: 978-81-208-0287-2

1 Indian Buddhism—*Hajime Nakamura*
2 Nagarjuniana—*Chr. Lindtner*
3 Chinese Monks in India—*Latika Lahiri*
4 Buddhism in Central Asia—*B.N. Puri*
5 Dharmakīrti's Theory of Hetu-Centricity of Anumāna—*M. R. Chinchore*
6 The Legend of King Aśoka—*John S. Strong*
7 Buddhist Insight—*George R. Elder*
8 Buddhism Transformed—*Richard Gombrich* and *Gananath Obeyesekere*
9 The Buddhist Tantras—*Alex Wayman*
10 The Lion's Roar of Queen Śrīmālā —*Alex Wayman* and *Hideko Wayman*
11 The Buddha Nature—*Brian E. Brown*
12 Evolution of Stupas in Burma —*Sujata Soni*
13 Buddhist Parables—*E. W. Burlingame*
14 The Debate of King Milinda —*Bhikkhu Pesala*
15 The Chinese Madhyama Āgama and the Pāli Majjhima Nikāya—*Bhikṣu Thich Minh Chau*
16 Sudden and Gradual—*Peter N. Gregory*
17 Yoga of the Guhyasamājatantra—*Alex Wayman*
18 The Enlightenment of Vairocana —*Alex Wayman* and *R. Tajima*
19 A History of Indian Buddhism—Tr. *Hirakawa Akira*, Ed. *Paul Groner*
20 Introduction to the Buddhist Tantric Systems—*F.D. Lessing* and *Alex Wayman*
21 Anāgatavaṃsa Desanā—Tr. *Udaya Meddegama*, Ed. *John Clifford Holt*
22 Chinnamastā—*Elisabeth Anne Benard*
23 On Voidness—*Fernando Tola* and *Carmen Dragonetti*
24 Nāgārjuna's Refutation of Logic (Nyāya) Vaidalyaprakaraṇa—*Fernando Tola* and *Carmen Dragonetti*
25 The Buddhist Art of Nāgārjunakoṇḍa —*Elizabeth Rosen Stone*
26 Discipline—*John C. Holt*
27 Philosophy and its Development in the Nikāyas and Abhidhamma —*Fumimaro Watanabe*
28 Untying the Knots in Buddhism —*Alex Wayman*
29 Early Buddhist Theory of Knowledge —*K. N. Jayatilleke*
30 Calming the Mind and Discerning the Real—Tr. *Alex Wayman*
31 A Comparative Study of the Prātimokṣa—*W. Pachow*
32 The Rise of Esoteric Buddhism in the Tibet—*Eva M. Dargyay*
33-35 Saṃyuktābhidharmahṛdaya (3 Parts) —*Bart Dessein*
36 A Millennium of Buddhist Logic —*Alex Wayman*
37 The Buddhist Pilgrimage—*Duncan Forbes*
38 Chanting the Names of Mañjuśrī —*Alex Wayman*
39 The Literature of the Personalists of Early Buddhism—*Bhikshu Thich Thien Chau*
40 The Laṅkāvatāra Sūtra—*D.T. Suzuki*
41 Studies in the Laṅkāvatāra Sūtra —*D.T. Suzuki*
42 The Vimalakīrti Sūtra—*Burton Watson*
43 The Gāndhārī Dharmapada—*John Brough*
44 Imaging Wisdom—*Jacob N. Kinnard*
45 Pain and Its Ending—*Carol S. Anderson*
46 Apparitions of the Self—*Janet Gyatso*
47-49 Rules for Nuns according to the Dharma-guptakavinaya (3 Parts) —*Ann Heirman*
50 The Chinese Hevajratantra—*Ch. Willemen*
51 The Historical Buddha—*H.W. Schumann*
52 Dana—*Ellison Banks Findly*
53 Hermeneutics & Tradition in the *Saṃdhinirmocana-sūtra*—*John Powers*
54 Skillful Means—*John W. Schroeder*
55 The Two Truths in Chinese Buddhism —*Chang-Qing Shih*
56 The Bodhisattva Path—*Jan Nattier*
57 Becoming the Buddha—*Donald K. Swearer*
58 Approaching the Land of Bliss —*Richard K. Payne* & *Kenneth K. Tanaka*
59 Indian Monastic Buddhism: Collected papers on Textual, Inscriptional and Archaeological Evidence— *Gregory Schopen*

Fig. 1. Lumbini – Mayadevi Temple rebuilding

Fig. 2. Devadaha – The River Rohini

Fig. 13. Vaishali – The Lion Pillar and Stupa

Fig. 14. Pava – Remains of the Malla Stupa